Education, Globalization and the Nation

Education, Globalization and the Nation

King Man Chong
The Hong Kong Institute of Education, China

Ian Davies
University of York, UK

Terrie Epstein
Hunter College, City University of New York, USA

Carla L. Peck
University of Alberta, Canada

Andrew Peterson
University of South Australia

Alistair Ross
London Metropolitan University, UK

Maria Auxiliadora Schmidt
Universidade Federal do Paraná, Brazil

Alan Sears
University of New Brunswick, Canada

Debbie Sonu
Hunter College, City University of New York, USA

First published 2016 by
PALGRAVE MACMILLAN

Palgrave Macmillan in the UK is an imprint of Macmillan Publishers Limited, registered in England, company number 785998, of Houndmills, Basingstoke, Hampshire RG21 6XS.

Palgrave Macmillan in the US is a division of St Martin's Press LLC, 175 Fifth Avenue, New York, NY 10010.

Palgrave Macmillan is the global academic imprint of the above companies and has companies and representatives throughout the world.

Palgrave® and Macmillan® are registered trademarks in the United States, the United Kingdom, Europe and other countries.

ISBN: 978–1–137–46034–9

This book is printed on paper suitable for recycling and made from fully managed and sustained forest sources. Logging, pulping and manufacturing processes are expected to conform to the environmental regulations of the country of origin.

A catalogue record for this book is available from the British Library.

Library of Congress Cataloging-in-Publication Data

Chong, King Man, 1974– author.
   Education, globalization and the nation / King Man Chong, The Hong Kong Institute of Education, China, Ian Davies, University of York, UK, Terrie Epstein, Hunter College, New York., USA, Carla Peck, University of Alberta, Canada, Andrew Peterson, University of South Australia, Australia Alistair Ross, London Metropolitan University, UK, Alan Sears, University of New Brunswick, Canada, Maria Auxiliadora Moreira dos Santos Schmidt, Universidade Federal do Paraná, Brazil, Debbie Sonu, Hunter College, City University of New York, USA.
      pages cm
   Includes bibliographical references.
   ISBN 978–1–137–46034–9
      1. Education and globalization.   2. Education and globalization—Case studies.
   3. Education and state.   4. Education and state—Case studies.   I. Title.
   LC191.C5228 2015
   379—dc23   2015020286

Contents

List of Tables

Acknowledgements

We wish to acknowledge the efficient and supportive approach of all at Palgrave Macmillan. We are grateful to Kim Peacock for producing the index to the book.

About the Authors

King Man Chong is a lecturer in the Department of Social Sciences and a research fellow of the Centre for Governance and Citizenship at the Hong Kong Institute of Education. His career focuses on citizenship education, on curriculum development of liberal studies and general studies in Hong Kong schools, and on the politics of Hong Kong SAR and Macao SAR.

Ian Davies is Professor of Education at the University of York, UK. He is also Director of the Graduate School in Education, Director of the Centre for Research on Education and Social Justice and the deputy head of the Department of Education.

Terrie Epstein is Professor of Education at Hunter College and the Graduate Center, City University of New York. She is interested in the relationships among children's, adolescents' and adults' social identities and their understandings of their nations' histories and contemporary societies. Her books include *Interpreting National History: Race Identity and Pedagogy in Classrooms and Communities* and *Teaching United States History: Dialogues between Social Studies Teachers and Historians* (edited), both published in 2009. Currently, she and Carla L. Peck (University of Alberta) are the recipients of an American Educational Research Association Grant for a conference entitled *Research on Teaching and Learning Difficult Histories: Global Concepts and Contexts*, to be held at the end of June 2015 in New York City.

Carla L. Peck is Associate Professor of Social Studies Education in the Department of Elementary Education at the University of Alberta and the editor of *Theory & Research in Social Education*. Her research interests include students' understandings of democratic concepts, diversity, identity, citizenship, and the relationship between students' ethnic identities and their understandings of history.

Andrew Peterson is Senior Lecturer in History and Civic Education and an ARC DECRA Research Fellow at the University of South Australia, Australia, conducting research on global learning in Australian high schools. His research covers civic, history and global learning, as well as the related fields of values education and the connections between schools and their communities. Peterson sits on the Editorial Board of the *British Journal of Educational Studies*. He is the handling editor and a member of the Editorial Board of the journal *Citizenship Teaching and Learning*. He is also the co-editor of a new journal launched in 2014 – *Journal of Philosophy in Schools*. He has published in numerous journals and books. His most recent book, co-authored with Paul Warwick, is *Global Learning and Education* (2014).

Alistair Ross is Jean Monnet Professor of Citizenship Education and an emeritus professor of London Metropolitan University, UK. He established and directed an EU thematic network, Children's Identity and Citizenship in Europe, from 1988 to 2008, linking 100 universities in 26 countries. He is researching young people's constructions of identity in Europe.

Maria Auxiliadora Schmidt has several degrees including an MA in Education (Universidade Federal do Paraná, 1985), a PhD in History (Universidade Federal do Paraná, 1997) and a post-PhD in Didactics of History (Universidade Nova de Lisboa-Portugal, 2001) (Capes scholarship). She is an associate professor of the Universidade Federal do Paraná, and coordinates the Laboratório de Pesquisa em Educação Histórica LAPEDUH (www.lapeduh.ufpr.br). She is a participant researcher in the Universidade do Minho, Portugal; a consultant of the Universidade Estadual de Londrina; a participant researcher in the Universidad de Barcelona; and a member of the assistant council of the Editora Grao and of the Revista de Investigación *Enseñanza de las Ciencias Sociales*. She is the editor of the periodic *Educar em Revista* and a member of the editorial council of the Editora da Universidade Federal do Paraná.

Alan Sears is Professor of Education at the University of New Brunswick. He is the editor of the journal *Citizenship Teaching and Learning* and is on the Executive Board of The History Education Network.

Debbie Sonu is Assistant Professor of Education in the Department of Curriculum and Teaching at Hunter College, City University of New York. Her research interests include urban schooling in the US, social justice teaching, youth culture, and curriculum studies. She uses qualitative methodologies to examine educational experience, seeking to understand how theories such as poststructuralism can provide alternative explanations for classroom practice. She is also interested in how singular meanings are made, particularly around the topics of peace, violence, and history, and how they govern within school relationships. Her work has been published in *Curriculum Inquiry*, *Journal of Teacher Education*, and the *Journal of Curriculum Theorizing*, among others.

1
Introduction

'Globalization' and 'nation' provide perhaps the most significant contexts, concepts and processes that inform educational thinking and practice today. In this book, we – a team of authors from around the world – have written collaboratively about several overlapping themes. We describe and discuss the sorts of education about – and for – the nation that occur within individual countries. We are interested in the links that are made in education between the nation as a distinct unit and its connections to other similarly distinct nations. As such we are exploring the role that education plays in internationalization (or, literally, what education does in terms of understanding and activity *between* nations). And, we are also keen to explore the issues that emerge from national and international initiatives and characterizations that are pertinent to globalization, which allows us to consider overarching and perhaps more inclusive conceptions of education that go beyond the nation state.

These themes are not mutually exclusive or treated in isolation from each other. Education *for* the nation may be seen as allowing for the consideration of multiple perspectives and the recognition and development of multiple citizen identities among learners. We recognize that the nature and purpose of education and schooling in different parts of the world may differ in very significant ways. We felt we had to develop an appropriate way of engaging with these complex matters. The process by which we worked together and the structure that governs the book are interlocking factors. This is a co-authored and not an edited book. From the beginning we had determined to avoid writing a set of highly individualized, separate chapters.

1

We wanted instead to establish a collegial dialogue that allows us to learn from each other and to generate a series of insights about how different practices and perspectives inform debates about education, globalization and the nation. Hence, in chapter 2 we explain and discuss key terms and explore the background to debates in national education, internationalization and globalization; we then provide a series of case study chapters in which we focus on individual countries and produce a case study of transnational educational action in the European Union; and we have a final chapter in which we present an overarching discussion arising from the individual case studies with a clear intention to influence thinking and practice by recommending strategies for the future. Chapters 1, 2 and 10 were written collaboratively by authors working in co-ordinated teams. The case study chapters were written by specialists, initially as drafts that were commented upon by others and then finalized. The discussions arising from the case study chapters were of great use in developing the frameworks for the other more generalized and overarching parts of the book.

It is necessary to explain the reasons for the case study chapters that were chosen and the structure that was adopted to inform the writing of each chapter. It is of course impossible to include every country in the world and our selection is somewhat arbitrary based on our current networks and knowledge of experts. We do not claim to be comprehensive either in achieving geographical coverage of nation states (this would clearly be impossible in one book) or in including examples from each continent or in illustrating all relevant themes and issues in debates about nations and citizenship and education. Our case study countries are Australia and its federal states; Brazil; Canada, its provinces and territories; China including particular mention of Hong Kong Special Administrative Region (SAR) and Macau SAR; the UK with special reference to England, Scotland, Wales and Northern Ireland; the US and its states; and, finally, the EU and its member states. All these countries have national populations within a nation state and have witnessed long-standing discussions in relation to national identity, internationalization and globalization. Within and across these cases there is a range of characterizations of the state and a variety of experiences in relation to national issues (e.g. there is a sharp contrast between the devolved UK, the federal US and Australia, provincial Canada and the newly defined Chinese state). In some ways our key criterion has been our preference to include a diverse range of case studies in which we have expertise. There is sufficient coherence in these cases to allow for discussion; there are sufficient differences across our cases to allow for a consideration of diversity (politically, culturally, economically and in other ways). We wish to aim for insightful but not comprehensive reflection, consideration of diverse but not isolated cases, and coherent and yet varied examples that relate to education within, for, about and across national citizenships. But all the cases mentioned so far have been to do with countries. As such it is necessary to offer further justification for our inclusion of a case study of the EU. The inclusion of the EU offers a particular and unique opportunity to examine the response of educational systems to emerging post-national characteristics. The EU is not, unlike the countries in our other case studies, a devolved or federal state. The possibility (or perhaps growing acceptance) that the nation is a social construct and that most European countries are not nation states, but include a variety of nationalities within a political unit, is leading to interesting developments in the re-appraisal of the role of the nation in national syllabi. And the various member states of the EU have all joined in the creation of a common additional citizenship that can be seen as something that consolidates post-nationalist identities (or the possibility of these). This possibility compromises the near-exclusive nationalist identities often seen to be required by the nation state and in turn begins to impact on the ways in which young people learn about their nation and the characteristics of the national identity they may construct.

Within each case study chapter we aimed for a coherent and consistent approach to key issues. So, we decided to include some background information about each case. We wanted to describe the social, political and cultural contexts so that we could be clear about what nations exist within each particular nation state. We have also included some historical background and highlighted the strategies (curricular and other) that are used for educating about and for the nation. This focus on curricular contexts means that we have given particular consideration to social studies programmes with an emphasis on citizenship education. We have finally in each chapter discussed likely and desirable futures so that we make clear what we feel will (and should) happen in the next 50 years.

In the final and main part of the book we look to the future. Principally, we wanted to develop not only some discussions but also some focused recommendations that could apply across more than one location. We did not want to pretend that individual differences do not matter but we prefer a logic of globalization to allow for some forms of consensus in a shared commitment to enhanced educational standards and common commitment to human worth, dignity and rights. Our recommendations fall principally into four areas: policy that is nationally framed but also in relation to international organizations such as the United Nations; research in which key issues are explored philosophically and empirically; teacher education so that we have a professional and inclusive approach to those who we see as one of the principal engines of reform; and work with young people within and beyond schools. Throughout we intend our recommendations to be seen as ranging widely across different contexts. So, an emphasis on professionals is not meant to be exclusive; a commitment to schools is signalling our educational ambitions and an inclusive approach to communities. We want this book to illuminate issues and to influence key opinion formers as well as the professionals and young people who are already engaged in building education about and for the nation in a globalizing world. And through the collaborative approach that has been adopted throughout the process of writing this book we wish to make our own small contribution to the ways in which people from around the globe can work together.

2
Key Contexts and Challenges

A quarter century ago, Benedict Anderson (1991) published what came to be a seminal book on understanding nationalism and nation states, *Imagined Communities: Reflections on the Origins and Spread of Nationalism*. Anderson argued that nations were not primarily bounded territories but 'imagined communities', created in the mind and heart through the mediation of a number of institutions and processes including schools, public monuments and historical sites, and patriotic ceremonies. It is evident from the case studies in this book that the process of imagining and reimagining communities continues but is not necessarily limited to the context of nation states. China, it appears, is very focused on incorporating the people of Hong Kong and Macau (SARs), as well as their numerous ethnic minorities, into one national imagined community. The EU, on the other hand, is focused on imagining a 'post-national' community of communities.[1] While the EU moves to a supranational understanding of citizenship, some in the UK imagine devolution of the federal nation state into smaller, more traditional entities. Consistent with Anderson's original analysis, this reimagining is being fostered through formal schooling, other public institutions such as museums, galleries and historic sites, and cultural ceremonies and traditions.

It can be seen from the chapters in this book that ideas of the nation and citizenship are contested and fluid, both within and between the models of education for citizenship described in each case study. It is also clear that there are common themes or elements related to globalization driving the evolution of policy and practice. Increasing cultural diversity and the increasing complexity of that diversity,

5

for example, is a key theme in all of the chapters. Kymlicka (2003) identifies three kinds of minorities that impact ideas of citizenship and nation in modern states: national minorities, immigrant minorities and Indigenous Peoples. The case studies contain examples of all three but also some that do not fit neatly into these categories. Afro-Brazilians and African Americans, for example, are not indigenous, can hardly be described as immigrants (at least for the most part) and lack the territorial and institutional heritage within their respective states to be seen as national minorities. Similarly, the people of Macau and Hong Kong are largely Han and therefore part of the ethnic majority of China and yet their particular histories and local identification raise issues for how they fit in with majority (or state) conceptions of citizenship and the nation. They are, in a real sense, minorities within the state.

Thus, in this chapter, in an effort to provide structure and context for the case studies that follow we explore themes that cut across all of these case studies. The themes we explore below include the influence of historical and political contexts on educating for and about the nation, teaching for the nation in diverse contexts, and tensions between patriotism/social cohesion and critical citizenship. In this book, we examine how these themes are manifest in particular jurisdictions and in so doing, we point to some key questions that continue to shape debates about what it means to teach for the nation in an increasingly globalized world.

Context matters

A central lesson from these case studies is that historical and social contexts matter in shaping both ideas about the nation and citizenship and the specific policies and practices that flow from those ideas. Several years ago, Sears et al. (2011) argued that citizenship education curricula around the world have taken on a 'generic' (p. 198) character. That is, rather than pay attention to particular social and political contexts including complex and messy ideas like identity, they tended to focus on generic processes of political and social engagement such as understanding how government works and developing skills related to active participation in society. Sears et al. (2011) go on to argue that these generic approaches are inadequate because while democratic citizenship does share generic features across jurisdictions, it is practised in particular times and contexts and one cannot be an effective citizen without understanding those. The case studies in this book illustrate this.

Virtually all of the jurisdictions, for example, have been shaped by their experience of colonialism but its effects are very different across contexts. *The question of whether or not colonized people, as inhabitants of colonized spaces, will ever be allowed to rise above their colonizers is a pressing question that many nations face.* Britain was the most powerful colonial power of the 19th and 20th centuries, and its more contemporary citizenship laws and policies have been significantly influenced by the results of decolonization and the desire of some British subjects from abroad to take up residence in the UK. Meanwhile curricula across the UK largely ignore colonialism and its effects. As the case study chapter points out, 'colonialism and decolonisation occupy only a very marginal place in the English curriculum'. England is not alone in this as a number of European powers push colonialism to the margins of the curriculum and even then they portray it in quite positive terms. It is interesting that Japan receives significant international criticism for what many see as the sanitizing of its part in World War II in school curricula, but most of Europe seems to do exactly the same thing with regard to colonialism (Yoshida, 2007). Like the UK, many European states have experienced significant immigration from former colonies and have struggled with issues related to integration and the fostering of engaged citizenship among these communities.

China's experience has been much different. The perceived humiliations of colonization have pushed it towards a much more aggressive and nationalistic orientation to citizenship. A key purpose for citizenship education is to re-establish national dignity and to promote international recognition of China as a significant actor in the world. One of the central ways of doing this was through developing elite sports programmes that put Chinese athletes at the top of the world in their respective fields. In addition, the complexities of incorporating the people of Macau and Hong Kong into the Chinese polity are a direct result of prolonged colonial control of those territories. The Macau and Hong Kong SAR governments have introduced nationalistic education to promote identification as a Chinese national citizen among students, though with different degrees of success between them.

This could be regarded as a form of re-engineering from local to national identification of minorities within a Chinese state.

Colonialism manifests itself differently again in the new world states of Australia, Brazil, Canada and the US. In these jurisdictions, inheritors of colonial power and the colonized (including both the descendants of slaves – slavery being a vestige of colonialism – and Indigenous Peoples) have been left to build nations together but that process has often been thwarted by continuing power differentials and the legacy of oppression. In all of these places, constitutional and legal frameworks promoting equality, equity and inclusion have been put in place, but practice on the ground often falls far short of those mandates.

Another important contextual factor shaping how the nation is taught is the impact of critical incidents. We write this in the shadow of the terrorist attacks that rocked Paris, France in January 2015. While it is far too early to predict the impact of those on French conceptions of the nation and teaching for and about citizenship, we do know that events like these have had significant effects on policy and practice in citizenship education in other jurisdictions. Indeed, some early responses from certain media organizations to the *Charlie Hebdo* attacks in Paris carry a 'if you're not with us, you're with the terrorists' tone, a message that immediately places some groups (mostly Muslim) on the 'wrong' side of the equation *and* the nation – a move that is full of assumptions and stereotypes and grounded in fear mongering and a nationalist agenda.

The bus and underground train bombings in London in 2005 precipitated significant national discussion about how British citizens could perpetrate such acts on their own people. National inquiries were struck examining the question of teaching 'Britishness' in schools, and reforms were made to the national curriculum with citizenship education paying more attention to both Britishness and diversity (Ajegbo et al., 2007; Goldsmith QC, 2008; Heath & Roberts, 2008; Kiwan, 2008).

Similarly, in the Netherlands, a series of events including the murder of a prominent film-maker, threats against politicians and the rise of right wing, anti-immigrant political parties precipitated 'a national debate about Dutch identity' (Doppen, 2010, p. 132). This resulted in a rethinking of the traditional policy of '*verzuiling* (pillarization) or the development of 'parallel societies known as *zuilen* (pillars)' (p. 133). As part of this policy, ethnic and religious communities were provided with state funds but largely left alone to run their own schools. Part of the rethinking has been work on developing 'a canon' (p. 139) of common events and understandings from Dutch history that should be taught to all students as part of an effort to foster social cohesion.

In a 2009 analyses of US history textbooks' and supplemental materials' portrayal of the 11 September 2001 World Trade Center attack, Hess (2009) found that the materials presented a range of political perspectives, from those that sought to commemorate and re-inscribe into young people's consciousness the nation's civic values to those that asked students to deliberate about the options the US should take in response to the attack. Overall, however, Hess determined that 'none of the curricula in our sample advocated civic responses that were even remotely linked to a thoroughgoing critique of either U. S. history relative to terrorism or the current structures of governance in the United States' (p. 146).

Critical incidents do not always involve real or perceived acts of terrorism but can include the release of a well-timed report. In the late 1970s and early 1980s, the US was reeling from an economic downturn and several humiliating rebuffs on the international stage (the Soviet invasion of Afghanistan and the US Embassy take over in Iran being two examples). The report from the US Commissioner of Education, *A Nation at Risk*, was released in this context and had enormous and enduring impact on the direction of educational policy and practice, particularly at the federal level. It laid the groundwork for a neo-liberal turn in American education that, among other things, severely constricted curricular focus to literacy, numeracy, science and technology. Subjects more traditionally related to citizenship such as social studies and history were pushed to the margins or twisted to serve very narrow economic ends.

Space prohibits a detailed examination of critical turning points in all jurisdictions profiled here, but the overall lesson is that particular historical and social contexts have significant impact in shaping policy and practice related to citizenship and citizenship education. In order to operate effectively, policy makers, teachers and individual citizens need to understand the civic contexts in which they live and work.

Teaching for the nation in diverse contexts

Across all of the case studies collected in this volume, a central theme coalesces around the question, *How do we teach for the nation when what it means to be [American, Brazilian, Chinese, etc.] is constantly in flux?* Even in jurisdictions where one idea of what it means to be a citizen of that jurisdiction dominates government discourse and policy development (e.g. China, the US), the reality of the ethnocultural diversity in each jurisdiction, which both indirectly and directly influences ideas of who is an insider and outsider to the nation (Bannerji, 2000), cannot be ignored, at least not in practice (even if it is ignored in policy).

Globalization, in addition to opening up markets and the exchange of ideas, has also accelerated the movement of people across the globe. The nations examined in this book have always had diverse populations; so, in many ways, the question of teaching for the nation in diverse contexts is a very old one. In almost every jurisdiction explored in this volume, early models of citizenship education focused on forming citizens of a certain type, and by this we mean citizens who learned how to become more like the dominant (usually White) group (Bhabha, 2001). However, this approach to citizenship education has become more tenuous due to increasing migration, but also due to internal rights movements that witnessed minority groups striving for more – and equal – recognition by the society in which they live. In some jurisdictions, the struggle for recognition of minority rights and equal citizenship has made more progress than in others; yet even in well-established democracies, rights and justice continue to be under threat. It is not hard to think of examples: in the US, numerous states passed 'voter identification' laws that purportedly were meant to target voter fraud, but instead had the real effect of systematically restricting African American and Latino suffrage (Childress, 2014). Similarly, in Canada, debates about religious freedom dominate political discourse and radio airwaves as politicians argue over what 'Canadian values' are, particularly as they relate to expressions of religious (and mostly Muslim) identity (Wherry, 2015).

That debates such as these continue to be pressing matters speaks to the increasing complexity of the diversity in each nation. Although ethnocultural diversity (not to mention gender, sexual and other forms of diversity) has always been present in one form or another in nations across the world, globalization has increased (the ease of) mobility in ways not seen before. With this increased movement of peoples across national boundaries from disparate parts of the globe, so too has the complexity of diversity in each nation increased. Add to this changing ideas about identity – that it is not static but rather fluid, plural (or potentially plural), layered and influenced by intra- and inter-group boundary negotiation as well as the context of one's circumstance (Hall, 2003; Jenkins, 1996) – it is no wonder that nations continue to wrestle with what it means to teach for and about citizenship within and across borders.

Contestations around issues of identity and belonging in the public domain have real impact on discussions focused on teaching the nation. In the US, for example, xenophobic attitudes towards immigrants, especially non-White immigrants, led the state of Arizona to ban a course on ethnic studies from school curricula (Gersema, 2012). In Texas, politicians passed legislation that mandated revisions to history textbooks with the end result being a diminished emphasis on the nation's slavery history and an increased emphasis on Christianity (Need to Know Editor, 2010). In Canada, the federal government cut funding to The Historical Thinking Project, a pan-Canadian initiative to reform history education in Canada, because it wanted to focus its energies and resources on celebrations and commemoration, not critical historical thinking (Peace, 2014).

Tension between patriotism/social cohesion and critical citizenship

In a 2014 keynote address to a conference sponsored by the Association for Canadian Studies, Peter Seixas (2014) set out the distinction between what he called '*celebratory heritage* and *critical history*' (p. 14, emphasis in the original). The former sets out to foster national unity and patriotism while the latter sets out to build critical understanding. Seixas argued that these orientations to education continually contest for space within the Canadian history curriculum. The Canadian case study chapter takes this up by pointing out that both 'the nation as unifying icon' and 'the nation as the site for engagement' have been dominant themes in Canadian curricular history. The other cases in this book make it clear this tension exists across jurisdictional contexts. The Australian case study, for example, with its substantial discussion of the curriculum wars around so-called 'black armband' and 'three cheers' history is a perfect example, as is the account of the battle around national history standards in the US.

Indeed, all of the jurisdictions profiled here are attempting to forge a sense of national citizenship amongst populations of disparate peoples. *How do nations deal with contested stories about the past?* Attempts to answer this question are summed up well by the American motto 'e pluribus unum': out of the many, one. In their study of 12 jurisdictions around the world, Reid et al. (2010) found the issue of fostering cohesion in diverse societies to be central. They concluded that most places fell somewhere along the continuum between jingoistic patriotism and diverse, critical citizenship, but they concluded that the focus of most was on fostering a common sense of national identity. They wrote that in virtually every one of the nations profiled, 'diversity is seen as a problem or issue to be managed in the service of the nation state. Nowhere is the potential for cosmopolitan or global citizenship explored in any depth' (p. 8).

The case studies here show a more complex picture. In virtually all jurisdictions, the tension exists, including Chinese attempts to implement a mandatory national and moral curriculum that proved too narrow for many residents of Hong Kong, who took to the streets in protest, and tensions in Europe between those promoting the post-national nature of the EU and political movements focused on returning to a more narrow nationalism. There are, however, examples of attempts to promote more complex and cosmopolitan conceptions of citizenship, including attempts in Brazil to find ways to move beyond past policies and practices that socially and politically marginalized indigenous and Afro-Brazilian populations, as well as attempts to find ways to implement the constitutional imperative to protect and promote 'indigenous and Afro-Brazilian culture'. In Australia and Canada, efforts have been, and are being, made to recognize the special relationship between indigenous and settler societies. In the case studies profiled in this volume, we note a shift, at least in some jurisdictions, that education for the nation involves moving from one storey to multiple stories of citizenship and belonging – if not officially, then at least in the vernacular.

Conclusion

The shift to more generic models of citizenship, noted above, stands in conflict with the changing nature of diversity with which all nations in this volume wrestle. By focusing on political processes and qualities of a 'good citizen', a generic citizenship education laid on top of an increasingly complex and diverse citizenry will be ill-fitting at best. *How can citizenship education be generic when people aren't?* As the case studies in this volume illustrate, education for citizenship in a globalized world needs to be as dynamic and flexible as the citizens it hopes to reach.

Case Studies

3
Australia

Andrew Peterson

Introduction

To ask what it means to educate for and about the nation in Australia raises immediate tensions concerning how the 'nation' is defined and understood. Approached from one perspective, Australia is a post-colonial nation established in 1901, one which therefore is historically speaking relatively new, and which because of its colonial past remains inextricably connected to the UK (e.g. the reigning monarch remains Australia's Head of State). The Commonwealth of Australia was established as a constitutional monarchy in 1901 following the federation of the six colonies – New South Wales, South Australia, Tasmania, Victoria, Western Australia and Queensland. The context in which Australia became a nation is important to understanding its sense of national identity:

> Australia grew as part of the British Empire. Unlike the USA, India or Britain's other far-flung possessions. Australia never managed a decent independence movement, let alone a liberation struggle. Australia was made a nation by an Act of the British Parliament in 1901. The creation of a nation in a struggle for independence is usually the pre-eminent moment for the definition of national character, language, culture and myths. Australia has missed out on this. (Castles et al., 1990, p. 9)

From this perspective, the birth of Australia as a nation was intimately bound with its colonial roots, meaning that nationhood and educating for the nation relate inherently to Australia's relationship with the UK.

Approached from another perspective, however, the land that is now known as Australia has been continuously inhabited by Indigenous Peoples (Aboriginal and Torres Strait Islanders) for at least 40,000–50,000 years. Prior to the arrival of the First Fleet of British ships which landed and founded the first penal colony at Botany Bay, Aboriginal Australians comprised approximately 500 nations, or clan groups, speaking more than 250 languages. At different times since the European settlement (or invasion depending on one's perspective), official policies towards Indigenous Australians have ranged from forced assimilation to integration and, more recently, to recognition and reconciliation. Developing a sense of Australian national identity which is inclusive of Indigenous Australians remains both a contested and pressing concern for politicians, public commentators and educationalists.

The complex external and internal relationships sketched briefly thus far prompt essential questions concerning what it means to educate about and for the nation in Australia, including the role of education in shaping and building identification with the nation. The purpose of this chapter is to explore these questions and to seek to explain and consider how complex questions of nationhood have directly influenced (and continue to influence) educational policies, curricula and initiatives within Australian schools. In doing so it is suggested that schools and teachers have had to grapple with significant questions about how they organize learning in their schools and classrooms. These have involved, for example, the connection between historical fact/narrative and multiple interpretations, as well as the possibility and desirability of teaching common, shared values in an increasingly diverse society.

Following this introduction, the chapter is formed of four sections. The first section establishes the *social*, *political* and *cultural context* by exploring two factors fundamental to understanding the nation in Australia: (1) relationship with the UK and (2) recognition of, and reconciliation with, Indigenous Australians. An understanding of these factors is central to comprehending the challenges faced by schools and teachers with regard to educating for the nation (though it should be noted that other factors, such as the impact of Asian migrant communities and Australia's economic relationship with Asia, are becoming increasingly important, and therefore are explored in brief in the conclusion). The section also explores the way in which educating for the nation has been central to the 'history wars' in Australia.

The second section presents the *historical background of educating for and about the nation* in Australia and analyses the ways that education became a key battleground for the history wars. The third section explores *education about and for the nation today*, focusing on the recently introduced national Australian Curriculum as well as the extent to which this too has been subject to the history wars. The fourth and concluding section identifies some possible trajectories concerning the *future of educating for and about the nation* in Australia.

Any attempt to provide a true depiction of the contested nature of Australian national identity, particularly in the scope of a single chapter, will by necessity have limitations. The choice to focus on specific aspects of Australian identity – most clearly the changing relationship between Australia and the UK and the need for recognition and reconciliation of Indigenous Australians – is made on the basis of what have been, and continue to be, some of the key issues facing those interested in educating for the nation in Australia.

Social, political and cultural context

As suggested above, if we are to understand educating for the nation in Australia today, we need to have a particular appreciation of two factors: the relationship with the UK and the recognition of, and reconciliation with, Indigenous Australians. This section illustrates the complexities and tensions associated with each of the factors in turn, focusing in particular on how they have been the subject of, and indeed been subjected to, political rhetoric within Australia. How Australians understand their nationality has been at the heart of what have been termed 'the history wars', which while originating in the wider social, political and cultural context have crossed over to shape educational debates and policies.

Australia's relationship with the UK

Over the last 30 years, a number of leading Australian politicians and policymakers have emphasized the need for young Australians to learn about the importance of Western civilization in shaping

Australia as a nation (see, e.g., Blainey, 1993; Donnelly, 2005; Howard, 1996, 2006). Central to this view has been the perception that Australia's national identity – its values, its culture, its history – cannot be understood without due recognition to its colonial relationship with the UK. For others, Australian national identity can only make sense through a breaking of colonial ties and through a forging of a sense of national identity independent of the UK which gives recognition to Indigenous Australians (see, e.g. Keating, 1992; Macintyre and Clark, 2004).

The complexity concerning Australia's relationship with the UK lies to a large extent in the political influences and connections between the two nations, which have continued since the establishment of the Commonwealth of Australia in 1901. The Australian political system which developed following Federation was one in which individual states retained their bicameral parliaments – whilst a new bicameral parliament, a High Court and the post of Governor General (the UK monarch's representative) were established at the federal level. Though there was a republican movement in Australia at this time, the establishment of the Commonwealth in 1901 did not lead to an increase in fervour to cut ties to the UK. Indeed, according to a number of observers, the engagement of Australia in World War I, and subsequently in World War II, served *both* to develop a new sense of Australian identity, such as mateship and the Anzac spirit, as well as further cementing the affiliation of many Australians to the UK (Alomes, 1988; Alomes and Jones, 1991; Knightley, 2000; McLachlan, 1989). For the journalist Paul Kelly (2011, p. 69), 'Australian nationalism originated in the belief in nation and in Empire'.

In the latter half of the 20th century, and into the 21st century, although significant vestiges of the intimate political relationship between Australia and the UK remained, there was a significant movement towards the forging of a new Australian national identity (to which I return below). Throughout the 1960s and 1970s, Australian politicians set about defining a clearer sense of their own national identity and place in the world, one which while not altogether forgetting their colonial roots did seek to break many of the strong connections with the UK (e.g. in 1974, "God Save the Queen" was replaced as the Australian national anthem). The following examples serve to illustrate the nature of this changing relationship, as well as some of the tensions to which it gave rise:

1. The pursuance of the 'White Australia' policy from Federation until the 1970s through which applicants from certain countries were given priority (DIBP, 2012). Speaking in 1941, Prime Minister John Curtin reinforced Australia's commitment to the policy acclaiming that Australia would 'remain forever the home of the descendants of those people who came here in peace in order to establish in the South Seas an outpost of the British empire' (DIBP, 2012). The post-war period witnessed its retraction and the opening up of immigration, particularly to migrants from Asia.
2. The Australian constitutional crisis in 1975 which highlighted the residual role of the UK monarch in the political system. The crisis, which saw the removal of the Gough Whitlam government from power, arose when the Liberal Opposition used their Senate majority to block bills financing the operations of the Labor government. With the Opposition pushing Whitlam to call an election for the House of Representatives, Whitlam instead visited the Governor General (the Queen's representative) Sir John Kerr to seek an election for half of the Senate. Kerr dismissed Whitlam, making the Opposition leader, Malcolm Fraser, prime minister while instigating a double dissolution of Parliament.
3. The 1999 referendum held to decide whether to amend the Australian Constitution, including for Australia to become a republic, thereby removing the British monarch as the Head of State. The public rejected the proposed republic (many republican supporters were not prepared to support a model that did not include a directly elected Head of State) with none of the six states returning a majority in favour of a republic.

This brief illustration highlights the complex and contested nature of the relationship between Australia and the UK. I return to these in specific relation to educating for the nation in the next section.

Reconciliation and recognition of Indigenous Peoples

The need for recognition of, and reconciliation with, Indigenous Peoples – Aboriginals and Torres Strait Islanders – remains the most central and compelling issue facing Australia today. How Australia views its relationship with its Indigenous Peoples (in both a historical and a contemporary sense) impacts significantly on its sense of national identity and what form educating for the nation should take.

Recognition and reconciliation are, of course, highly sensitive, but as the Governor General Sir William Deane (1996, p. 19) reflected:

> It should, I think, be apparent to all well-meaning people that true reconciliation between the Australian nation and its indigenous peoples is not achievable in the absence of acknowledgement by the nation of the wrongfulness of the past dispossession, oppression and degradation of the Aboriginal peoples. That is not to say that individual Australians who had no part in what was done in the past should feel or acknowledge personal guilt. It is simply to assert that our identity as a nation and the basic fact that national shame, as well as national pride, can or should exist in relation to past acts and omissions, at least when done or made in the name of the community or with the authority of government.

There is not enough space or scope in this chapter to do full justice to the experiences of Indigenous Australians in the period between British settlement and the present day. Other histories of this period exist (see, e.g., Broome, 2010; Muecke and Shoemaker, 2004). Instead, the intention here is to give a sense of these experiences, as well as the issues to which they give rise, in order to provide a basis for the analysis in the next section which focuses more specifically on educating for the nation.

Before 1967, the Australian constitution included a number of clauses that restricted recognition of Indigenous Australians and placed significant limitations on their citizenship. For example, the Constitution provided:

> 51. The Parliament shall, subject to this Constitution, have power to make laws for the peace, order, and good government of the Commonwealth with respect to: . . . (xxvi) The people of any race, *other than the aboriginal people in any State*, for whom it is necessary to make special laws.

> 127. In reckoning the numbers of the people of the Commonwealth, or of a State or other part of the Commonwealth, *aboriginal natives should not be counted*. (National Archives of Australia; emphasis added)

Provisions such as these meant that Indigenous Australians did not experience full citizenship. They were subject to the laws of individual states, but not those at the federal level, meaning that Indigenous Australians did not enjoy full voting rights, were not included in census data and were not able to access a variety of federal welfare programmes. Indeed, in order to enjoy greater citizenship rights, Indigenous Australians were required to obtain a Certificate of Exemption from state governments as part of an assimilation policy. On being granted a Certificate of Exemption (termed 'dog tags' by many Indigenous Peoples), Indigenous Australians were able to vote and access education and other welfare services in return for renouncing their heritage. This required them to give up their culture and to avoid contact with Indigenous Australians other than their immediate family in order to assimilate. Speaking about her Certificate, Mary Terszak, a Nyoongah woman from south-west Western Australia who was a member of the Stolen Generations (see below), has explained:

> I was two years as an Aboriginal child and then all taken away. I now . . . stand here not as the person that I was born to be – I am changed, programmed into . . . white society . . . And I used to joke and say to the other girls 'I'm white cause I've got proof', you know. (National Museum Australia, n.d.)

In the 1967 Referendum, 90.77% voted in favour of the words 'other than aboriginal people in any State' and the whole of section 127 being removed from the Australian Constitution. Political leaders at the time were aware that the outcome of the referendum would have significant repercussions for how Australia – as a nation – was viewed. In campaigning for a Yes vote, the then leader of the Opposition Gough Whitlam claimed that if Australians failed to vote in favour, 'the rest of the world will believe that we have neither comprehension nor compassion' (cited in Hocking, 2008, p. 298).

Australia's sense of national identity is also impacted on by the Stolen Generations. The Stolen Generations refer to Aboriginal and Torres Strait Islander people who as children were forcibly removed under duress from their families and communities and placed into either institutional care or adoption with non-Indigenous families between the late 1800s and 1970s. Enforced by Australian governments (federal and state/territory), children were removed (or stolen) on the pretence that they were 'at risk' within Indigenous communities. Underpinning the rhetoric of risk was an expressed commitment to assimilation, though later the term 'integration' was preferred (van Krieken, 1991). In the early 1950s, the Federal Minister for Territories, Paul Hasluck (1953, p. 16, see National Inquiry into the Separation of Aboriginal and Torres Strait Islander Children from Their Families, 1997), claimed that 'assimilation means, in practical terms, that, in the course of time, it is expected that all persons of aboriginal blood or mixed blood in Australia will live like other white Australians do'.

Drawing on extensive testimony evidence, the 1997 Report of the National Inquiry into the Separation of Aboriginal and Torres Strait Islander Children from their Families – *Bringing Them Home* – established a platform for greater recognition of the Stolen Generations and the need for reconciliation. While some have questioned its quality as a work of history (see, e.g., Pearson, 2008), the report reinforced the pressing question of whether the Australian government should apologize for Stolen Generations. Throughout his term in office, John Howard refused to apologize for the Stolen Generations. In 2008, Prime Minister Kevin Rudd led an apology on behalf of the Australian government and Parliament. In the apology, Rudd (2008) referred to the Stolen Generations as a 'blemished chapter in our nation's history'. Prefacing the apology to Indigenous Australians, Rudd made clear that the time had 'come for the nation to turn a new page in Australia's history by righting the wrongs of the past and so moving forward with confidence to the future'. Rudd concluded the apology by suggesting that Australians could now lay claim to a 'future where all Australians, whatever their origins, are truly equal partners, with equal opportunities and with an equal stake in shaping the next chapter in the history of this great country, Australia'. The national apology had significant 'symbolic value' but also had 'practical effect' in providing a point of reference and influencing subsequent government policies and programmes (Gooda, 2011, p. 6).

The extent to which the Australian nation can be said to have turned a new page, and indeed can lay claim to a new future, remains questionable. Aboriginal lawyer and founder of the Cape York Institute for Policy and Leadership Noel Pearson (2008), for example, made clear his 'worry' that the apology would 'sanction a view of history which cements a detrimental psychology of victim-hood – rather than a stronger psychology of defiance, survival and agency'. Pearson also questioned the extent to which the apology was valid in the absence of compensation. Many more issues remain that bring into question the extent to which Australia has truly recognized Aboriginal and Torres Strait Islanders. Despite the rhetoric of commitment and the passing of the Aboriginal and Torres Strait Islander Peoples Recognition Act in 2013, a referendum to recognize Aboriginal and Torres Strait Islanders within the Constitution has not taken place and at the time of writing does not seem likely in the lifetime of this Parliament (the Act has a two-year sunset clause). In addition, Australia remains the only former British colony not to have a treaty with its Indigenous Peoples (Auguste, 2010). For many, a treaty – or treaties – between the Australian government and Indigenous peoples will help to secure sovereignty and self-determination. Chair of current Prime Minister Tony Abbott's Indigenous Advisory Council, Warren Mundine (2014) has called for treaties between the government and each of the nations or language groups that still exist and existed prior to European settlement on the basis that they would create 'rights for Aboriginal people that have been denied to us in the past and those rights would include recognition of customary law, the right to land, the right to make decisions over Aboriginal people and the right to raise our own economy'.

The History Wars

The factors considered in this section so far evidence the high profile of contested notions of national identity in Australia since Federation. Over the last three decades, these debates have been primarily played out through the discourse of the Australian 'history wars' (Macintyre and Clark, 2004). The history wars themselves have been shaped in turn by competing discourses concerning the 'black armband view of history'.

First used by leading historian Geoffrey Blainey (1993), the 'black armband' view of history posits that too much emphasis is placed on the more shameful aspects of Australia's past – predominantly the experiences and treatment of Indigenous Australians – thereby underplaying the more positive aspects of colonization. The term 'black armband' itself derives from the wearing of black dress and black armbands by Indigenous Australians during key commemorative events (such as the bicentenary of James Cook's landing in 1970 and the bicentennial celebrations of the landing of the First Fleet in 1988) (McKenna, 1997). Critiques of the black armband view took issue with the work of the historians such as Manning Clark (1988), who had spoken of the need to take the 'blinkers off our eyes' and to recognize the 'great evils' that the 'coming of the British' had brought to Australia, particularly in regard to its Indigenous population (cited in McKenna, 1997; see also Macintyre and Clark, 2004; Taylor and Collins, 2012). For example, Blainey (1993, p. 10) argued that:

> To some extent my generation was reared on the Three Cheers view of history. This patriotic view of our past had a long run. It saw Australian history as largely a success. While the convict era was a source of shame or unease, nearly everything that came after was believed to be pretty good. There is a rival view, which I call the Black Armband view of history. In recent years it has assailed the optimistic view of history. The black armbands were quietly worn in official circles in 1988. The multicultural folk busily preached their message that until they arrived much of Australian history was a disgrace. The past treatment of Aborigines, of Chinese, of Kanakas, of non-British migrants, of women, the very old, the very young, and the poor was singled out, sometimes legitimately, sometimes not . . . The Black Armband view of history might well represent the swing of the pendulum from a position that had been too favourable, too self congratulatory, to an opposite extreme that is even more unreal and decidedly jaundiced.

Similar views were expressed by the academic Keith Windschuttle (1996) who in his book *The Killing of History* took issue with those who rejected the concepts of historical truth and objectivity and who sought instead to construct history around multiple perspectives.

The view that many within Australia were too quick to focus on the more regrettable aspects of its past found expression within the political rhetoric of the Liberal-National leader Howard both prior to and after his election as prime minister in 1996. During his time as prime minister between 1996 and 2007, Howard consistently argued for a rebalancing of Australian national identity (Curthoys, 2007). For Howard, while Indigenous perspectives and histories were important, so too were Australia's ties to the UK, to Western civilization and to Judeo-Christian values.

To understand Howard's approach to Australian national identity, we need to locate it against the view of national identity and history expressed by his immediate predecessors, Labor prime ministers Bob

Hawke (1983–1991) and Paul Keating (1991–1996). During his premiership, Hawke sought to refocus Australia as an outward-looking nation with meaningful political and economic connections beyond the UK, in particular with both the US and Asia. In the face of criticism (including from Blainey) that increasing number of Asian migrants into Australia would be destructive of national identity, Hawke contended that multiple identities were possible alongside, and were not detrimental to, a common understanding of being Australian (Curran, 2004). Under Hawke, there was also a strong commitment to reconcile with Indigenous Australians, particularly regarding land rights, though, despite his promise, Hawke did not deliver a treaty between Australia and its Indigenous Peoples (Alomes, 1988; Korff, 2014). This commitment was taken up by Keating during his period in office. In his highly significant Redfern Park speech, Keating (1992, pp. 227–228) went further than any previous prime minister in publically acknowledging that the situation faced by Indigenous Australians was a direct result of the actions of the European Settlers:

> We took the traditional lands and smashed the traditional way of life. We committed the murders. We took the children from their mothers. We practiced discrimination and exclusion. It was our ignorance and our prejudice. And our failure to imagine these things being done to us.

In 1992, a similar acknowledgement of Australia's shameful past had formed part of a High Court ruling (*Mabo v Queensland, No. 2*) that gave recognition to Indigenous ownership of lands and overturned the understanding that pre-1788 Australia had been *terra nullius* (Curran, 2004). In one of the judgements made by the High Court in reaching this verdict, Justices Deane and Gaudron denoted 'a national legacy of unutterable shame' (cited in McKenna, 1997). Speaking about the 1993 Native Title Act, which recognized and protected Indigenous land, Keating argued that to deny what had happened to Aboriginal Australians was to 'deny a part of ourselves as Australians' (cited in Knightley, 2000, p. 315).

Keating saw that the forging of a new national identity in Australia could only meaningfully occur if there were lasting reconciliation with Indigenous Australians (Curran, 2004; Kelly, 2011). For Keating, Australia needed to forge a new sense of national identity that reconciled with and included Indigenous Australians, and which also transcended its colonial past. This form of 'aggressive Australianism' was both radical and controversial for the extent to which it openly eschewed and dismissed the need for continued ties to the UK (Curran, 2004, p. 255). Keating expressed this in the following terms:

> I want us to leave home. Of course, we do not remain there in any substantial material way – but we are there emblematically and to a degree psychologically, and it would be better for us . . . if we removed the emblems and exercised the doubts. We need very badly that spirit of independence and faith in ourselves which will enable us to shape a role for ourselves in the region and the world. (cited in Curran, 2004, pp. 280–281)

As Keating has subsequently reflected, it was him who 'pressed the starter's pistol on the history ways, no doubt about that' (cited in Kelly, 2011, p. 63).

As suggested previously, during his term in office, Howard sought a rebalancing of Australian identity, one which recognized Indigenous Australians while also celebrating Australia's relationship with the UK (it is worth pointing out that though it is not given attention here, Howard's conception of Australian identity also include a neo-liberal sense of self-reliant individualism [Johnson, 2007]). In his general policy manifesto – *Future Directions* – Howard (Liberal Party of Australia, 1988, pp. 92–93) stated his commitment to seeking a common sense of national identity as 'One Australia', including recognizing a shared sense of history. According to Howard, government policy under Hawke had led to a context in which Australian national identity had become obfuscated and in which 'confidence in their nation's past' had been 'under attack' from 'professional purveyors of guilt'. For Howard, this resulted in Australians being 'taught to be ashamed of their past, apprehensive about their future, pessimistic about their ability to control their own lives let alone their ability to shape the character of the nation'.

Speaking in Parliament in 1996, Howard (1996) addressed the central issue of the history wars directly:

> I profoundly reject . . . the black armband view of Australian history. I believe the balance sheet of Australia history is a very generous

and benign one. I believe that, like any other nation, we have black marks upon our history but amongst nations of the world we have a remarkably positive history. I think there is a yearning in the Australian community right across the political divide for its leader to enunciate more pride and sense of achievement in what has gone before us. I think we have been too apologetic about our history in the past. I believe it is tremendously important, particularly as we approach the centenary of the Federation of Australia, that the Australian achievement had been a heroic one, a courageous one and a humanitarian one.

The form of Australian national identity that Howard wished to – and indeed did – promote was one that recognized and celebrated its colonial past, and which adopted a critical stance towards multiculturalism. For Howard, multiculturalism became problematic if it limited the possibility of a singular, common and shared understanding of Australian identity (Curran, 2004).

The history wars that shaped Australian political discourse about national identity in the 1990s and 2000s remind us that nationhood is a fluid and dynamic concept in the Australian context, shaped and refined through a range of contested political and social processes and relationships. The fluid nature of the nation is inherently connected to how Australia (and Australians) views itself in relation to its past and its future, particularly with regard to its colonial past and its recognition and reconciliation of Indigenous Peoples. The attention being paid to national identity translated into education, with the school curriculum being identified as a key battleground for the history wars.

Historical background – educating for the nation

The history wars have played, and continue to play, an important role in Australian education. On one level, the history wars have raised questions about content, processes and outcomes. For example, what forms of national identity should young Australians be taught? What direct and indirect pedagogies are useful for teaching national identity? What sort of citizens young Australians should become? These questions are pertinent at a number of levels – educational policymakers, curriculum writers, schools and teachers. They have led, however, to wider questions about the role of different jurisdictions in the education system. The history wars in Australia have directly informed the development of a national Australian Curriculum at a federal level as a replacement for curricula at the level of individual states and territories. The purpose of this section is to analyse the way in which the history wars have impacted on educating for the nation in Australia, particularly in relation to the teaching of history, values and civics and citizenship education.

A key aspect of Howard's rhetoric about national identity was to depict a crisis concerning the teaching of history in Australian schools and to challenge the way national identity was being constructed within classrooms. Howard's concern was twofold. First, that in most states (with the exception of New South Wales and Victoria), history was not a discrete curriculum subject, and second, that schools were teaching a particular, negative interpretation of Australia's past:

> I think we've had too much . . . we talk too negatively about our past. I sympathise fundamentally with Australians who are insulted when they are told that we have a racist bigoted past. And Australians are told that regularly. Our children are taught that. Some of the school curricula go close to teaching children that we have a racist bigoted past. Now of course we treated Aborigines very, very badly in the past . . . but to tell children who themselves have been no part of it, that we're all part of a racist bigoted history is something that Australians reject. (Howard, cited in McKenna, 1997)

Howard's response to this 'crisis' was to advocate a more objective, fact-based approach to the teaching of history, one that paid greater attention to the importance of Western civilization and shared Australian values. Speaking on a visit to Gallipoli in 2000, for example, Howard remarked that there had been 'perhaps too much of an emphasis on issues rather than exactly what happened' in history teaching in Australia (cited in Clark, 2008, p. 1).

Stemming from his critique of state curricula, Howard launched a 'root and branch renewal of the teaching of Australian history in our schools' during his Australia Day address in 2006 (Howard, 2006). At the Australian History Summit that followed, progress was started in producing an Australian-wide national curriculum for history.

Key recommendations from the summit included that history be sequentially planned for throughout primary and secondary education and that it be compulsory for all students in Years 9 and 10 (14- to 16-year-olds) (Bishop, 2006). An Australian History External Reference Group (including Geoffrey Blainey) was commissioned to produce a *Guide to the Teaching of Australian History in Years 9 and 10*. In the Guide's foreword, Howard (DEST, 2007, p. 3) set out the connection between history education, citizenship, values and national identity, arguing that 'teaching young Australians about our shared past plays an important role in preparing them to be informed and active citizens' and that 'it provides them with a better appreciation of their heritage and of the national community of which they are a part'. The Guide (DEST, 2007, p. 6) premised the importance of history education in relation to the nation:

> The history of Australia provides the single most important disciplinary perspective from which students can know, understand and evaluate the development of the nation in which they live. It helps them learn about Australia's democratic traditions, its institutions, its sense of national identity, the life and values of its citizens and its cultural diversity. These understandings should be informed by a sense of relevant local, regional, state, national and global contexts and influences, an awareness of the past and present experiences of distinct groups within Australian society, and the heritage and influence of Australia's Indigenous peoples. The story of Australia encompasses settlement and expansion, consolidation and enrichment, struggle and triumph, dependence and self-determination, and war and peacetime. An historical perspective allows students to appreciate Australian social, political, economic, religious and environmental values and how they have changed over time.

Though it did not have traction in terms of implementation (owing to Howard's defeat at the federal election in 2007), the Guide represented a significant outcome of the history wars and brought questions concerning interpretations of Australia's past squarely into educational discourse.

Howard's attempt to influence the teaching of Australian history sat alongside his commitment to reforming the teaching of

Australian values. This commitment was based on the perception that Australian public (government) schools were 'too politically correct and values-neutral' (Crabb and Guerrera, 2004) and manifested itself in the funding of a large-scale Values Education Program in Australian schools. A *Values for Australian Schooling* poster containing nine values was produced to be displayed in all public schools. Prefaced with the statements that 'these shared values . . . are part of Australia's common way of life, which includes equality, freedom and the rule of law' and that 'they reflect our commitment to a multicultural and environmentally sustainable society where all are entitled to justice', the nine values are: 'care and compassion', 'doing your best', 'fair go', 'freedom', 'honesty and trustworthiness', 'integrity', 'respect', 'responsibility' and 'understanding, tolerance and inclusion' (DEST, 2005, p. 4). According to Reid and Gill (2010, p. 7), the values education programme represented a 'form of coercive federalism where federal funding for schools was made conditional on the implementation of a number of federal initiatives, including the requirement that all schools must hang the values poster in the school foyer'. Similarly to the interventions in history teaching, the federal government was seeking to use education and schooling to promote a particular understanding of national identity that prioritized the significance of Western civilization and the democratic values of the UK.

Throughout the Howard period, civics and citizenship was not a discrete subject within the curricula of individual states. There had, though, been a good deal of political interest at the federal level in the teaching of civics and citizenship since the late 1980s, and it remained a stated aim of the curriculum more generally. A Senate Committee enquiry on *Education for Active Citizenship* (SSCEET, 1989) 'painted a bleak picture' of the low level of political knowledge and understanding among young Australians, and indeed Australians more generally (Hughes et al., 2010, p. 297). The Senate Committee (1989, p. 7) argued, for example, that it regarded 'the retreat into apathy and ignorance as opening the way for a victory of self-centredness over a sense of community responsibility', citing 'a remarkable level of ignorance in the Australian population about even quite elementary of politics and government' (p. 9). On this basis, the Senate Committee recommended that 'the Commonwealth initiate a national program in education for active citizenship, directed at the whole community' and that 'the Commonwealth designate education for active citizenship as a priority area for improvements in primary and secondary schooling', with the latter being to be strongly encouraged among 'State and non-governmental school authorities' (1989, p. 6).

It is notable that in its 1989 report and in a follow-up report in 1991, the Committee (1989) referred throughout to education for *active* citizenship, and had very little to say about national identity, focusing instead on the need for all Australians to possess knowledge of the democratic system and to be confident in participating within it in order to address the civic deficit. The *Civics Expert Group* that was established in light of the Senate enquiries by the then Labor government also made great play of a 'civic deficit' in their report *Whereas the People: Civics and Citizenship Education in Australia* (CEG, 1994). In one of their most pointed assertions, the CEG (1994, p. 18) suggested that there was 'widespread ignorance and misconception of Australia's system of government, about its origins and about the way in which it can serve the needs of citizens'. The perception of low levels of political understanding among young Australians was also supported by academic literature on education for citizenship around this time (Kennedy et al., 1993; Print, 1995a, 1995b). Again, education for *active* citizenship was identified as crucial in addressing this gap, with the CEG (1994, p. 6) explaining its intention that the objective of education for citizenship should be not only to 'enable Australians to discharge the formal obligations of citizenship, such as voting and compliance with the law', but 'more than this . . . should include those measures that would help Australians become active citizens'. Where the CEG did refer to national identity, this was in general and uncontentious form. Reference was made to 'basic liberal democratic values' and also to the 'rich diversity of Australian society' (CEG, 1994, p. 7). Mirroring the idea of forging a new sense of Australian identity promoted by Prime Minister Paul Keating, the report presented the balance between shared values and diversity as a challenge for Australia's future, also making clear that 'it is no longer possible to assume the old values that once bound Australians together as a community' (CEG, 1994, p. 7). The approach adopted by the CEG was one of critically examining Australia's sense of national identity and the issues involved, rather than promoting a particular, fixed interpretation of Australian identity.

The work of the CEG informed the development of units for teaching Civics and Citizenship in Australian schools. Funded at the federal level, the *Discovering Democracy* unit provided for the teaching of Civics and Citizenship but without its establishment as a curricular subject (the curriculum remained under the jurisdiction of the individual states/territories). While the *Discovering Democracy* units and their associated professional development for teachers perhaps moved beyond being 'minimal guidance', their impact was limited by their non-compulsory nature. According to research conducted a year after the *Discovering Democracy* materials were sent to schools, their use by teachers was 'haphazard at best', with the 'adoption and use' of these materials within schools being 'somewhat superficial' (Print, 2001, p. 141). The Evaluation Reports of the *Discovering Democracy* programme paint a similar picture, and point to the 'great variation . . . found both in the depth and breadth of implementation of the program' (ECG, 1999, p. 7).

The *Discovering Democracy* materials contained units on the nation, though these focused on students learning the factual basis of the development of the Australian nation with some exploration of critical issues facing Australia as a nation. While the units for secondary students did include some centrally contested questions (e.g. Should Australia become a republic? What kind of country do we want Australia to be?), these were presented mainly through the prism of students' own views rather than through critical engagement with the sorts of issues central to the history wars. Indeed, the materials were resoundingly criticized for their 'minimalist approach' and for their 'heavy reliance on an "historical knowledge" approach, at the expense of "active citizenship"' (Criddle et al. 2004, p. 36; see also, Gill and Reid, 1999; Robinson and Parkin, 1997). Hughes et al. (2010, p. 302) have argued that 'if recent measures of student outcomes are any guide to teacher inputs, then young Australians have learnt little from Discovering Democracy'.

The success of *Discovering Democracy* was prohibited by the lack of effective teacher professional development and pre-service teacher education. Research conducted nationally in Australia shortly before the *Discovering Democracy* materials were sent to schools indicated that even amongst teachers of Studies of Society and Environment (or its equivalent), 54% were completely unaware of the *Discovering Democracy* programme (Print, 2001). Data collected as part of the International

Association for the Evaluation of Educational Achievement (IEA) civic education teacher survey in the late 1990s indicate that while the teachers most likely to be involved in its teaching (those teaching Studies of Society and Environment and English) were committed to education for citizenship, 'only third . . . had had any training in discipline areas related to civics during their initial teacher training courses' (Mellor, 2003, p. 8).

For all of the debate and contention at policy and curricular level, little research exists about how young Australians actually experienced teaching and learning about national identity. In their study of how 11- to 12-year-olds understood being Australian, Howard and Gill (2005, p. 47) report that for this group the feeling was of being 'safe, free and proud', but that this was both 'partial and idealistic'. They also report that young people commonly spoke about being Australian in terms of 'symbols, lists or stereotypes' (Gill and Howard, 2009, p. 55). The young people saw Australia as a peaceful nation and as not being involved in war, seemingly unaware of its military engagement in Afghanistan. In a large, nationwide study of the teaching of History in Australian schools funded by the Australian Research Council in the mid-2000s, Clark (2008) found that while students saw some value in learning about key aspects of the nation's history – such as federation – they generally saw this as boring and repetitive. Perhaps of more concern:

> It's not just federation – topics such as Indigenous history or the goldrushes are just as likely to be taught and retaught without consistency. Many history classes learn patchy, repetitive versions of the past that chop and change between eras and events. There's no guarantee that students have any equivalent knowledge or historical understanding. (Clark, 2008, p. 141)

These findings, coupled with the research cited above, suggest that if any direct teaching about and for national identity was occurring in Australian schools, then this was piecemeal and sporadic, with little consistency.

In the last two decades of the 20th century, educating for the nation became a key concern within public discourse. History, values and education for citizenship were seen as key tools for teaching young Australians about their national identity. Moreover, the perception that educating for the nation was in some form of crisis, and needed refocusing and rebalancing was a key factor in the development of a federal national curriculum that has in turn influenced debates concerning what educating about and for the nation should mean in Australia today.

Educating about and for the nation today

A key argument of this chapter has been that to understand educating for and about the nation in Australia today requires an appreciation of wider debates concerning national identity. These debates continue to inform and shape current contestations around the content of the Australian Curriculum, meaning that teachers in Australian schools are working in the context of significant disagreement about the purpose and nature of educating for the nation. Reflecting the continuation of the history wars, contestation hinges on the relationships explicated in the previous sections of this chapter. Moreover, they require educators to examine what educating for and about the nation means in the context of the 21st century, particularly with regard to the balancing of singular, objective grand narratives of Australia's past and recognition of multiple, contested perspectives.

In 2009, the Australian Curriculum and Assessment Reporting Authority (ACARA) was established by the Labor government to plan for the new, and first ever, Australian national curriculum. The curriculum has been in development and implementation since this time. A number of core elements of the curriculum relate firmly to educating for and about the nation. Most clearly, and building on the focus placed on history education under Howard, is the place within the curriculum for History as discrete subject. One of the first phase of subjects to be developed and implemented (alongside English, Mathematics and Science), History education forms one of four subjects within the wider Humanities and Social Science learning area and is compulsory for years from Foundation (5 years of age) to Year 10 (16 years of age). Civics and Citizenship, developed in the third phase of subjects, also forms part of the Humanities and Social Sciences and is compulsory from Year 3 to Year 8. Sitting across the curriculum are three cross-curricular priorities and seven general capabilities. Of the former, Aboriginal and Torres Strait Islander histories and cultures and Asia and Australia's engagement with Asia, both relate to educating about and for the nation, as does the general capability Intercultural Understanding. Rather than detail the curricular content and focus of each of these in turn, the focus will be on the extent to which these subjects have become part of a renewed history wars.

The History curriculum was developed by an advisory group lead by a leading Australian historian, Stuart Macintyre. Macintyre had been a protagonist in the history wars having published a book – *The History Wars* – that had been critical of Howard's understanding and representation of Australian history and which advanced a more historically insightful understanding of Australia's past. The Shaping Paper (NCB, 2009, p. 5) that informed the development of the History curriculum adopts a critical perspective, making clear that students would be expected to 'develop a critical perspective on received versions of the past'. The Shaping Paper continues:

> We fail students – both those who have arrived recently and those with many earlier generations in this country – if we deny them a familiarity with the national story, so that they can appreciate its values and binding traditions. We fail them also if we do not foster the skills of historical understanding that equip them, by the end of their studies, to take an active part in the debates over the legacy of the past, to understand and make use of new sources of information, to distinguish the unimportant from the important, to find truth and meaning in history and contribute to democratic discussion of national issues. (NCB, 2009, p. 12)

During the process of its implementation in the early 2010s, the approach and content of the History curriculum once again became the focus of criticism. The executive director of the Institute of Public Affairs, John Roskam, for example, claimed that the curriculum ignored key elements of Western civilization, citing the absence of the English Civil War as evidence that 'Australia's cultural and political heritage is being evaporated' (Roskam, 2011, p. 34). Again the history wars were at play (Taylor and Collins, 2012).

Having been critical of its content while in opposition, the Liberal-led Coalition government announced a review of the curriculum shortly after winning the 2013 federal election. In launching the review, the Minister for Education, Christopher Pyne (2014), suggested that there was a lack of balance and objectivity to the current History curriculum:

> I . . . want the curriculum to celebrate Australia, and for students . . . to know where we've come from as a nation . . . There are two aspects to Australia's history that are paramount. The first, of course, is our Indigenous history, because for thousands of years Indigenous Australians have lived on this continent. The second aspect of our history is our beginnings as a colony and, therefore, our Western civilisation, which is why we are the kind of country we are today. It's very important the curriculum is balanced in its approach to that. It's very important the truth be told in our history. So, yes, the truth of the way we've treated Indigenous Australians should be told in our curriculum. But also the truth about the benefits of Western civilisation should be taught in our curriculum. And I think that there is some fair criticism that the curriculum is balanced one way rather than the other.

One of the two men placed in charge of the review, former teacher and head of the *Education Standards Institute* think tank, Kevin Donnelly, has been critical of the teaching of history in Australia. In 1997, Donnelly contended that as it was currently framed the teaching of history in schools 'belittles Australia's Anglo/Celtic [*sic*] history and traditions' and that it is 'wrong to simplify the situation by making today's students feel guilty about something over which they had no control' (cited in Clark, 2006, p. 14). In 2005, Donnelly (2005, p. 56) claimed that 'subjects like history and civics are rewritten to embrace a politically correct, black armband view' and that 'across Australian schools, in areas like multiculturalism, the environment and peace studies, students are indoctrinated and teachers define their role as new-age class warriors'.

At the timing of writing, the final report of the review has just been published, and again evidences the continuation of the history wars and the contested nature of educating for and about Australian national identity. The review is explicit in its view that the Australian Curriculum does not adequately provide for the socialization of students into an overarching narrative of Australian identity. It asserts, for example, that 'whereas the history associated with Western civilisation and Australia's development as a nation is often presented in a negative light, ignoring the positives, the opposite is the case when dealing with Indigenous history and culture', and on this basis recommends both that the curriculum should 'properly recognise the impact and significance of western civilisation and Australia's Judeo-Christian heritage, values and beliefs' and that it should 'better acknowledge the strengths and weaknesses and the positives and negatives of both Western and Indigenous cultures and histories' (Australian Government, 2014, p. 181). Explicit within these recommendations is that students, particularly at primary ages, should be taught historical knowledge rather than historiography. It is clear from the review that the relationships, discourses and contestations explored in this chapter are of continued importance in thinking through educating for and about the nation in Australia.

Conclusion: the future of educating for and about the nation

This chapter has explored meanings of educating about and for the nation in Australia over the last three decades. It has sought to demonstrate the centrality of two relationships that have shaped, and continue to shape, what it means to be an Australian – that between Australia and its colonial roots and that with Australia's Indigenous Peoples. These relationships are contested in terms not only of their respective importance to Australian identity but also in the ways in which they are interpreted within the history wars. Given the extent to which the history wars have dominated teaching for and about the nation in Australia, it seems likely that they will continue to impact on policy, curricula and the work of schools. Importantly, educational work in this area will connect to the question of whether recognition and reconciliation of Indigenous Australians within the Constitution and through an official treaty eventuates, though how this will take shape within the Australian Curriculum is currently unclear.

It is also worth pointing to one further relationship that, while not explored in detail here, has to some extent impacted on Australia's sense of national identity and looks set to do so increasingly over the next decade – the relationship with Asia. At least since Hawke, Australian prime ministers have sought to focus Australia as a key nation within the Asia-Pacific. Rudd (2012), for example, suggested that Australia should become the 'most Asia-literate country in the collective West'. The current prime minister, Tony Abbott (2013), has adopted a similar stance, suggesting that there was a prescient need for 'more Australians who can speak Asian languages, catch cultural meanings and navigate local networks', suggesting that this 'means starting with children at school'. The need to teach young people to be 'Asia-literate' has found increasing representation in education discourse, with 'Asia and Australia's engagement with Asia' forming a cross-curricular priority within the national Australian Curriculum. Multiple reasons are provided to support the need for young Australians to learn about Asia. In part, these are geographic, but largely they focus on the importance of the Asian economy (more than half of Australia's current trade is with the Asian region; Milner, 2011) and the idea that the 21st century will be the 'Asian century'. The question of how to develop Asia-literacy through individual subject disciplines and cross-curricular themes is one which will challenge policymakers, education scholars and teachers over the next decade. According to the Asia Education Foundation (2014, p. 2), 'five-year-olds who start school in Australia today enter their adult lives just at the time China and India become the world's top economies. Our students' future will be shaped by these global geopolitics and shifting patterns of global mobility, trade, technology and youth cultures'. This reminds us that at the heart of educating for Asia-literacy is, once again, the question of how Australia views itself as a nation, particularly as a nation within a globalized world.

4
Brazil

Maria Auxiliadora Schmidt

Introduction

The analysis of the relations between globalization, education and the Brazilian nation is very complex, and in this chapter, I approach these matters from a particular perspective. The issue will be analysed in terms of the challenge to achieve through education in Brazil a democratic, socially fair, multicultural and multiethnic nation. I discuss how Brazil, when constituting itself as a nation, has operated in the context of social inequality and ethnic diversity, how the country is trying to seize the opportunities and face the challenges associated with these things and which future possibilities exist.

In 2015, Brazil is a country with over 200 million inhabitants, with about 8.5% living in extreme poverty. Economically, the country is part of the group of major emerging national economies known as BRICS (Brazil, Russia, India, China and South Africa). Politically, it has been constituted since 1889, as a federal republic with 26 states and a federal district.

Since the end of the military dictatorship period, which lasted from 1964 to 1984, the country has been consolidating, with some successes and some difficulties, a project aimed at the achievement of becoming a democratic nation. Historically and currently, one of the challenges facing the Brazilian nation is seeing education as a means of struggling against poverty and social and cultural inequalities. The richest 10% of society receives about 75% of the national income, with 90% of the population accounting for the remaining 25%. The country has not managed yet to overcome the obstacles related to inequalities of income and wealth. One of the key challenges is the universality of quality education: there are, at least, 33 million Brazilians who are considered to be functionally illiterate.

The socio-economic context should be seen in relation to Brazilian cultural diversity. One can speak not just about one Brazil but rather about diverse 'Brazils', with an ethnic and a cultural plurality which has been one of the opportunities and challenges in the construction of national identity, and, therefore, in the various projects for the Brazilian citizen's education.

From the point of view of these considerations, understanding the relationships between education, globalization and nation in Brazil is complex. It is necessary to take into consideration the historical process of the formation of the nation, with the participation of the Indigenous Peoples, as well as Africans and Europeans, and the role of continental and diversified dimensions of education. The analysis of the specific relations between education and nation formation requires an in-depth examination of the history of Brazilian education. To understand the interfaces between this issue and the processes of globalization, it would be necessary to answer a multiplicity of questions which involve, mainly, the specific relationships between the Brazilian educational policies, the government and the agreements with the transnational agencies, including the World Bank and International Monetary Fund. These matters cannot be considered fully without reflecting on the problems related to the imposition of conditions for financing education and the transferring of educational ideas not compatible with Brazilian reality and the interests of those involved in social movements in Brazil.

In light of the above, this chapter contains five main sections: the historical context of the Brazilian nation and its relations with education, dictatorship and democracy and what they mean for education and the Brazilian nation, education and the construction of a multiethnic and multicultural nation in Brazil, strategies and educational policies for the consolidation of a multicultural and multiethnic nation, and perspectives and challenges for the future.

The historical context of the constitution of the Brazilian nation and its relationship with education

The construction of the idea of a nation in Brazil was a process which lasted throughout the 19th century, marked by various characteristics, including the fight for national independence (1822), the abolition of slavery movement (1888) and the search for a national identity. Politicians and business people were involved in this process. It is worth highlighting that the permanence of a slavery regime for a period of 388 years marked in an indelible way the social relations in diverse segments of the Brazilian society.

One of the issues to be highlighted in the process of nationalization is that those people who were considered to belong to ethnic 'minorities' were excluded from any educational project after slavery was abolished in 1888. The 'African' was not considered capable of paid work which was, since the middle of the 19th century, being made available to European immigrant groups, principally Germans and Italians. These immigrants were encouraged to come to Brazil where they would find a 'true paradise'. Their role was to contribute to the whitening of Brazilian society and as a mechanism to de-escalate explicit forms of social conflict after the end of slavery. This process made it difficult for Black peoples to become integrated into the national identity and citizenship that were being created. The Brazilian writer José Murilo de Carvalho (2002) characterized citizenship in Brazil as something that was exclusively for White peoples.

The second half of the 19th century is considered as the period of new discovery. It saw the construction of national symbols and heroes, the valuing of nationalist literature about nature as well as art production, all of which contributed to national identity formation. The urge to know and identify the ethical and the anthropologically singular Brazilian population's composition emerged as the dominant preoccupation in this period. This preoccupation can be observed in the writings of foreign travellers who pointed out the great racial miscegenation which existed in the country and which Schwarcz (1993) called 'the miscegenation show'.

According to Sobanski (2008), from the point of view of Brazilian historiography since the end of 19th century:

> What one intended was to create a historical narrative which would justify a model of Brazilian nation, understood as an extension of the Western Europe history. The proposals understood the nationality as summary of the white, indigenous and black people races, with predominance of an ideology of white people's superiority. (p. 35)

From the point of view of education for the formation of the Brazilian citizen, the conflicts that emerged from the predominance of the European culture and involved the indigenous and African cultures led to the adoption by some of the principles of 'racial democracy', which was developed by the Brazilian sociologist Gilberto Freyre. In one of his principal works, *Casa-Grande e Senzala*, Freyre (1988) opposed Brazil's whitening racial doctrines, which had been defended since the 19th century by those who favoured the ideas and practices associated with social eugenics. He argued that racial determinism did not influence the country's development. In his opinion, the African people's cultures were as complex as that of the European, but superior to those of Indigenous Peoples. The African's cultural consistency permitted a homogeneous miscegenation between the two cultures. This perspective has given birth to the so-called 'racial democracy myth' in Brazil. It allowed, according to Freyre, the perspective to develop that Brazilian slavery was less bad than that which happened in the US. This difference occurred, according to Freyre, because the Brazilian elites had created a humanized slavery, influenced above all by the cultural and moral history of the Portuguese people and their descendants in Brazil, thus making Brazilian society racially democratic. This perspective was adopted as a guide for the education of children and young people, mainly spread by didactic manuals published in Brazil since 1940. In the same way, it was the 'Brazilian racial democracy' which has coloured the ways in which Brazil has been recognized and represented by other countries:

> It is still the pacific racial living image, coined by Freire, which appears designed in Disney's Zé Carioca, in the Carnaval exported by the tourist agencies, in the image of a crook who every time moves away from reality. It is this negative, exotic representation of the country which becomes a form of show. It is not in vain that on postcards Brazil is still presented as a multicolour country. (Schwarcz, 1993, p. 49)

Representing the new Brazilian historiography, Ricardo Benzaquem de Araújo (1994) states that, while exalting cultural miscegenation, Freyre transferred an idealized vision of the African's presence, omitting the exploitation, the racism and the discrimination resulting from the process of slavery. I agree with Benzaquem (1994) about the difficulty of defining the place of Black people in Brazilian society, as evidenced by the successive laws which have been proposed by the Brazilian government. The laws oscillate between the labels of 'Afro-descendant' and 'Black people'. However, since the beginning of the 21st century, advances have been made, such as the growing acceptance of Black people's involvement in political life at the level of the Brazilian state.

The installation of the Brazilian Republic in 1889, as well as the 1891 Republican Constitution, revealed some expansion of political rights, including the right to elect and to be elected as national representatives. However, women secured the right to vote only in 1934, together with illiterate people, and in practice, these rights are not always used. The 1891 constitution did not grant social rights, particularly those relating to employment. It is worth highlighting that the country remained without any legislation around working conditions until 1943, when the laws which regulated paid work in Brazil were established.

The establishment of the Republic essentially was concerned with the construction of the Brazilian nation within the parameters of modernity. It included the creation of a public educational system. The period between the beginning of the Republic in 1889 and the third decade of the 20th century saw a good deal of activity by intellectuals who argued for the development of an educated society. The struggle for the political and cultural modernization of the country, however, was made difficult by the existence of an agro-exporting economic system and a political structure based on the power of large landowners. In this period, the majority of the Brazilian population lived in the countryside in situations of poverty and illiteracy.

It is not surprising, therefore, that the fight for the expansion of elementary and secondary schools and the struggle against illiteracy united representatives of the secular and catholic liberal sectors of society. The period between 1889 and 1930 is known as the phase of 'enthusiasm for education', as many people, despite at times significant differences of principles, believed in the redemptive power of education, 'to mould a new citizen, who is a builder of a new country' (Bittencourt, 1990, p. 95). An attempt was being made, through education, to develop a national unit for the construction of a modern country, with a homogeneous culture. However,

[t]he educational plans of the politics to transform the fundamental teaching into uniform and a transfer of a homogeneous culture came across with several obstacles in a period of the 1920's and 1930's. The diversity of the clientele, of the teaching board, of the space not only urban but rural, made fundamental school a place of difficult definition. (Bittencourt, 1990, p. 96)

One of the initiatives put forward to make culture and the citizen's ideal more cohesive was the creation and the introduction of the school subject Moral and Civic Instruction into the fundamental school curriculum. The key reform of Brazilian education, known as Reform Rocha Vaz, in 1925, brought in its article 55 the definition of what would be the contents of this school subject: notions of civility, sociability, work, truth, justice, equity, agreeability in manners, kindness, cleanliness, hygiene, love to the family and to the native country and altruism (HORTA, 1994). This school subject was introduced in the context of a debate between liberals and the Catholics, the consequence of which was the elimination of religious (Catholic) teaching until 1930 when it became compulsory. The strong influence of the Catholic educators established the moral foundation of the Brazilian citizenship formation, based on nationalism and on Catholicism. Today, Brazilian public schools are still obliged to offer religious teaching of an ecumenical character, but the students cannot be obliged to attend it.

Dictatorship and democracy: meanings for education and for the Brazilian nation

The period between 1937 and 1945, called Estado Novo, with the government of President Getúlio Vargas and the period between 1964 and 1984 of the Brazilian military dictatorship were marked by political and social exclusion. This made the construction of Brazilian citizenship to be rather fragile.

Since the beginning of the dictatorship of Estado Novo, the concepts of native country, race and religion were the basis of the Brazilian principal document (Magna Carta) of 1937. These concepts were also added as content in the compulsory school subjects, including moral and civic education, physical education and choral singing (music was considered to be a form of education for patriotism).

Civics, known as love for patriotic things, was also learned in the school subject history of Brazil.

After the dictator Getúlio Vargas's deposition in 1945, a new constitution for the country was written. The constitution of 1946 excluded the civic basis of the former document and valued freedom of thought and pedagogical ideas. However, between 1946 and 1961, the clash between the liberal educators and the Catholic educators made it difficult to change educational legislation, and reforms did not happen until 1961. These educators discussed issues such as the end of the obligation to provide religious teaching and the school subjects moral and civic education and choral singing. At the heart of these debates was support for or opposition to the principle of secularism as part of the education of the Brazilian citizen. The law of Brazilian education of 1961 still reveals a strong influence of Catholic thought.

Between 1946 and 1964, Brazilian society re-established the democratic experience. In this period, there was a struggle around ideas of nation and, thus, of education. Debates about the nation were influenced by the project of developmental democracy, which gave birth to the construction of the new capital city in Brasília and to the big expansion of the industrial park of the country, always dependent on foreign capital. This new nation demanded a citizen who knew how to live in an industrialized and a democratic society which can be exemplified in the proposal of education, defended by the Brazilian educator Anísio Teixeira. He was a student of John Dewey in the US, and his proposals, influenced by the ideas of the Escola Nova pedagogical movement, were significant in the development of several governmental educational strategies. They contributed to the opposition shown to Catholic educators' ideas and helped to broaden the principle of secular education in Brazil.

However, the idea of nation was also discussed in relation to other matters, including development and underdevelopment, domination and dominated. The principle of redemptive education has influenced most Brazilian educators, who adopted the ideas of Paulo Freire's pedagogy, defended, mainly, in his work *Pedagogy of the Oppressed*. For Freire (1987), due to the fact that Brazil identifies itself as a developing nation, the Brazilian government should take as a starting point the struggle against poverty and illiteracy as social issues which guide for actions and strategies of public policies for national education.

These ideas emerged from the demands from Brazilian people in the struggle for their emancipation from social and cultural disadvantage. The proposal was adopted mainly by sectors of the Brazilian Catholic Church, engaged with the social struggles and which were seen in the context of commitment to a theology of freedom.

These projects of nation, education and citizen are seen in several interconnected ways in Brazilian society and resulted in important debates and some successful outcomes. However, a political strike in 1964, made with the support of the US, installed a military dictatorship in Brazil for 20 years (1964–1984). The consequences for the ideal of nation and of free and democratic education were profound.

In the highest point of the so-called Cold War, the ideal of a democratic nation came to be seen officially as an anti-communist nation. Gradually, from the use of a strong repressive system, the armed forces imposed censure, political persecution and torture. Several educators were dismissed from universities and exiled, as was the case of Paulo Freire.

In 1971, the military dictatorship consolidated its educational project for the nation based on what it saw as principles of civics and love for the native country, implanted by the education law 5692. The bedrock of anti-communism was expressed by the ideology of national safety. This approach connected to teaching and learning in various ways. The school subjects of history and geography were replaced by the teaching of social studies based on the North American model of the spiral curriculum. The school subject moral and civic education became compulsory again, including in universities. A new school subject called Brazilian social and political organization was created with the objective to ensure that learners accepted the values of anti-communism and of national security. The curricula, didactic manuals and teachers of these school subjects were kept under severe censure and control by the central military government. Several Brazilian historians, sociologists and philosophers were persecuted; most of them arrested and some are considered as political disappeared people.

In 1984, after the end of the military dictatorship, the teaching of history in the schools returned and a debate started for the writing of a new Brazilian constitution and a new education law. This debate involved various segments of Brazilian society, and among the claims was the need of the country to consider itself as a democratic, multicultural and multiethnic nation.

Education and the construction of a multicultural and multiethnic nation in Brazil

With the end of the military dictatorship in Brazil (1964–1984), Brazilian society was mobilized for the creation of a new constitution, within democratic boundaries and principles. Promulgated in 1988, the new constitution indicated the basics for combating prejudice and racism, as highlighted below:

1. Article 3, interpolated propositions I, III and IV: 'constitute elementary objectives of the Federative Republic of Brazil to build a free, fair and solidary society, as well as to promote everybody's welfare, without prejudice of origin, race, gender, colour, age and any other forms of discrimination and to eradicate the marginalization and to reduce the social inequalities'.
2. Article 4, interpolated propositions II and VIII: the Federative Republic of Brazil, in the international affairs plans, must care for the observance of the principles of human rights prevalence and to repudiate terrorism and racism.
3. Article 5, interpolated propositions XLI and XLII: consecrates the principle of equality; punishment for any attacking discrimination of the elementary rights and freedom, and enunciates that racism constitutes a crime which cannot be bailed and not prescribed, subject to imprisonment penalty, under the terms of law; and paragraph 2nd: consecrating the right incorporation comes from international agreement.
4. Article 7, interpolated proposition XXX: in the social rights field, it forbids the salary difference, the exercise of responsibilities and the criteria of recruiting by reason of gender, age, colour or marital status.

(BRASIL Constituição, 1988)

The new constitution incorporated demands from parts of Brazilian society who were looking forward to changes in the realm of social and cultural relations. In 1978, the Unified Black People's Movement against racial discrimination was created in Brazil. Its representatives argued for linguistic shifts to be made in order to avoid the injustice of the past. To avoid the myth of racial democracy, terms such as 'racial prejudice' and 'racial discrimination' were debated with the aim of better describing and thereby helping to create a fairer society.

In 1996, the constitutional principles related to education for the nation were expressed by the law 9394/96 of the Guidance and Foundations of National Education. This law kept the multicultural and multiethnic principles and also indicated the need to establish basic curriculum content for Brazilian schools. These contents were established by means of National Curricular Parameters, in 1997, 1998 and 1999. It is important to highlight that these curricular parameters, as well as all the pedagogical guidance from the Brazilian government, from this date on, are based on the foundations of pedagogy of competences and on the necessity to prepare Brazilian citizens to be prepared for employment and other engagement with the economy. As such, it is clear that there is continuing commitment to education for development, suggested in the documents of the international agencies, World Bank and International Monetary Fund, which state that education is the main weapon against poverty.

Debates were stimulated by the Black people's movements which were organized in several regions of Brazil as well as in the international context. There are demands for actions against racism. The racial issue in Brazil has become the focus of attention of the society and the government. This has happened mainly after the former sociologist and the then president of the Republic, Fernando Henrique Cardoso, recognized in 1995 the widespread existence of racism and racial inequalities in the country. This statement was accompanied by the first specific public politics for the Black population, whose objective was the modification of this situation.

From 2001, Brazil approved policies of affirmative action for Black people. The racial issue was included in the agendas and proposals of various candidates for president in 2002. The elected president of the time, Luiz Inácio Lula da Silva, created, on 21 March 2003, the Special Secretariat of Racial Equality Promotion Policies (SEPPIR). The article 2nd of the Law of Creation attributes to SEPPIR the function to assist the President in the formulation, coordination, articulation, promotion, follow-up and evaluation of all racial equality policies developed by the federal government. President Lula also recognized officially that there is racial discrimination against Black people in Brazil, giving continuity to the rupture with the previous official characterizations in which Brazil was said to be a racial democracy. Under the pressure of the Black people's social movements, President Lula not only created SEPPIR but also sent to the Brazilian National Congress

Law number 3.627, of 20 May 2004, which 'institutes Special System of Vacancies Reserve for students who came from public schools, in special Black and Indigenous People, in the federal public institutions of university education and gives other providences'. This project and others are on course in the National Congress and have led to wide-ranging discussions, debates and academic and political disputes.

The problems related to the Brazilian educational situation have been affecting the access to – and their success within – schools of disadvantaged children and young people. Additionally, there are difficulties faced by Brazilian schools regarding financial resources that are available for technological maintenance and innovation, as well as the qualifications and quality of teaching staff in order to achieve basic levels of quality education. There are significant challenges in relation to access to university teaching and, particularly, for those who belong to ethnic 'minorities'. These topics play an important role in Brazilian educators' discussions. Hasenbalg and Silva (1990) called attention to the fact that

> when it comes to the access to the school system, a bigger proportion of non-white children enter school later on. Besides it, the black and brown people's proportion who do not have any access to school is three times bigger than the white people's one. These inequalities cannot be explained either by regional factors or by family's socio-economic situation . . . Although a better socio-economic situation reduces the children's proportion who do not have access to school, not depending on their colour, there still persists a clear difference in the general levels of access among white and non-white children, even in the higher level of per person family income. (p. 99)

In July 2004, the Brazilian government created, in the Education Ministry, the Secretariat of Continued Education, Literacy, Diversity and Inclusion. The principal objective of this body has been to contribute to the inclusive development of the teaching systems, to highlight the need to value differences and diversity and to promote inclusive education, human rights and socio-environment sustainability.

The Brazilian government's proposal, Education for the Ethnic and Racial Relations, is based on the conception of political consciousness and diverse history, of the strengthening of identities and of rights and of the actions to combat racism and discrimination. From this perspective, the National Plan of Implementation of the National Guidance for the Education of the Ethnic-Racial Relations and for Teaching of Afro-Brazilian and African History and Culture was created to make educational public policies for racial equality. Affirmative actions for the elimination of ethnic-racial inequality were proposed as an important mechanism, taking into consideration that today 51.7% of the Brazilian population identifies as Black (or brown) people, and of the illiterate people over 15 years old 68.3% are Black, and of those people who have studied for fewer than four years at school 64.6% are Black, according to the Census IBGE/2010 (Geography and Statistics Brazilian Institute). The availability of didactic–pedagogic materials and of reference works about history and Afro-Brazilian and African History and Culture is one of the strategic axes for the implementation of the Law number 10.639/03, which made compulsory the inclusion of topics related to Afro-Brazilian culture and African history in Brazilian schools.

In 2005, the Affirmative Action Programme was created for black people to enter public universities (UNIAFRO). This Programme had as its objective to offer financial support to the Afro-Brazilian Studies Nucleus, which was created inside the Brazilian public universities. The objective of UNIAFRO is to support actions related to the public schoolteachers' professional development and to create didactic materials for the re-education of ethnic-racial relations and the history of Afro-Brazilian and African culture.

In Brazilian universities, the quotas for the brown or Black admissions were inaugurated by the Law number 3.708/01, disciplined by Decree number 30.776/02, which reserved quotas up to 40% for Black people in the universities of the state of Rio de Janeiro, which implemented them in 2003. The initiative was followed by Bahia State University (Uneb), by Brasilia's University (UnB) and by Bahia Federal University, among other institutions. Today, the majority of Brazilian public universities adopt the quota system for this population, including representatives of the indigenous population.

Among other actions aim for the inclusion of Afro descendant and Indigenous People was the Diversity Programme in the University created on 13 November 2002. Its objective was to implement and evaluate strategies for the promotion of access to university teaching of people belonging to disadvantaged social groups, especially Afro descendants and Brazilian Indigenous People.

In partnership with United Nations Educational, Scientific and Cultural Organization (UNESCO) in 2013, the government started a project to publish the Synthesis Collection of the Africa General History Collection and didactic materials for teachers and students to be distributed in 2014 to public sector schools. In this same year, the Education Ministry (MEC) launched the Academic Development Programme which takes the name of a great Black politician Abdias Nascimento. In 1980, with the re-democratization of the country, Abdias Nascimento, a federal deputy, formulated the first project of law proposing compensatory action for Afro-Brazilians in several areas of the social life, providing reparation for centuries of discrimination. The project was not approved by the National Congress, but the claims continue. The objective of the project proposed in 2014 is to provide education and professional development for students who identify as Black, brown and indigenous students as well as others.

Despite these measures, there have been historical and contemporary claims by the Black people's social movement and progressive sectors of the civil society that policies, programmes, projects and governmental actions related to affirmative action/character for Black people are being very slowly implemented and have been the object of many debates and discussions. One of the main discussions happened when the system for vacancies reserved for Black people started to be implemented in public universities (the so-called quota system for Black people), and since 2003, this has been the object of juridical contestations.

In a general way, one observes a broadening of governmental initiatives in the field of affirmative action for Black people, including, for example, the concession of fiscal benefits for private universities which adopt racial quotas – by means of Programme University for Everybody (ProUni) – a juridical regularization of lands occupied by communities reminiscent of *quilombos* (settlements created by Black people who were fugitive slaves or former slaves) and the creation of quotas for Black people in public service. The dynamic characteristic of this process has also relied on the special programmes of investment in the consolidation of African history and culture, as a compulsory curricular component in the Brazilian schools.

Strategies for the consolidation of a multicultural and multiethnic nation

The existence of organized social movements has been an important factor in the construction of Brazil as a fairer and plural nation and in the proposition of alternative forms for education. Since the end of military dictatorship, it is noticeable that the No Land Movement – MST (Movimento dos Sem Terra) – has been created. This phenomenon can be characterized as a mass popular movement involving trade unions and having a political character. Its main focus is to fight for land and agricultural reform. It emerged from land occupations which were made by groups of workers who had been banned from the countryside by the process of mechanized agriculture, between 1978 and 1979. MST was created in 1984. These groups live in campsites where they organize their schools with their own pedagogical approach, mainly based on Paulo Freire's pedagogical principles. Today, there are about 1,800 schools in the campsites and settlements of MST across Brazil, with approximately 160,000 children who are called 'small no land'. The students are the children of workers as well as of the unemployed and of people who have been many times excluded from society. The campsites, which have not yet been established in definite settlements, have itinerant schools which follow the children to where their parents move.

From the beginning of the 21st century, in the context of the re-democratization of the Brazilian society, the actions of the Black People's Movement intensified as did the increase in academic work which questioned, for example, the existence of an immediate and direct association between prejudice and slavery. These works show the organic relation between racial discrimination and the dependent and globalized type of capitalist development existing in Brazil.

In this context, two specific state policies are relevant to the struggle of the Black and indigenous population for access to formal education. These policies deserve to be highlighted and point to challenges and ways for the future. The first of them led to the questioning of the state, in that there was an emphasis on the need to revise the ways in which multiethnic and multicultural principles apply to Brazil's history, as well as recognition of the need to include African and indigenous history in national curricula proposals. As a result of this struggle, Law number 10.639/03 was created – National Curricula

Guidance of the Ethnic-Racial Relations Education for the teaching of Afro-Brazilian and African History and Culture – which altered the existing education law in Brazil and made it to be compulsory to include these topics in national curricula and in didactic manuals. This law also altered one of the most traditional commemorative dates of Brazil, which was 13 May, used to commemorate the abolition of slavery by Princess Isabel, during the period of the Brazilian monarchy. As it can observed in one of the articles of the above-mentioned law, the commemorative date was changed to become 20 November, as commemoration of the death of a Black people's hero, Zumbi dos Palmares.

In 2008, with UNESCO support, the Brazilian Education Ministry proposed the document, 'Contributions for the implementation of the LAW 10.639/03'. According to this document:

> The Law 10.639/2003 can be considered an arrival point of a black people's historical fight to be seen portrayed with the same value of other peoples who have come to here, and a departure point for a social change. In the educational politics, the implementation of the Law number 10.639/2003 means deep rupture with a type of pedagogical posture which does not recognise the differences resulting from our national formation process. For beyond the positive impact together with the black people's population, this law must be faced as an elementary challenge of the politics group which aim for the improvement of quality Brazilian education for everybody. (UNESCO/MEC, 2008)

This same document makes reference to the importance of the Didactic Books National Programme – PNLD. This programme makes possible the evaluation of teaching and learning resources produced by various publishing companies in Brazil. If the books are approved, they are distributed for free by the government for Brazilian public school children and young people. Among the criteria for approval are the following:

1. To promote positively the image of the Afro descendants and descendants of the Brazilian indigenous ethnics, considering their participation in different works, professions and power spaces;

2. To promote positively the Afro-Brazilian and the indigenous peoples' culture, giving visibility to their values, traditions, organizations and socio-scientific knowledge, considering their rights and their participation in different historical processes which have marked Brazil's construction, valuing the cultural differences in our multicultural society;

3. To approach the topics of ethnic-racial relations, of prejudice, of racial discrimination and of the correlated violence, aiming for the construction of an anti-racist society, solidary, fair and equal.

(BRASIL/MEC/FNDE/PNLD, 2014)

In relation to the inclusion of African history as a compulsory curricular content in these resources, there is still the persistence of severe problems due to the predominance of the traditional historical narrative based on Eurocentric historical perspectives and time periods: antique history, medieval history, modern history and contemporary history. Not only in the university course curricula for history teachers in the elementary and secondary schools but also in the manual contents, Brazil's history is 'integrated' in this linear and Eurocentric history division.

The need to create new theoretical perspectives, which would directly result in teachers' professional development, led to the creation of universities with differentiated curricula and with new approaches, like the University of Latin America Integration, in Foz do Iguaçu, South of Brazil; the University of International Integration of Afro-Brazilian Portuguese Speakers, in the Northeast; and the University of Amazonian Integration, in the North region.

These universities have proposals of integration of the Brazilian nation with other Latin American, Amerindian and Portuguese African nations. In addition to the differentiated curricula, they have their proposals as references in the so-called theory of 'Colonial tour' ('Giro Colonial'). The 'Colonial tour' defends, among many proposals, the perspective of the decolonization of the theory based on the reflections for an epistemic diversity, beyond global capitalism. As Castro-Gómez and Grosfoguel state, we see the transition of modern capitalism for the global colonial system from the focus that we call here decolonial, the contemporary global capitalism means again, in a postmodern way, the exclusions provoked by epistemic, spiritual, racial/ethnic and of gender/sexuality hierarchies developed in modernity (Castro-Gómez and Gosfoguel, 2007, p. 13).

On the one hand, the multicultural and multiethnic perspective of the Brazilian nation is a conquest of claims of various indigenous nations which are part of the Brazilian population. They look for recognition in their rights to culture and to the access of the cultural wealth of the nation, including bilingual education and the schools aimed at these children. On the other hand, the Afro-Brazilian population has been demanding inclusive actions and, because of that, has gradually conquered space in universities and in the struggle against discrimination and prejudice. Finally, one can observe the valuing of Brazil as a nation whose identity is linked to other Latin American nations and also to Portuguese African peoples.

However, this historical moment points towards issues about the future of the ideal of the nation and of the ways forward for Brazilian education, mainly regarding the way in which the country faces the economic and cultural determinations of the globalization process.

Challenges for the future

The proposals for the nation which have developed in Brazil during the last 50 years mirror the historical duality existing in the country. On the one hand, a representation of nation is riddled with the idea of a country in growing development, with significant opportunities for individual employment and for the economy as a whole. This nation has a project of education based on the principles of pedagogy of competences which look for preparing everybody to be prepared, with professionalism and competence, for the employment market, in a multicultural and multiethnic perspective. On the other hand, there is also a representation of 'nation' from disadvantaged, poor and oppressed people, of the ones without rights and without justice. They fight for an education based on the pedagogy of emancipation and of the human freedom whose objective would be to construct a fairer and more equal society.

The document of the World Bank, *Education Sector Strategy Update (ESSU): Achieving Education for All, Broadening Our Perspective, Maximizing Our Effectiveness*, published in 2006, updated the orientations and predictions for the relationship between education and development in emerging countries, mainly as a factor of poverty reduction, already made public by the Bank in 1990. This agency emphatically defends a policy of results and the culture of evaluation of students and teachers, as Roger Dale (2004) explains in his work *Globally Structured Agenda for Education*.

There are, however, difficult questions to be addressed. What and how should we consider in relation to the future of education for the nation, in view of the diversity and complexity of Brazilian society? How will civil and political society in Brazil be able to maintain the dialogue with the international agencies which find capital for Brazilian education, in the sense of maintaining integrity and sovereignty of its proposals, for example, revitalizing Paulo Freire's thought in curricular strategies and proposals? Will education be able to contribute to the development of the country, as the proposals of the international agencies affirm? And what kind of development, for what kind of nation?

Our expectation, and one that is held by many Brazilians, is that education will help Brazil in the future to consolidate itself as a modern nation that is democratic, multicultural, and multiethnic with social justice for all. And we hope it may be a political project for the nation, in which there can be an appropriate melioration of the role of powerful interest groups.

5
Canada

Carla L. Peck and *Alan Sears*

In November 2014, the Association for Canadian Studies (ACS) hosted a national conference with the theme '(Re) Making Confederation: (Re) Imagining Canada'. The meeting was held on the 150th anniversary of the first conference held to discuss the confederation of the British colonies that came together to form Canada. The keynote address focused on educating about and for the nation with a specific focus on the difference between *'celebratory heritage* and *critical history'* (Seixas, 2014, p. 14, emphasis in the original). The former uses iconic representations and stirring celebrations to foster a strong sense of national identity and social cohesion amongst citizens of a nation state, while the latter focuses on building critical understanding of the nation and its history. The speaker argued that these very different visions of history education, one promoted by the federal government and the other by a national history education project, have been contending for dominance in the field in Canada over the past decade. Indeed, in recent years, both academic and popular sources have been inundated with claims that the government intends to 'rewrite history' (Ibbitson, 2013) to promote its own iconic vision of the nation (Brean, 2013; Conrad et al., 2013; Curtis, 2013; Geddes, 2013; Pashby et al., 2014).

The surprising thing is not that attempts are being made to politicize Canadian history in general and the teaching of the nation in particular to the advantage of one particular ideological orientation, but the assumption that this is something new. Ken Osborne's (2000, 2004, 2005, 2011) large body of work demonstrates that school and public history has been heavily contested ground in Canada for well over 100 years, and central to those debates have been questions about how to teach about the nation – or nations – of Canada. Similarly, a persistent issue for Canadian citizenship education has been the search to discover, or create, some sense of shared national identity (Sears, 2010; Sears et al., 1999).

In this chapter, we examine the idea of nation in the Canadian context and the ways it has been dealt with in education. We begin by setting the context: examining the multinational nature of the Canadian state and how that has impacted the ways Canadians think about themselves and their nation. We move on from there to consider the history of education about the nation in Canada focusing on various recurring themes that alternatingly crescendo and fade over time. From there, we go on to consider how contemporary structural and cultural realities shape teaching about the nation and the general features of current policy and practice in the field. Finally, we look ahead and propose both likely and preferred futures for citizenship education.

Social, political and cultural contexts of citizenship education in Canada

Canada is widely acknowledged as a multinational state and has had deep diversity and the presence of many nations since before it became, officially, a country. The work of political philosopher Will Kymlicka (1998, 2003) has been influential in understanding the complexity of Canada as a country composed of 'nations within', and notes that Canada is distinct among Western nations with regard to addressing this complexity and 'the extent to which it has not only legislated but also *constitutionalized*, practices of accommodation' (p. 374, emphasis in original).

According to Kymlicka (1998), two categories of minority groups are particular to Canada's diverse population and history. The first, 'national minority', is defined as 'historically settled, territorially concentrated, and previously self-governing cultures whose territory has become incorporated into a larger state' (p. 30). He later subdivides this group into two discrete categories: 'substate nations' and 'indigenous peoples' (Kymlicka and Opalski, 2001, p. 23). In Canada, the Francophone Québécois and Aboriginal peoples would fall into these categories, respectively. A recent study described them, and others, as 'distinctive "communities of memory"' within the wider Canadian state (Conrad et al., 2013, p. 102). Historically, the Canadian government has been willing to negotiate with these two distinct national minorities in terms of the rights and privileges to which they lay claim.

Minority groups who do not meet the above-mentioned criteria are known primarily as 'immigrant or ethnic groups', despite the fact that, for many generations past, the descendants have not actually been immigrants. Recent immigrants to Canada are also included in this category. These groups are composed of people who have made a conscious choice to come to Canada and 'knew that they were entering a new society with its own established laws and institutions' (Kymlicka, 1998, p. 7). Further, 'historically, immigrant/ethnic groups have sought and achieved social and political integration in Canada – not self-government – although they have also wanted some accommodation of their ethnocultural distinctiveness' (p. 8). The main difference between national minorities and immigrant/ethnic groups is that the former have historically and constitutionally acknowledged (but still contested) inherent rights, and the latter do not.

Like other Western nations, Canada has moved away from policies designed to assimilate Indigenous Peoples and stamp out minority nationalisms. However, Kymlicka (2003) argues that Canada's approach to 'managing' diversity is unique in several ways. He posits that, while accommodation of diversity 'reflects underlying sociological and political factors that affect all Western democracies, . . . Canada is distinctive in having to deal with all three forms of diversity [immigration, Indigenous Peoples and sub-state nationalities] at the same time' (p. 374). Canada's approach to diversity is also made distinct by virtue of the fact that the accommodation of diversity is enshrined in the constitution.

Constitutional reform since 1867 has broadened the range of national minorities accorded constitutional recognition and protection and has also embedded multiculturalism as an interpretive frame for the constitution (Kymlicka, 2003; Kymlicka and Norman, 2000). For example, Aboriginal rights, including treaty rights, are affirmed in the Constitution Act of 1982. The Act also establishes English and French as the official languages of the province of New Brunswick, largely to protect the place of the Acadian people who have a definite understanding of themselves as a national group within Canada. Central to the Act is *The Canadian Charter of Rights and Freedoms* with a clause that states, 'This Charter shall be interpreted in a manner consistent with the preservation and enhancement of the multicultural heritage of Canadians' (Department of Justice, 1982). *The Charter* also has a clause that recognizes and protects Canada's official language minorities and their educational rights to French first-language schooling (outside Québec) and to English first-language schooling (in Québec).

Contemporary factors related to globalization, including changing patterns of migration and citizenship, have created 'a growing awareness of the multiethnic nature of most contemporary nation-states and the need to account for this aspect of pluralism in public policy' (Johnson and Joshee, 2007, p. 3). Jaenen (1981, p. 81) suggests four factors in Canada's history that uniquely suit it for pluralism: the English–French dualism, which has been 'a fundamental characteristic of Canadian society' since the Loyalist migration at the end of the 18th century; the more diverse British, rather than exclusively English, nature of early Anglophone Canada; the separation of church and state and relative religious liberty that has always existed in Canada; and the fact that control over education was made a provincial, rather than a federal, responsibility.

The end result of this complex historical development of the nation combined with the constitutional issues described above means that there is little consistency from province to province when it comes to citizenship education in Canada, both in how it is approached and the degree to which departments of education have committed to implementing citizenship ideals into their policies, curricula, schools, materials and teaching practices. These factors also make it very difficult to make any claims about citizenship education on a national level. Below, we explore what we see as major themes running through citizenship education across the country.

Historical context of teaching the nation in Canada

Many histories set out a chronological account of phenomena over time, often with a subtle (although sometimes quite overt) sense of progression from darkness into light. Things are better now than in the past, we know more now than we did then and are closer to getting it – whatever 'it' is – right than were people in the past. It is tempting to approach this section of the chapter that way, setting out the progression of citizenship education in Canada from a process of didactic indoctrination into single, iconic views of the nation to the more progressive and nuanced approaches more common today. While that might be the easiest way to proceed in our view, it fundamentally distorts the nature of the field.

Rather than a linear progression, we argue that the history of teaching about, and for, the nation in Canadian schools is more like a complex symphony. Tchaikovsky's *1812 Overture* is a good example. It merges Orthodox hymns, Russian folk music, La Marseillaise, the stirring anthem 'God Save the Tsar' and cannon fire to tell the story of Napoleon's march into and retreat from Russia in 1812. These musical themes blend and clash, crescendo and fade over the course of the piece. Sometimes, one is clearly dominant, at others two or more compete for superiority, and occasionally they blend into a smooth harmony. Similarly over time, there have been recurring themes in education about the nation in Canada that have surged and diminished sometimes in competition with each other and sometimes merging in harmony. The major themes are set out in Table 5.1 and discussed below. It is important to remember that the themes identified in the table rarely, if ever, exist in isolation or ideal form. They almost always appear in combination, and their manifestation is therefore nuanced in important ways. It often takes close analysis to recognize the underlying features described here.

The nation as a unifying icon has been a dominant theme in this symphony. As an immigrant country with the kind of deep diversity described above, Canada has consistently struggled with the challenge of fostering social cohesion across regions and peoples, and this has been reflected in education about the nation. As Osborne (2011) points out, 'From the 1890s to the 1970s Canadian history education in English-speaking Canada was dominated by the theme of nation-building, intended to instill a sense of pan-Canadian identity in the young' (p. 55). While this motif has always been present in Canadian citizenship education, times of national significance or perceived threats to the nation have caused it to surge to the forefront. One of the earliest of these was the period immediately following World War I. Significant labour strife culminated in a general strike in Winnipeg in March of 1919 that included a violent confrontation between strikers and police resulting in the death of two strikers, numerous other injuries and the arrest of the leaders of the strike. All of this took place in

Table 5.1 Conceptions of the nation in Canadian citizenship education

	Nation as a unifying icon	Nation as the site for engagement	Nation as the pluralist ideal	Nations together
Central purpose of the nation	To unite disparate people in a common vision and project	To engage citizens in actively shaping the common good	To provide opportunity for different individuals and collectives to live together justly, peacefully and productively	To provide a framework for the national minorities within to share power and live together
Focus of citizenship education	To develop in citizens a common understanding of and commitment to the nation and its institutions	To develop citizens who are committed to, and equipped for, engaging at local, national and international levels to make the world a more just and prosperous place	To develop citizens who understand their own values and worldviews, understand and respect the values and worldviews of others, and can think through complex and diverse value positions on the issues of the day	To develop citizens who understand and support the national aspirations of various groups and can work within and across boundaries to create a healthy and just society

the context of a Western world worried about Bolshevism and led to the convening of the National Conference of Moral Education in the Schools in Relation to Canadian Citizenship in Winnipeg in October of the same year (W. F. Osborne, 1919). The lieutenant governor of Manitoba opened the conference with a stirring call for Canadians to shake off their ambivalence to the nation: 'It is high time that Canada should love itself and thus avoid that chaos and intellectual and moral stagnation and bankruptcy in idealism that comes from lack of self-love' (Aikins, 1919, p. 2).

The energy from the conference was taken up by a range of groups, including a number of federal members of parliament, to conclude 'that a crisis of citizenship threatened the stability of the social order and the destiny of the nation' (McLean, 2007, p. 7). Motions were presented in both the House of Commons and the Senate in support of establishing a national system of education to address this threat, but these met with considerable opposition, and no such system has ever been established.

Crises like these have arisen a number of times in Canadian history, pushing teaching the nation as an iconic unifying force to the centre of the civic education agenda. Space does not allow for a detailed examination of them all, but we will highlight two because their causes were rather different than the one described above. In the mid-1960s, Canadian nationalism, at least in English Canada, was surging while, at the same time, a burgeoning sense of a more localized and particularistic nationalism was also taking hold in the province of Québec. The centennial of Canada's establishment as an independent country occurred in 1967, and the following year, Pierre Trudeau was elected prime minister. His government pursued an overtly national-ist agenda, including passing legislation to limit foreign ownership of companies operating in Canada and setting quotas for the broadcast-ing of Canadian material on radio and television. At the same time, *La Révolution tranquille* (the Quiet Revolution) was leading many Québécois to push for greater provincial autonomy within Canada and, in some cases, outright independence (Conrad et al., 2013). In the midst of this nationalistic surge, a substantial study entitled *What Culture? What Heritage?* painted a bleak picture of the teaching of Canadian history in schools across the country (Hodgetts, 1968).

Drawing from a number of data sets, including surveys, class-room observations and analysis of curricula and textbooks, Hodgetts reported that in the programmes of both official language communities, 'much of the standardized Canadian history taught in the schools is antiquated and fundamentally useless' (Hodgetts, 1968, p. 19). Perhaps the most damning indictment was the description of the almost totally different civic education offered to French and English students. A. B. Hodgetts, the study's principal investigator, wrote, 'Canadian studies in the schools of both linguistic communities do so little to encourage a mutual understanding of their separate attitudes, aspirations, and interests' (p. 35).

Hodgetts's study fell on fertile soil and created significant panic about the state of teaching the nation in Canadian schools. Various private interests and the federal government combined to provide significant funding to establish the Canada Studies Foundation (CSF), which produced teaching materials and provided in-service teacher education from 1970 to its demise in 1986. Fostering 'pan-Canadian understanding' was identified as the key objective of this work (Hodgetts and Gallagher, 1978, p. 1).

During the same period, concerns were also raised regarding teaching about Canada and using Canadian materials in post-secondary education. In the mid-1970s, the Commission on Canadian Studies issued a bleak report arguing that Canadian universities were teaching very little about Canada and neglecting Canadian cultural products in their curricula (Symons, Page, and Commission on Canadian Studies, 1975). Like Hodgetts's report, this caused considerable consternation and led to the forming of the ACS, which in turn helped to lead a transformation of university programmes and curricula to include more focus on Canada.

With the perceived demise of separatism in Québec after the mid-1980s, the focus of curriculum reform shifted to more interest in diversity and global affairs, but before turning to that we will explore one more surge of the nation as a unifying icon theme. Again, the theme exploded on the scene with the publication of a book, this time one with the inquisitional title *Who Killed Canadian History?* For historian Jack Granatstein (1998, p. 3), the author of the polemic, almost everyone involved in education in Canada seemed 'to be engaged in a conspiracy to eliminate Canada's past'. Except on reading further, it is clear the past has not been eliminated but changed. Instead of a single grand narrative focused on 'the European civilization on which our nation is founded' (p. xiv), Granatstein argued that school and university history had been hijacked by feminists, multicultur-alists and others seeking to 'subdivide it into micro-histories, alter, and bury it' (p. 148). For Granatstein, returning to a single, heroic Eurocentric version of Canadian history was imperative. 'We have', he extolled, 'a nation to save and a future to build' (p. 149).

Leaving aside the accuracy of Granatstein's claims, and there is a good reason to question them (e.g. K. Osborne, 2000; Stanley, 2000), his book and the far-ranging response to it provoked a revival of interest in teaching Canadian history. Granatstein went on to help found the Dominion Institute, an institution dedicated to promoting his preferred approach to this enterprise. Margaret MacMillan (2008, p. 19), herself a prominent Canadian historian, derisively described the Institute as having 'shown great entrepreneurial talent for mak-ing Canadians feel guilty about how little they know about their own past'. That guilt was often parlayed into significant curricular reform. As this major theme played on over the years, another competed for attention across the country, that of the nation as the pluralist ideal: the place where different individuals and collectives live together justly, peacefully and productively.

On 8 October 1971, the then prime minister of Canada, Pierre Elliot Trudeau, rose in the House of Commons to announce his govern-ment's response to a set of recommendations contained in the report of the *Royal Commission on Bilingualism and Biculturalism*. The speech dealt with recommendations in *Volume IV* of the Commission's report concentrating on 'the contribution by other ethnic groups to the cultural enrichment of Canada and the measures that should be taken to safeguard that contribution' (Trudeau, 1971).

The prime minister's purpose was largely to allay concerns of some non-English and non-French Canadians that their cultures might be threatened or diminished in the rush to implement official bilingual-ism across the country. Trudeau asserted that 'although there are two official languages, there is no official culture, nor does any ethnic group take precedence over any other'. He went on to say, 'A policy of multiculturalism within a bilingual framework commends itself to the government as the most suitable means of assuring the cultural freedom of Canadians.' The address concluded with Trudeau setting out the four pillars of that new policy, including the commitment of resources to help sustain large and small cultural groups within Canada, assistance in overcoming barriers to 'full participation in

Canadian society', the promotion of 'creative encounters and inter-change among all Canadian cultural groups in the interest of national unity' and, finally, government programmes to assist immigrants in the learning of English and/or French.

As discussed above, for much of its history, the Canadian state has been preoccupied with creating an overarching sense of national identity that might be shared by all Canadians. The federal govern-ment has been thoroughly engaged in that effort, and the devel-opment of the multiculturalism policy of 1971 was a part of that endeavour. The document tabled with Trudeau's (1971) speech made the claim that 'Canadian identity will not be undermined by mul-ticulturalism. Indeed, we believe that cultural pluralism is the very essence of Canadian identity'. A number of scholars have argued that this 'pluralist ideal' (Sears et al., 1999, p. 113) was not only federal policy but caught the imagination of many Canadians (Joshee, 2004; Kymlicka, 2003).

The period following the initial articulation of the multicultural-ism policy also saw a shift in approaches to diversity education from more assimilationist models to ones more focused on inclusion and social justice. Joshee (2004) documents these changes in detail, argu-ing that for many years the general trend was in this direction. In an extensive review of research in the area, Bickmore (2014) concludes, 'research shows that Canadian citizenship education about intercul-tural diversity and equity issues is increasingly inclusive and justice-oriented in policy pronouncements' (p. 258).

Indeed, there is a plethora of literature documenting the explo-sion of attention to diversity in Canadian education in the 40 years since Pierre Trudeau set the course with his speech to the House of Commons (Bruno-Jofré and Aponiuk, 2001; Peck et al., 2010; Joshee, 2004; Joshee and Johnson, 2007; Sears, 2010). While pluralism and inclusion are central to the rhetoric of social studies and citizen-ship education policy and programmes across Canada, it has often largely been an iconic rather than a deep pluralism. From the 1970s, the idea of education as a doorway for individuals and groups to feel included in the mainstream civic life of the country in Canada has extended to at least attempt to include the voices of 'Aboriginal Peoples, women, diverse ethnic groups, disabled people, gays and lesbians' (Sears et al., 1999, p. 113). This has resulted in a widespread policy framework that promotes the 'pluralist ideal', but there is little evidence it has been translated into significant understanding of diversity amongst students or teachers (Peck et al., 2008; Peck, 2010; Varma-Joshi et al., 2004).

Kymlicka (2003) argues that this iconic vision plays directly into how Canadians see the nation. Many like to think of Canada as 'a young, modern society, free from the old hierarchies, cultural prejudices and embedded traditions of the Old World. It is, Canadians like to think, a classless, meritocratic and democratic society, open to newcomers and to new ideas' (p. 362). While he argues this is more myth than reality, it is often presented as the latter. A recent study, for example, found a group of Ontario history teachers 'emphasized Canada as a nation that stands for peacekeeping, multiculturalism, civility and commitment to the common good' (Faden, 2012, p. 183).

Partly in response to increasing attention to diversity, recent intrusions of the federal government into public history have been characterized by some as a 'rebranding of Canada' along the lines of the nation as an icon described above in order 'to encourage social cohesion in the twenty-first century' (Conrad et al., 2013, p. 153). In a study of curricula and policy in two large provinces, Pashby et al. (2014) found 'that the opportunities within educational curricula advocating liberal social justice discourses are taking a background to those that promote social cohesion and a narrow vision of Canadian identity and history' (p. 4). This is part of a worldwide trend emphasizing social cohesion in citizenship education (Reid et al., 2010). One theme fades, while the other rises.

These two motifs, the nation as the unifying icon and the nation as the pluralist ideal, have been dominant in the history of Canadian citizenship education. While they seem at odds with each other, there is an interesting harmony between them, in that both portray themselves as focused on fostering national unity. For proponents of the former, unity is nurtured when all citizens unite around a common, largely heroic, conception of the nation state. Advocates of the latter, on the other hand, see unity emerging when different peoples see their own stories and experiences cast as part of the national framework. While these two themes have dominated, others are present as well. We turn to an examination of these now.

Over the past 15 years, there has been a move to 'a generic, participation focused approach' to citizenship education in Canada and around the world (Sears et al., 2011, p. 299). Central to this is an activist conception of citizenship in which every citizen, or group of citizens, will have the knowledge, skills and dispositions needed to participate in the civic life of the country and feel welcome to do so. It is important to note that what citizens are being included in is not citizenship in the ethnic or sociological sense of belonging to a community but, rather, they are being included in the community of those who participate, who join in a process. A key feature of this approach to citizenship education is its almost blatant denial of national identity as a key aspect of citizenship. The nation is not primarily an iconic symbol around which to unite, nor a pluralist community emphasizing different voices, but a context for civic engagement.

The move to a generic, participation-focused approach has been driven by both ethical and pragmatic concerns. Policymakers and educators were and are genuinely concerned that a focus on identity, particularly any sense of national or collective identity, marginalizes and excludes some people and groups. Approaches that recognize and attempt to include multiple understandings of identity and nation often get subverted because they are complex, difficult to deal with and have the potential to generate conflict. In studies of policy and practice in several Canadian provinces, Bickmore (2005) found that schools and teachers generally avoided difficult issues with high potential for conflict, including those involving ethnicity and identity. Instead, they focused on what she calls 'harmony building' and 'individual skill building' approaches rooted in conflict avoidance. The first includes attention to the 'appreciation of diverse cultural heritages' (p. 165) but does not explore the real difference between and among those heritages. Current Canadian social studies curricula share this commitment to a civic republican approach to citizenship education focused on fostering both agency (the sense that individual citizens can make a difference) and responsibility (the obligation to engage and make a difference) (Hughes and Sears, 2008). Even Quebec has recently moved away from a focus on promoting a deep sense of provincial identity to a more generic and participatory citizenship education (Éthier and Lefrançois, 2011; Létourneau, 2011).

Finally, we turn to the theme of Canada as a nation of nations. This is hardly a new idea in Canadian history. Following rebellions in the colonies of Upper and Lower Canada in the mid-1830s, Lord Durham (1839) was dispatched to sort things out and famously wrote in his report, 'I expected to find a contest between a government and a people: I found two nations warring in the bosom of a single state.' Durham's proposed solution was to work to assimilate one of the nations into the other and thereby eliminate the problem.

Durham's inclination lies at the root of attempts to create a single, iconic Canadian identity and has sometimes had disastrous consequences for minority groups. It has been particularly devastating for Canada's Aboriginal Peoples who have been subjected to several overt attempts to exterminate their languages and cultures in order to assimilate them into the Canadian mainstream. Education has been an important vehicle in these attempts, including the Indian Residential Schools, which for years separated young Aboriginals from their families and communities in order to 'take the Indian out of the child' (Battiste, 2013; Galloway, 2013). Battiste and Semaganis (2002) describe traditional approaches to schooling for Aboriginal students as 'cognitive imperialism', arguing it was, and largely still is, an attempt to extinguish 'Aboriginal conceptions of society' (p. 93).

For other groups, the attempts at creating a single national identity may have been less insidious, but they were certainly not benign. Charles Taylor (1993) describes the process as 'English Canada bent on whipping everyone into line' (p. 32) and argues it is both ineffective and unnecessary. In the latter part of the 20th century, he began arguing for a more nuanced and complex understanding of Canadian citizenship, making the case that members of some collectivities understand their citizenship as multilayered. They are at one in the same time citizens of a sociological nation such as an Aboriginal First Nation or 'la nation canadienne francaise' (p. 31), and citizens of the nation state of Canada. Other Canadians, Taylor contends, understand themselves as citizens in the more liberal sense of being individual members of the polity unmediated by any particular group affiliation. For Taylor, the educational problem is not how to forge a single sense of citizenship but, rather, how to foster mutual understanding among citizens about these different ways of thinking about their affiliation to the polity.

While Taylor's ideas were quite controversial when first suggested, they have become fairly widely accepted. In November of 2006, for example, Members of Parliament passed a motion in the House of Commons which stated, '[t]hat this House recognize that the Québécois[1] form a nation within a united Canada' (*CBC News*, 2006).

This gave parliamentary and state recognition to the multinational nature of the Canadian state, something Québec nationalists, as well as Aboriginal leaders, political scientists and social theorists, had been advocating for some time. There is a growing body of work in Canada and around the world demonstrating young people often have quite cosmopolitan identities and are able to negotiate these quite well (Peck, 2010; Osler, 2009; Osler and Starkey, 2003).

This theme has been slower to move into the educational system in Canada but has begun to make some headway in recent years. Educational scholars are writing about decolonizing education (Battiste, 2013), indigeneity (Orr and Ronayne, 2009) and Treaty Education (Tupper, 2012), and curricula across the country are beginning to focus on teaching about the multinational nature of the Canadian state and the complexity of civic identity in the country.

In Alberta, for example, all social studies curricula have to pay substantial attention to both Francophone and Aboriginal perspectives across a range of topics and issues (Alberta Education, 2005). More specifically, one of the outcomes in the grade 11 curriculum calls for students to 'analyze nationalism as an identity, internalized feeling and/or collective consciousness shared by a people (French Revolution and Napoleonic era, Canadian nationalism, Québécois nationalism, American nationalism, First Nations and Métis nationalism, Inuit perspectives)' (Alberta Education, 2007). Saskatchewan is arguably the province that has gone furthest down this road, particularly when it comes to teaching about Aboriginal peoples. The province has developed outcomes and indicators for Treaty Education designed to foster 'partnerships between First Nations and non-First Nations people in Saskatchewan in the spirit of the Treaties' (Government of Saskatchewan, 2014). One of the four overall mandated outcomes of this initiative is that 'by the end of Grade 12, students will appreciate that Treaties are sacred covenants between sovereign nations and are the foundational basis for meaningful relationships that perpetually foster the well-being of all people' (Saskatchewan Ministry of Education, 2013).

Even with this rise in interest in teaching about Canada as a multinational state and Canadian citizenship as complex and fluid, there remains a significant thrust to develop a single, iconic understanding of the country and its people rooted in a shared European (largely British and French) heritage (Pashby et al., 2014). Indeed, all of the themes discussed here exist to some degree in educational systems across the country, and they often exist in harmony with one another. It is possible, for example, to incorporate the pluralist ideal with the idea of multinationalism, or to harmonize a commitment to civic engagement with pluralism.

Structures of the educational system that impact teaching the nation

There are a number of features of the education system that impact teaching about the nation, including the diffuse authority structures resulting in a strong regional rather than national focus in social studies and history curricula, the generally low level of priority accorded to citizenship education across the country and the range of public and private players involved in the field. We will provide a brief overview of each area.

The Canadian constitution gives authority for education exclusively to provincial governments. The provinces guard this power jealously and resist any overt attempts by the federal government to intrude in this policy area. While many nations with similar constitutional structures have active federal departments of education and there is no constitutional or legal prohibition on Canada doing the same (Ungerleider, 2003), no federal office of education has ever existed. Comparing Canada to other OECD (Organisation for Economic Co-operation and Development) countries in this regard, Robertson (2006) points out, 'every other nation, including those which, like Canada, are structured as federations had devised a vehicle for articulating, debating, and adopting national policies and for coordinating education research' (p. 410), but Canada has not.

Educational policy and curricula are developed at the provincial or regional level, and that has a number of important implications for the issues raised in this chapter. First, it is always risky to speak about education in the national sense. While there has long been a sense of general curricular continuity across the country (Tomkins, 1986), there are important differences in approach. Quebec, for example, has taken a very different slant on education for and about diversity, preferring the concept of interculturalism to multiculturalism and drawing subtle differences between the two (McAndrew, 2001). One of the differences is the overt acknowledgement in interculturalism of a dominant public culture that frames civic life. In the case of Québec, it is Francophone culture. As stated above, some western provinces, most notably Saskatchewan, have a significant focus on education about Aboriginal Peoples, while there has been relatively less focus on that in the Atlantic Provinces.

The second structural component that greatly impacts the teaching about and for the nation is the generally low priority given to social studies in general and civic education in particular in Canadian education. The recently revised social studies curriculum in the province of Ontario boldly proclaims that 'citizenship education is an important facet of students' overall education' (Ontario Ministry of Education, 2013, p. 9) and that echoes similar pronouncements in other provinces. Unfortunately, these rhetorical commitments to citizenship education are virtually never matched with concomitant resources to enact them in substantial ways. As in many jurisdictions, an overweening focus on literacy and numeracy has caused a narrowing of the curriculum, pushing many other subjects, including citizenship, to the margins. While this is an international phenomenon, a comparison of civic education in four democracies (Australia, Canada, England and the US) found Canada lagging behind the other nations examined (Hughes et al., 2010). The title of one article sums it up well, in terms of significant progress in citizenship education – 'Canada dabbles while the world plays on' (Hughes and Sears, 2006).

While the federal government has no official role in education in Canada, it is one of several key players working hard to shape the teaching of the nation in Canadian schools and public educational settings. Working through a range of 'policy instruments' (Sears, 1997), it has worked since at least the early 20th century to shape citizenship education in ways consistent with its vision for the country. One of the primary instruments for doing this is the provision of financial inducements to the provinces in exchange for them adopting particular programmes. 'The most significant program, in terms of money and effect on school systems in the area of citizenship education that was established and maintained through federal-provincial agreements was the Bilingualism in Education Program begun in 1970' (Sears, 1997, p. 7). This initiative was designed not only to foster language proficiency but also to reinforce Canada's identity as a bilingual–bicultural nation.

When unable to exercise influence through the means of official agreements, the federal government developed a number of 'ways around' (Sears, 1997, p. 10) constitutional limitations on its educational role. One of these was the provision of educational materials to teachers and schools and another was the direct delivery of in-service teacher education programmes. Elections Canada, for example, is one of dozens of federal institutions that provides free, high-quality teaching materials for teachers interested in the teaching aspects of Canadian democracy. In addition, many teachers have attended workshops or much longer courses provided by federal actors on teaching things like second language, multiculturalism and Canadian history.

Perhaps the most common policy instrument in the federal government's arsenal has been the use of 'surrogate organizations' (Sears, 1997, p. 11) to carry its message to schools or directly to young people outside of school contexts. The CSF and the ACS discussed above are two examples of this. In 1956, the director of the Citizenship Branch of the Department of Secretary of State identified 60 surrogate organizations with which the Branch worked to provide citizenship education programmes to Canadians, 'including: the Canadian Council of Churches, B'nai Brith, the Canadian Legion, and the YM-YWCA' (Sears, 1997, p. 11). That work has expanded greatly since the 1950s and continues apace today.

Finally, Margaret Conrad and her colleagues in *The Pasts Collective* document a range of both government and non-government actors who seek to shape education about the nation in Canada today. They describe the 'extraordinary expansion of history-related cultural institutions, including museums, historic sites, libraries, archives, and arts councils' (p. 155). In addition to these largely publicly funded initiatives, 'private interests such as the CRB Foundation, Canada's History Society, and Historica-Dominion Institute have sought to introduce selected, carefully framed, often politically driven of ideologically conscious themes into the public conversation about history' (Conrad et al., 2013, p. 155).

Current approaches to civic education

The past 15–20 years have seen the development of a widespread consensus across democratic countries in several key areas relating to citizenship education. This consensus has four attributes: a pervasive sense of crisis about disengagement from civic involvement, particularly among young people (and, in recent years, with particular concerns about young immigrants); a commitment to citizenship education as a key means for addressing that disengagement; focusing citizenship education on a generally civic republican conception of citizenship with an emphasis on civic responsibility and engagement; and proposing constructivist approaches to teaching and learning as models of best practice in civic education. In terms of official policy and programmes, Canada shares in all aspects of this consensus (Hughes and Sears, 2008; Sears, 2010). In addition to these general trends are several specific developments related to citizenship education.

The first of these is the general move to focus on the teaching of the disciplinary structures of thinking related to the various subjects that are central to citizenship education. The best developed and influential of these is the historical thinking movement. There are a number of specific frameworks for historical thinking, but common to them all is an emphasis on developing student competencies with the key disciplinary processes of historical work – students are expected to know not only *what* historians know but also *how* historians know (Lévesque, 2008; Stearns et al., 2000).

The model of historical thinking that is most influential in driving policy and curricular reform in public schooling across Canada is that developed by Peter Sexias and his colleagues at the Centre for the Study of Historical Consciousness at the University of British Columbia and articulated through the Historical Thinking Project (HTP). The HTP sets out a framework of six historical thinking concepts that are designed to help students think 'about how historians transform the past into history and to begin constructing history themselves' (Seixas and Morton, 2013, p. 3). This framework is being integrated into curriculum and policy documents across Canada (Sears, 2014).

Amidst much debate and controversy, in 2007, the Québec government introduced a new 'History and Citizenship Education' curriculum that had two central goals: 'to lead students to understand the present in light of the past' and 'to prepare them for enlightened participation in community life' (Létourneau, 2011, p. 84). These two goals are grounded in the assertion that 'history is the discipline that allows students to understand the present by studying the past' (Duquette, 2014, p. 141).

The controversy hinged on proposed (and eventual) revisions to the history curriculum that would see it expand its view beyond Francophone–Anglophone relations in Canada's past to a more inclusive history curriculum that reflected the contributions of the many diverse groups in Québec's (and Canada's) past, present and future and which required students to engage in the practices of the discipline of history rather than commit to what Létourneau (2004) has called a national narrative of *la survivance*. Although history curricula across Canada have always had an implicit relationship with citizenship education (K. Osborne, 1987), with its new history curriculum Québec makes the link much more explicit. Still in its infancy, research into the effects of the new curriculum tends to focus more on historical thinking competencies than on citizenship goals (Éthier and Lefrançois, 2010).

'Roots of Empathy' is an extracurricular programme in use across Canada and throughout much of the Western world. It was created and first implemented in Ontario in 1996 and has now been established in every province (excluding the northern territories) (Roots of Empathy, 2012). Although not in use in every school in Canada, according to the Roots of Empathy website, almost 480,000 students in kindergarten to grade 8 have taken part in the programme. The programme's goals are to 'foster the development of empathy; develop emotional literacy; reduce levels of bullying, aggression and violence, and promote children's pro-social behaviour; increase knowledge of human development, learning, and infant safety; and prepare students for responsible citizenship and responsive parenting' (Roots of Empathy, n.d.) through the development of relationships between the students and an infant and her/his parent, who visit the students' classroom several times throughout the year. Working primarily in the affective domain, the Roots of Empathy programme has been shown to positively influence children's prosocial behaviour and reduce aggression towards others (Santos et al., 2011; Schonert-Reichl et al., 2012). However, questions remain for us about the programme's effectiveness in terms of its goal to 'prepare students for responsible citizenship', and we could not find any research that speaks to this component. Responsible citizenship appears to be an ethereal goal promoted through group work and consensus-building classroom discussions rather than one that is directly taught and measured by the programme.

Another pan-Canadian initiative is the inclusion of a service-learning component as a required but extracurricular element of students' learning. Like the Roots of Empathy programme, service-learning or community involvement initiatives are implemented sporadically across the country. Some provinces such as British Columbia and Ontario require evidence of participation in a community service in order to graduate. According to Schwarz (2011), the Ontario programme is unique in that students are free to decide how and with what organization(s) they will fulfil this requirement, 'provided their proposed placement type is listed on the school board's catalogue of approved activities'. Whether connections are made between the extracurricular service activities and the official social studies or history curricula is left to teachers to decide, which means that the potential for meaningful learning about the kind of citizenship qualities one can gain from such experiences is left to chance. To be sure, there are benefits to both approaches, but the elements of constructivist teaching, which all curricula in Canada claim to uphold, make clear that learning about such concepts is not developmental – that is, a person does not grow into a reflective and active citizen just because she or he grows older – constructivist teaching principles tell us that 'the most important single factor influencing learning is what the learner already knows. Ascertain this and teach him [sic] accordingly' (Ausubel, 1968, p. vi). Thus, we would like to see more explicit attention to students' prior knowledge about citizenship, including community involvement, in teaching, learning and curriculum development (Peck et al., 2008).

Conclusion: looking forward

Attempting to describe the essence of citizenship education in Canada, Ken Osborne wrote, 'Perhaps the most fundamental fact about Canada is that it is a country that is continually debating the terms of its own existence. It has been doing so ever since 1763. To participate in this debate, to avoid false solutions, to accept that there might in fact not be any once-for-all solutions at all, and above all not to turn one's back on its frustration, is perhaps the ultimate exercise in democracy' (2001, p. 54). The themes we have taken up in this chapter demonstrate the veracity of Osborne's argument. The main approaches to teaching about the nation – as heroic icon, pluralist ideal, site for civic engagement or nation of nations – reflect some of key positions in this ongoing debate. We concur with Osborne that the purpose of civic education is to induct students into this ongoing debate in an informed and engaging way. We hope they leave school not frustrated with the 'conundrum of Canadian identity' (Seixas, 2014, p. 14) but committed to participating in the ongoing national conversation about what it is and should be. In order for that to happen, we hope to see some current trends continue and new developments come to fruition.

One very positive trend is the 'rapprochement' (Christou and Sears, 2014) between history and citizenship education. For various reasons, the two have been 'at war' for a number of years, resulting in a depoliticized and uninteresting approach to history in schools and a decontextualized citizenship education (Sears, 2011; Sears et al., 2011). As described above, new initiatives in history education are very consistent with contemporary trends in citizenship education, and we hope the relationship between the two fields will continue to be strengthened in Canada.

A critical element of the capacity to deliver quality programmes in citizenship education is the development of highly capable teachers with both subject matter and pedagogical knowledge. Canada fails in this regard in several ways. First, we know of no initial teacher education programmes that provide for a specialty in citizenship education. Most have a more general focus on social studies or one or more of its constituent disciplines. Second, teachers, particularly elementary teachers, in several parts of the country tell us they have little opportunity for in-service education in areas related to citizenship education. Finally, out-of-field teaching is relatively common in Canadian secondary schools, and that is particularly true of subjects that are not part of provincial and international assessments, including social studies and citizenship. There are signs that the first two are being addressed, and a major new collection on teacher education related to history teaching is a promising development in that area (Sandwell and von Heyking, 2014).

As stated above, citizenship is generally a low-status subject area in Canadian schools. A significant new initiative in Ontario called Measuring What Matters is calling that into question. The project seeks to broaden the areas deemed critical for educational success. In describing the project, the organization responsible writes, 'Literacy and numeracy are essential for further learning and success in life, but we need evidence of success and opportunities in other important areas like health, creativity, citizenship, social-emotional skills, and the quality of the learning environment' (People for Education, 2014). The project is still in infancy, so it remains to be seen how much impact it will have, but it has attracted positive attention from researchers, policymakers and the public.

Educators have a propensity to 'search for panaceas' (Hunt, 2002), for the one programme or initiative that will create a golden age of achievement and satisfaction with the system. Citizenship education in Canada has not been immune to this tendency. But just as Osborne suggests that the debates among Canadians about the essential nature of the country probably have no 'once-for-all solutions', we contend citizenship education is best served by ongoing discussion and debate rather than by forced consensus. We hope this chapter will contribute something of substance to that process.

6
China

King Man Chong

This chapter analyses what sort of education about and for the nation takes place in China and its SARs of Hong Kong and Macao, and what connections there are between national and internationalization initiatives and globalization. The situation in China is complex. For example, protests and conflicts in Tibet and Xinjiang Uyghur seem to arise out of ethnic tensions and inequities in terms of social mobility and the use of regional resources, in addition to attempts to align education across the whole of China. Given the available space in this chapter, the situations of Tibetans and the Uighurs in China and their meanings of 'education for the nation' are not covered in great detail. Hong Kong and Macao have experienced different development pathways from that of China since 1841 and 1557, respectively, and in this chapter, their versions of education for the nation will be discussed within their own specific contexts. Chinese nationalist theorists have sought to defend Chinese sovereignty against external threats in the early 20th century. Disputes over status and equality led to a national revolution against foreign imperialism, and these issues created implications for education about and for the nation. World War II (WWII) further drew China into a devastating nationalistic war against the invasion of Japan. After 1949, China entered into a far-reaching social revolution in history amid the struggles for national sovereignty and independence, and felt that its nation-building could not be completed without socialist engineering in education. The 'Open Door and Reform' policy reoriented the nation into pragmatic approaches and education for socialist patriots became a focus in school education. The 2000s saw China greatly increasing its economic powers, and in education, there has been a stronger emphasis and control on ideology and patriotic education in Chinese schools.

This chapter first discusses the historical background of Chinese nationalism so as to contextualize the subsequent analysis. Next, it reviews the development of Chinese education before moving on to discuss education for the nation, that is, what are the patterns of patriotic and socialist education that cultivate a young socialist Chinese patriot. Then, this chapter discusses what issues emerge from national and international initiatives in China and characterizations that are pertinent to globalization.

Historical contexts – nation and Chinese nationalism

Nationalism is one of the most powerful forces in human history, even though it is a relatively modern phenomenon that followed the birth of the nation states in Europe (Teng and Darr, 2012). According to Isaiah Berlin (1979), nationalism has been one of the greatest social and political phenomena of the last two centuries, and it is very likely to remain a permanent feature in the foreseeable future. Broadly speaking, there are three influential theories of nationalism, classified as functionalist, culturalist and constructivist. Ernest Gellner (1983) articulates a functionalist theory of nationalism in which economic development and modernization create the need for a unified knowledge through standardized education. The cultural and linguistic diversity in traditional agrarian societies disintegrates as a result of this educational standardization within the state. The modern and standardized educational system also creates social mobility between classes, a homogeneous high (literate) culture, and thus a common national identity which is imposed and protected by the nation state, in order to more smoothly make the transition to a modern, developed economy (Gellner, 1983). Anthony D. Smith (1995, 1998) focuses more strongly on the cultural origins of nationalism. He argues that the functionalist view may be useful for analysing industrial societies, but it fails to explain nationalism in pre-industrial, non-industrial and post-industrial societies. For Smith, nationalism is derived from premodern origins, such as kinship, religion, belief systems, and common historic territories and memories, and is thus defined as 'ethnosymbolic' or even 'primordial' (Smith, 1983).

Smith also sees most nations as having deep historical roots in ancestry, culture and shared history. States also harness existing ethnic and cultural identities through symbols, and the better a state can do this, the better it can legitimate itself (Hastings, 1997). The above discussions on cultural origins of nationalism (Smith, 1995) – that economic development creates the need for a unified knowledge through standardized education (Gellner, 1983) and that states utilize existing ethnic and cultural identities through symbols (Hastings, 1997) – could be useful for understanding the case of China too, since the nation has existed before the modernization drive at the fall of *Qing* (Manchu) dynasty Empire in 1911. The following will discuss China's nation and nationalism.

The concept of 'nation' is commonly used in informal Chinese discourse as equated with 'state' or 'country', but it is not identical to 'state'. A useful differentiation would be that the people in a nation state consider themselves as a 'nation', but united in the political and legal structure of the 'state'. The concept of 'nation' in China is complicated in the sense that China is made up of *Han* as the major ethnic nation and a multiplicity of about 55 minor ethnic nations who live in more than half of the area of the modern China, with many of them having their own languages. However, when one talks about 'nation' in China today, it usually refers to the *Han* majority, and others are referred to as ethnic minorities. The saying of *Zhonghua Minzu* (the literal meaning is 'Chinese nations') is commonly used to refer to all nations living in China. It should also be noted that China has been governed by the *Han* majority since the downfall of *Qing* dynasty in 1991. But in the preceding imperial dynasties, the *Han* majority had already been mixed up with other ethnic minorities both within and outside the constant changing borders through wars, migrations and marriages. Thus, the concept of 'nation' in China has its specific developments. Another significant achievement of Chinese imperial dynasties was that a sense of cultural superiority has been accepted by the Chinese people, and so the modern times of suffering from humiliations made it hard for Chinese (Fairbank, 1987).

Nationalism has been an important theme in Chinese political discourse for more than a century (Zhao, 2013). The *First Opium War* in 1839–1842 was regarded as a turning point in modern Chinese history when the Chinese nation was gradually downgraded to the status of an 'inferior people' (Wang, 2011, p. 6) and bullied by the Western imperial powers, Russia and Japan. In their colonial plunder and seizure of new markets, the imperial powers launched aggressions against China and forced the corrupted and incompetent *Qing* dynasty government to sign several unequal treaties with them, thus pushing China into a semi-colonial and semi-feudal society (Wang, 2011). As a consequence of China's defeat in the first Sino-Japanese War (1894–1895), which was a shock and wake-up call for Chinese, most Chinese elites became convinced that only by giving up its traditional imperial identity and becoming a nation state could China endure, and only by joining the emerging Western world order did China have any hope of recovering its past glory (Xu, 2008). The unfolding project of Chinese nationalism was thus an arduous and tortuous one as China engaged in a dual task of nation-building and state-making in a single endeavour (Shen and Chien, 2006), which was different from what John Breuilly (1982) noted that there has to be a modern state before a nation comes into being. China's survival 'appeared to require organizing the population into a collective force and reforming the imperial order into a nation state, in the modern sense' (Shen and Chien, 2006, p. 49). Zhao also summarized (2013, p. 535) that 'with a deeply rooted suspicion of the Western powers, Chinese nationalism is powered by a narrative of China's century of shame and humiliation at the hands of imperialist powers and calls for the Chinese government to redeem the past humiliations and take back all lost territories'. Thus, the keywords in understanding the driving force of nationalism in China are 'humiliation' and 'national dignity' (Berlin, 1997).

The authors (Anderson, 1991; Huntington, 1993; Said, 1995) of constructivist view saw nationalism as a product of elite manipulation of mass publics. They argued that national identities are constructed through printed national languages that connect people speaking different dialects. According to Anderson (1991), the rise of the printing press was a critical element in the advent of nationalism because people were able to imagine those who could read their language as members of their nation. In China, Macao serves a good example of this where Portuguese printing press brought about the Portuguese colony's development before the printing press made their way into Hong Kong (Li, 2010; Willis, 2002). In creating the imagination of a nation, due to the advocacy of Liang Qichao in the late 19th century, 'the Cavour of China', the term *guomin* (citizens) was accepted by late *Qing* dynasty intellectuals as a key concept in their articulation of the nationalist project (Shen and Chien, 2006). Propaganda on this concept of *guomin* was thus gaining momentum in the late 19th century. According to this *guomin* concept, if China was to be spared its imminent doom, Chinese must be turned from their debased status of being 'subjects', who lacked political subjectivity, into modern 'citizens' who actively took part in politics. In addition, the new Chinese state and the people were conceived as complementary and mutually reinforcing and so the concepts of nation and state would then converge to designate the same thing (Shen and Chien, 2006), thus nationalism as a doctrine of 'the political and the national unit should be congruent' (Gellner, 1983). This was the first time such modern concepts came into Chinese knowledge.

Berlin (1997) argued that a wounded or outraged sense of human dignity and the desire for recognition are the driving force of nationalism. This desire for recognition characterizes not only nationalism but all emancipation movements. In order to save China and recreate the glory of China, various political forces had put forward solutions and different means, especially that the early 20th century brought into China a great stimulus of foreign thought (Fairbank, 1987). Also, the 'struggle to restore "national dignity" in China had introduced a radical episteme of equality which gradually displaced the hierarchical ethics of an empire' (Fitzgerald, 2006, p. 112). The period between the downfall of the imperial *Qing* dynasty in 1911 and the centralized power established by the Communist Party of China in 1949 was a period of 'maximum susceptibility and response to foreign theories of social order' (Fairbank, 1987, p. 287). However, Socialism/Communism was finally adopted by the Communist Party of China, which was founded in 1921, as a way to save the nation, when China was nicknamed as the 'sick man of East Asia' and in need of being strong again (Xu, 2008). Throughout the early history of Chinese Communist Party, there were several political messages that help to build up Marxism, Socialism and Communism, for example, Marxism saves China from Western imperialist subjugations, it is the historical development that the Chinese people have chosen Marxism, the political party of the Chinese working class – the Communist Party – took Marxism as its theoretical basis and ideological guide, and Marxism as an ideological weapon combined with Chinese people could be a tremendous dynamic revolutionary force which changed China's historical destiny (Wang, 2011).

There were whole-nation attempts to raise the Chinese profile in the international arena too. Modern sports have played a significant role in constructing identities and ideologies since their gradual emergence in the mid-19th century (Xu, 2008) and the political functions of sports became pronounced during the 20th century. China was obsessed with Western sports at the turn of the 20th century, and this relates to China's search for national and international identity (Xu, 2008). The establishment of a Nationalist government in China since 1911 and unification again after an interim warlord period, where different factions of warlords fought against each other between 1916 and 1928, had made this nation-saving idea through sports possible. The Nationalist Party's military man Chiang Kai-shek raised the profile of sports when he became the national leader in 1925. From 1928 to 1945, Chiang made many speeches about the importance of citizens' physical condition to the nation's destiny (Xu, 2008); hence, sports had been used as a political tool for nation-building. In the 1930s, 'training strong bodies for the nation' became a widespread slogan. Subsequently, between the 1930s and 1940s, Chinese scholars, politicians and educators put their nation-saving ideas by sports into practices (Xu, 2008).

The founding of the People's Republic of China (PRC) in 1949 saw China engage itself in a series of radical mobilization such as Land Reform Campaign, which took away land ownership from the landlords to the state, and Great Leap Forward, which changed China from a predominantly agrarian society to a modern and industrial society, in the 1950s and 1960s. China was isolated and poor by the time Chairman Mao died in 1976 (Xu, 2008) after the break-up with the USSR. China was also a giant power trying to establish its influences among the newly decolonized African countries. But after the economic reform which was led by the political leader Deng Xiaoping in 1978, China began to increase its contacts with the Western world. Deng instructed the concept of 'seeking truth from facts' when he met the head of the Ministry of Education in 1977. In basic terms, it meant that the practical conditions of China should be the basis for economic policy, not inappropriate and idealistic dogma (Allen, 1997). This has begun an era of an ideology of pragmatism in post-Mao politics (Allen, 1997; Dickson, 2003). The political education in schools also underwent a reorientation in teaching ideologies of pragmatism. Yet, the Four Cardinal Principles were also stated by Deng in 1979 for which debate was not allowed, which include upholding the socialist path, the dictatorship of the proletariat, the leadership of the Communist Party of China, and upholding Mao Zedong Thought and Marxism–Leninism (Allen, 1997). Hence, the teaching of Chinese youths would need to uphold such cardinal principles, and the education system was under strict ideological control.

Beijing government, indeed, used the so-called gold medal strategy to demonstrate China's rise in power and wealth (Xu, 2008). Since the 1980s, sport events such as the Olympic Games and soccer World Cup, which have the capacity to move markets, make peace and shift national moods (Kempe, 2006), had been used as a way to raise the profile of Chinese nation in the world. The idea that winning is everything has also entered the Chinese mindset when the government mobilized the nation's resources to achieve victories through administrative, legal and political means (Xu, 2008). The taking part by China in the 1984 Los Angeles Olympic Games was a landmark after it rejoined the International Olympic Committee in 1979. In 1992, Deng pledged for continuous openness and reform following from the closing door in the aftermath of the military crackdown on the student movement in 1989. Since then, China became a rising power on a level with Japan (Fukuyama, 1992). China has also become more open in its approach to the world. In education, teaching materials about the Olympics were developed for teaching in schools, and this is an example of bridging learning about the world and the national pride of a new China. When sports as a nationalistic project unfolds, a loss in a major sports event could have a negative impact. When Chinese national soccer team loses a World Cup elimination match, its stock market, on average, loses nearly half a percentage point in value the following day (Kempe, 2006). But the Beijing Olympics Games in 2008 further demonstrated immensely Chinese political, economic and cultural significances and accentuated the significance of sports as a political endeavour in the minds of Chinese leaders (Xu, 2008).

Finally, in assessing Chinese nationalism today, by using the 2008 China Survey, Tang and Darr (2012) examine Chinese respondents' feelings towards their country. They compare Chinese nationalism with that of 35 countries and regions in the 2003 National Identity Survey and found that China shows the highest level of nationalism.

Nationalism in contemporary China is also better predicted by the political and economic characteristics of an individual rather than cultural attributes (Tang and Darr, 2012). Indeed, driven by nationalist sentiment, a yearning to redeem the humiliations of the past, and the simple urge for international power, China is seeking to replace the US as the dominant power in Asia (Bernstein and Munro, 1997; Gries, 2004). Yet, as regards the question as to whether Chinese nationalism was affirmative, assertive or aggressive, there are different views, with the prevailing perception being negative. Many scholars (Chang, 1998; Friedman, 1997; Sautman, 1997; Yu, 1996) see Chinese nationalism as a worrying phenomenon, and some even view China as a dangerously aggressive force that may threaten the peace and stability of the region and the world. But Zhao (2004, 2008) argued that while the Chinese government was hardly exploiting national-ist sentiment, it was able to control its expression, practise a prag-matic nationalism based on a sober assessment of China's domestic and global challenges tempered by diplomatic prudence. This posi-tion differed from those scholars who held that Chinese national-ism was a reckless and aggressive new nationalism (Zhao, 2013). On the domestic front, the rhetorical conventions of radical nationalism ironically work against the Communist. The emphasis on equality and dignity that carried the Communist to power 'surfaces daily in private conversations about privilege and rank, about corruption and nepotism, and about the arbitrary exercise of power in local commu-nities' (Fitzgerald, 2006, p. 113). Chinese found their daily lives to be dominated by party officials who have converted public goods into private assets and who compel those beneath them to submit to their arbitrary authority (Fitzgerald, 2006).

The two SARs, Hong Kong and Macao, were established in 1997 and 1999, respectively, after the resumption of sovereignties by China under the political arrangement of 'One Country, Two Systems' and guiding principles of 'ruling by local people' and 'high degree of autonomy'. Both places were governed under *Basic Law* for which the Hong Kong version set the model for Macau (Bray, 1997; Yee, 2001). Both cities also had been under Western colonial rule and influ-ences, as a 'meeting-point between East and West' (Clayton, 2009, p. 3) where traders and missionaries had been at the forefront to make them into global cities (Wei, 2014). In colonial Hong Kong, the government granted public funds to schools (Bickley, 2002) for procurement of teachers, buildings, textbooks and equipment (Sweeting, 1990, 2004), and used a 'depoliticized' approach (Morris, 1997) to govern society and education, such as forbidding the talks of politics in schools, so that many people had only a vague sense of their national identity (Ng, 2011). Education, indeed, is a tool for transmitting the ideology of a country. After the 1990s, Hong Kong developed into a cosmopolitan city that emphasizes civic concepts such as civil and political rights, as well as equality, regardless of race, ethnicity and gender, while that of Macao developed into an internationally famous city for entertainment and gambling (Wei, 2014). Concepts of environmental citizenship (Martinsson and Lundqvist, 2010) also appeared in the Hong Kong school curriculum. However, the concept of ethnic nationalism (Smith, 1991) is still relevant to Hong Kong and Macao, especially since China advocates ethnic-based nationalism. How Hong Kong and Macao SARs cultivated education for the nation will be discussed later on.

Education development in a nation-building China, with the concept of nationalism underpinning the nation-building movement since the late 19th century, and the implications for education for the nation will be discussed below.

Education development in a nation-building China

The dynastic Chinese education system had traditionally been ruled by Confucianism except in a few dynasties. Confucianism is a human-centred system that ignores or even rejects religious beliefs and practice (Reed, 1997). Confucianism exhorts people to be obedient to state rulers and the state itself, and it emphasizes values such as knowledge, loyalty, respect, obedience, humility, benevolence, kindness and courtesy. The impact of Confucianism on both dynastic and modern China is that one of the most essential roles of government is to educate the people and provide moral/political guidance through moral persuasion (i.e. telling people what sort of conduct or character is right and virtuous) with a paternalistic fervor which limits individual liberty or autonomy. The usual contents of such moral persuasion would be that the government always acts virtuously and legitimately and the populace is asked to follow suit. The secular nature of the Chinese system, coupled with the belief that moral leadership was an essential function of government, had facilitated the creation and implementation of moral/political education in China (Reed, 1997), though it is always tempting to ask about the degree to which the norms and values of Confucian education were actually realized in different parts of China. Furthermore, in contrast to the Western distinction between individual autonomy and the society (Bellah et al., 1986), there has been a tendency to define the individual in social terms, thus blurring the individual/society distinction (Reed, 1997). This has further given rise to a sense of merging individual morality and the bigger political morality in school's education.

In the early 20th century, there was a tremendous stimulus achieved through foreign ideas that were brought into China (Fairbank, 1987). The May Fourth Movement was a nationalistic response in 1919 which highlighted democracy and science, as well as the importance of civic and moral education, in cultivating the citizens to save the country from foreign threats (Lee, 2001). Since the late 1920s, the Nationalist government had assigned high importance to the urban professional middle class whose power lay not so much in property but in mastery of science and technology, finance and law, education and culture, all of which were vital to a modernizing state (Yip, 2003). These professionals shared a common modernist and nationalist ideology that drew on Western ideas in order to develop China. The Nationalist government also needed writers and intellectuals (meaning middle-school graduates or above in China) to further educational progress and propagating Nationalist ideology in education (Yip, 2003). Thus, there existed an interdependent relationship between the government and the urban middle class in which the former needed the services of the latter while the latter drew on the patronage of the former.

During the war against Japanese occupation between 1937 and 1945, the Chinese Nationalist government's education system was threatened. It relied upon voluntary charitable organizations participating in relief work for children by setting up children's homes, kindergarten and primary school education (Ministry of Education [ROC], 1990), as well as Christian missionaries and Catholic churches which provided clinics, hospitals, schools, orphanages, and other social services for refugee children (Whyte, 1988). WWII dealt a serious blow to the gains made by the professional middle class in the 1930s when the country enjoyed relative stability. The Nationalist government retreated to the undeveloped interior (Yip, 2003). Yet, an unexpected outcome of this refugee migration during the war was to bring educational and cultural benefits to the interior Chinese provinces. The relocation of many prestigious Chinese universities and colleges, and thousands of students, teachers, professors and educators, had greatly increased educational and cultural opportunities for the interior provinces (Yip, 2003). Cities such as Kunming and Chongqing took on a political, economic and cultural character that brought them closer to the developed coastal regions. The Nationalist government's support of normal, vocational and middle schools in the interior provinces further assisted the provision of elementary and secondary education in the whole of China (Ou, 1977).

The post-WWII turmoil of civil war between Nationalist and Communist parties and the incompetence of the Nationalist government further weakened the professional middle class in China (Yip, 2003). Thousands of refugee students and intellectuals already had joined the Communists in northern China under the belief that only the Communists could offer the nation an escape from its despair. This withdrawal of intellectuals' support had in part led to the final collapse of the Nationalist government (Yip, 2003). Once the Chinese Communist Party was in power after 1949, education became a political tool to cultivate socialist youths who shouldered the responsibilities of achieving the socialist ideals and devoting to the Communist Party line (Fairbank, 1987), although it should be noted that Confucianism exerted influences on morality, ethics, values and character development until the devastating campaign of Cultural Revolution which started in 1966. Since intellectuals were in large part teachers, the whole educational system became an area for revolutionary action. To Chairman Mao Zedong, the intellectuals' work was essential to the socialist revolution. The official position was that as peasants were amalgamating with workers to do labour and became members of the proletariat, so the same applied to the intellectuals (Fairbank, 1987). The Communist Party was concerned about whether the revolution would succeed if intellectuals were still following the Confucian model of censorial remonstrance and students were still learning classical and liberal ideas. Mao wanted the intellectuals to support the regime and education that would remould the masses. Therefore, Chinese schools educated its young citizens through socialist patriotic education, which emphasizes loving the party-state and the country (Fairbank, 1987).

The modern Communist Chinese education system thus developed in a highly centralized form with a top-down management style. Communist party cadres usually act as the principal of each school and stand for the party in administration and monitoring. There have been policies of establishing key-point schools where the best students, teaching staff and equipment could be concentrated in order to maintain high standards and produce a trained elite (Fairbank, 1987). A national examination at the end of secondary education has been functioning so that the percentage of graduates who passed on from middle schools into universities became the hallmark of a school's excellence (Fairbank, 1987). But there seems to be less overt ideological control over the schools since the late 1980s, and the teachers have assumed less of the function of state ideological actors. Chinese teachers usually teach according to the official approved textbooks, which originated from the Soviet example of regularizing teaching plans, materials and textbooks (Fairbank, 1987). Moral education guidance was carefully prescribed in textbooks and based on Confucian principles such as loyalty, respect and obedience. In recent years, the Communist government has come to regard Confucian principles as useful to supplement the Communist ideologies as a basis for Chinese organization and culture, and so Confucius Institutes are founded overseas with the support of the government (Paradise, 2009).

Since 2000, China has also opened up its education system in many ways, which includes allowing students to apply for universities in Hong Kong, Macao and the once so-called 'imperialist' Western countries. This in turn has created pressures for the mainland Chinese universities to improve their international prestige. China has also allowed foreign students studying in Chinese schools and universities so as to enable cultural exchange and learning about the Chinese language. But even with such opening up, throughout traditional Confucian China, Communist Maoist thought, post-Mao and post-Deng eras, moral actions in China have been defined as those that contribute to quality of the 'community', which is defined as the clan or village, the collective, or the state.

Education for the nation: patriotic education in Communist China, National Education in Hong Kong SAR and Macao SARs

Patriotism is regarded as an important glorious tradition in China, which propelled the Chinese society to move forward and act as a spiritual pillar for different Chinese nations, that is, *Zhonghua Minzu*. In the early years of Communist China after 1949, 'revolution' figured strongly in the education system, and a link was created between education and political ideals. Mao Zedong once said, 'Our educational policy must enable everyone who receives an education to develop morally, intellectually and physically and become a worker with both socialist consciousness and culture' (Cleverley, 1985, p. 139). The Red Guards movement in 1966, which was led by inexperienced youth, symbolized one of the high tides of learning revolution by making revolution. The whole Chinese education system was shut down. However, the Red Guards movement was immensely destructive to the Chinese society, as it had led to open and active warfare between organized groups, which were less institutionalized and the hardest to control (Fairbank, 1987). In short, Mao's generation had run the gamut of breaking down Confucianism to the acceptance of progress evolution and social Darwinism, adding on it fervent nationalism and reappraisal of Chinese tradition in order to save the nation (Fairbank, 1987). On the other hand, the secular nature of educational model, its combination of the political and the moral, and its belief in the efficacy of education as a means of moulding character and curing societal ills also remained (Reed, 1997).

Moral/political education in China faced new challenges after the 'Open Door and Reform' policy in 1979. Factors such as the economic policy of 'Commodity Socialism' in the post-Mao era, disillusionment with the Communist Party's leadership, and the open door policy itself have all conspired to bring about what some commentators call 'the death of ideology' in the 1980s (Reed, 1997). Entering into the 1990s, patriotism was spelt out in *Guidelines for Patriotic Education for Chinese Schools* by the Central Committee of Communist Party of China on 23 August 1994 (Zhao, 2004) in order to tighten up ideological control. This guideline on patriotic education emphasized the importance of upholding the guidance of Socialism with Chinese characteristics by the political leader Deng

Xiaoping, upholding the party line, bringing benefits to the modernization of Socialism, promoting reform and openness, protecting the country, national reputation, dignity, unity and interests, as well as promoting the unification of the motherland. These were regarded as guiding principles of patriotic education in China and were adhered strictly by all schools through a top-down approach.

The Chinese-national-flag-raising ceremony is treated as something which is very important. For Chinese people, the raising of the Chinese national flag and playing of the national anthem is often a stirring moment. The national anthem was originally written for a film against a background of imminent foreign invasions in 1935, but then it was adopted as the national anthem after the establishment of the PRC in 1949. This history is an extremely important part of learning in Chinese schools. In Communist China, students are arranged by teachers to observe the flag-raising and national-anthem-singing ceremony in schools with utmost respect on Chinese national anniversary and important historical days. The Chinese flag stands for the whole collective well-being and future of China. Students are taught to sing the national anthem enthusiastically while raising the national flag. Also, flag-raising guard teams are selected from the students to train them to perform the rituals of ceremonies. Since 1997, the Chinese government has established centres of education for patriotism in major cities, which number about 353 throughout China. These serve to cultivate socialist spirits among all Chinese students through arranged visits by the schools, as well as open to the public. At such patriotic education centres, the history and struggles of Chinese Communist Party, the patriotic war against the Japanese invasion (but not mentioning the Nationalist Party's efforts), the development of ideology of Marxism, and the political, social and economic achievements of China are told to the visitors.

There are no shortage in Chinese schools of reminders and education for the Chinese people about the humiliation of being invaded by foreign countries. Starting from the two Opium Wars in the middle of the 19th century, the Invasion by Eight Nations Alliance in 1900 and then the Japanese invasion during the WWII, they are all regarded as national humiliations by China. In particular, the anti-Japanese invasion is treated as a significant patriotic struggle. On 2 September each year, the Chinese officials organize large-scale mobilization to remember the wars against the Japanese invasion. There is even a saying of 'The 8-Year War of Resistance' to signify this sentiment of anti-Japanese war with an aim to remind the general public of the national shame.

In 2009, the Beijing government tightened up the patriotic education in China. The General Office of the Communist Party of China forwarded the requirement of 'Opinions from the Publicity Department of the Communist Party of China of Carrying out mass patriotic education activities to celebrate the 60th anniversary of the founding of New China'. The Opinions asked for pushing further patriotic education to different regions and administrative departments in April 2009 (*China Education Daily*, 27/4/2009). This notice also urges people to start campaigns of mass patriotic education, which will be helpful for motivating patriotism and national spirits, enhancing confidence in overcoming difficulties, unifying the people's power, moving forward the economy and society, and concentrating efforts on reform and open door policy and modernization of Socialism. It can be seen that the current Chinese government has put an emphasis on the importance of promoting patriotic education in the Chinese society.

Patriotic education, in fact, has always been in the school curriculum through the subjects of Thinking and Morality subject in primary and junior secondary, and Ideological and Political subject in senior secondary schools, which are mandated by Ministry of Education and usually follow the directives and instructions from the Central Communist Party. While the Thinking and Morality subject combined morality, psychological health, law and national conditions (i.e. *Guo qing* education), the Ideological and Political subject combined Marxism, Chinese political system, socialist political thoughts and political culture, citizen's political life, and socialist road with Chinese characteristics as contents. The education authorities also ensure that patriotism and socialist ideas are adopted in teaching materials and implemented in classroom teaching. In February 2013, the Ministry of Education issued *"Instruction on delivering 'Recommendations on Thinking and Morality courses in Junior High School and Ideological and Political courses in High School to act the spirit of the 18th Party Congress'"* (Ministry of Education, 2013), which emphasized how school education can follow the socialist spirits in the decisions made by the Chinese Communist Party.

In Hong Kong and Macao SARs, they have adopted different development pathways. While the colonial Hong Kong government adopted systematic regulations over the schools by giving funding to schools organized by charity associations, religious bodies, provincial origin bodies and professional organizations, the colonial Macao government adopted a freehand approach over schools in which religious, local charity and pro-Chinese government schools co-existed with certain degree of autonomy. Education for the nation thus showed diversified developments. Whereas the government and aided schools in Hong Kong did not spend much efforts on education for the nation under an apolitical and 'depoliticized' orientation which forbid the teaching of politics in schools, the pro-Beijing government 'Leftist schools' had traditionally adopted a more explicit pro-Chinese government attitude. Yet, Chinese culture is by and large an uncontroversial topic in many Hong Kong schools since a Chinese cultural identity was found to be acceptable. Chinese History as a subject was introduced in Hong Kong schools to address Chinese history and politics since 1945 but leaving behind national identification (Kan, 2007). The schools in Macao had largely adopted a conservative orientation in their teaching where Chinese culture and Chinese national identity were taught in schools. Just before the handover of sovereignty back to China, Macao education authority issued the revised *Framework for Moral and Civic Education* in June 1999 after reviewing the needs of Macao society, especially regarding the passivity of Macau's citizens in learning about their society, political environment, and civic rights and responsibilities (DSEJ, 1999).

After the return of sovereignty of Hong Kong to China in 1997, and Macao back to China in 1999, both SAR governments adopted a clearer stance towards cultivating students' Chinese national identification. The concept of 'Nation' is central to any nationalistic attempts in Hong Kong, as both governments have enforced a policy of promoting a sense of Chinese national identity to forge closer ties between themselves and China, although the education reform also acknowledges that Hong Kong is facing tremendous challenges posed by a globalized economy (Sweeting, 2004). This nationalistic aim in education, though not directly, linked up with an increasing number of emigrants from Mainland China to both cities since the handover of sovereignties. While the Hong Kong SAR government regards unification with China as an important constitutional change and so Moral and Civic Education was identified as one of *Four Key Tasks* in education reform (CDC, 2002), the Macao SAR government has implemented Moral and Character Education as a required subject for its primary and secondary schools. The Moral and Character Education for primary schools in Macao identifies understanding and preserving Chinese culture and moral values, knowing about the relationship between Macao and China, loving China, and fostering a spirit of contributing to the nation among its subject aims (DSEJ, 1999, p. 7). For Civic Education, which is regarded as a subset of Moral and Character Education, it further lists out understanding Chinese culture and cultivating national consciousness among the aims for primary education (DSEJ, 1999, p. 81). Civic Education is important to Macao's schools in the sense that it could cultivate civic consciousness so that a foundation for adaptation to complex social and political environments can be established (DSEJ, 1999, p. 80). Macao also utilized its long-standing close relationships with the nearby provincial governments in China and Chinese festivals by organizing celebrative events in order to enhance students' Chinese national identification.

Hong Kong and Macao SARs, however, showed a divergent development since 2012 when there was a mass protest against the Hong Kong SAR government's introduction of a mandatory Moral and National Education curriculum in all government and aided primary and secondary schools. A mandatory approach to introduce a curriculum that aims at fostering a Chinese national identification was not welcome by Hong Kong students and parents, who favoured individual autonomy rather than an imposed collective sense of national identification. Education for a nation is thus left to the individual school's own decision. But in Macao SAR, the education for a nation has not met with much fierce opposition as that of Hong Kong SAR. The possible reason may be that Macao has been a place for peace and was seldom disturbed by excessive violence, and there were long periods of silent understanding between Macao, Lisbon and Beijing before the handover (Ptak, 2014). This understanding lingered on well into in the Macao SAR era.

Education for a globalized world: the impacts of an ideological world outlook

The political curriculum in Chinese primary and secondary schools has usually centred on restoring 'national dignity' in 21st-century China, and thus they perceive the world as how to protect China itself against foreign Western powers. The new Communist China has successfully introduced a radical concept of equality (Fitzgerald, 2006), but it might also concede that the rights-based concepts based on the principle of equality were first hijacked by the modernizing Nationalist and Communist movements in the Republican era in the first half of the 20th century, and the 'Nationalist elites nevertheless popularized the discourse of equality through repeated attacks on domestic status hierarchies institutionalized in the family and in Confucian ritual and learning' (Fitzgerald, 2006, p. 112–113).

The treatment of WWII in education, in particular, has caused much uneasiness and even tension between China and Japan. Whereas there were very few pages allocated to the narration of wars, especially in terms of Japanese motives and reasons for going to war with its Asian neighbours in the Japanese history textbooks, it is commonly treated as Japanese militarism in Chinese textbooks (Nuhoglu and Wong, 2006). The 'Nanjing massacre' by Japanese armies in 1937 was also given much coverage in Chinese school textbooks as a cause for the Sino-Japanese War in the WWII; in particular, the education authority of Nanjing city regulated that upper primary, junior and senior secondary must spend at least four teaching hours on this event and adopt the Nanjing massacre history textbooks approved by the authority (*Beijing Times*, 20/11/2014). Apart from that, the Western powers' scramble for concessions by China in the late 19th and early 20th centuries were also given much curriculum weight to remind students of the national humiliations.

The Communist Party of China, indeed, has transformed its views on the world in different stages. When it first established itself since 1949, connections were made with the USSR in order to learn about the industrialized Communist model. The class struggle theory was also adopted in the education, in which proletariat and capitalist classes are taught as in antagonism and the capitalist Western powers were taught as finally to be overthrown while the socialist countries are taught as forming into a united front against the capitalist countries in Chinese schools. But when China broke up with the USSR in the late 1960s, China went on its own Communist road by building up its relationship with the Third World. So, in the school education, Chinese students learnt about diplomatic relations with the developing countries, especially the comradeship with the Third World, and to guard against the 'imperialist' intentions of Western capitalist countries when they grow up.

Under Deng's leadership in the late 1970s, Socialism was seen as having a distinct and different political make-up than before. The Socialist China took a conscious approach to economic development by aiming to 'realize common prosperity step by step' and by distributing resources fairly (Allen, 1997), or, in other words, a big government was adopted. By implication, capitalist political systems were just less socially consciousness, less rational and were characterized by smaller governments (Allen, 1997). Also, capitalist countries were no longer always treated as 'evil empires' which aimed to jeopardize the Chinese socialist roads. Therefore, the attacks on imperialist Western capitalist countries in education have become lesser since the 1980s.

A reforming China entered the 1990s and 2000s with a need to modernize its education system. Chinese education is coping with new demands in a globalized age which emphasizes critical thinking and multiple perspectives (Hahn, 1998), as well as preparing the students for globalization (Giddens, 2002). Meanwhile, Hong Kong and Macao SARs have been reformed since the early 2000s too, with Hong Kong focusing on all-round development, generic skills, reading to learn, information technology, special education needs and lifelong learning, so that the students can cope with globalization (Education and Manpower Bureau, 2001). Hong Kong and Macao SARs are on the road to balance the need of coping with globalization while building up students' national identification.

Issues emerging from national and international initiatives and characterizations that are pertinent to globalization

The overarching ideology of Socialism would always be the focus when we analyse the education for the nation and international initiatives in China. But one major issue is that following from an opening up of Chinese national system which allows educational exchanges and interactions with the outside world, can the top-down management in education be sustained over the years? Given that flexibility is needed in the process of interacting with the outside world, such cultural exchange and interactive learning in individual schools with outside world may come into conflict with a management system that is accountable to the party secretaries at district, township/county and city levels and requires individual schools to complete a lengthy process in gaining permission. What matters may not be just the time consumed, but also the ideologies that may be at risk when opening up for exchanges with the outside world, which will be discussed below.

The second issue that arises from Chinese national and international initiatives related to globalization is the ideological conflicts underpinning the learning messages. Learning about and interacting with the outside world may be seen as allowing for the consideration of multiple perspectives and the recognition and development of 'global citizens' among the learners. The discussion of individuals within nation states but acting through national-level civil society associations and organizations have pushed the Transnational Corporations to fulfil their global responsibilities in many parts of the world (Henderson, 2000). But, under socialist ideologies of education, it would possibly create ideological conflicts when it comes to what would be the ideal citizens that should be cultivated in education. A socialist 'good citizen' would be one who upholds the paramount importance of state-led Socialism and Communism, patriotism, and national sovereignty in the strictest sense of not any interference from outside is permitted. However, in a decentralized, pluralistic, multipolar and globalized world, especially given the discussions of global citizenship such as ideological pluralism (Schattle, 2008), and global culture, global ideology, global rights and responsibilities, global participation through the international NGOs, the Chinese socialist and patriotic principles would possibly lead to a clash of ideologies among the learners themselves when they realize the possibilities of multiple perspectives. There has been a common practice of asking the participants (e.g. school students) to reflect on the experiences after interacting with foreigners after cultural exchanges or overseas study occasions. This reflective practice was intended to clarify what have been learnt about outside world, in fears that this may affect students' orientation in upholding supremacy of socialist principles. Thus, it is interesting to see how an open China responds to the clash of ideologies in education.

The third issue is the potential contradiction between passive and active citizenship, albeit in a general sense. While China has been educating its citizens on values such as patriotism, loyalty, filial piety and obedience, which are usually associated with passive citizenship, any potential initiatives to cultivate citizens who are willing to participate in the community and public life would usually meet with ideological obstacles and challenges, unless these are geared towards preservation and unity for a socialist cause. The Chinese government has set a common goal for the country and its citizens, which is development of Socialism as the medium-term goal and Communism as the long-term goal. It has also determined and promoted beliefs about a 'correct' pathway for reaching the goal. Therefore, any initiative and campaigns that calls for voluntary participation, unless politically mobilized or sanctioned by the Party, would not be allowed. Although there are volunteer services in China such as charities and green groups, they are mostly under the auspices of the authorities and so the Chinese civil society struggles to grow. Individuals are not given the rights and opportunities to take up their active citizenship, not to mention the limited role of schools in educating students into active citizens who are prepared to take part in civic life.

Finally, similar to a question about the degree to which the norms and values of Confucian education were actually realized in such a vast geographical China, patriotic or socialist education for a Chinese nation may also face the question of how much of an inescapable gap there is between what is taught, what is learned and what is practised. For example, moral learning is always difficult to be assessed because an individual can demonstrate an understanding of moral principles and even display the desired moral behaviours, but one can only rarely assess the motives that underlie the behaviours (Reed, 1997). It could be argued that the effectiveness of educating for a nation in China may bear a risk of superficial 'lip service' among the populace.

Conclusion

The issue of educating for the nation will likely continue to be a major concern given China continues to open up itself in a globalized world. Of course, nationalism has been a whole nationwide project after the fall of the imperial *Qing* dynasty and then the building up of a republic in the early half of the 20th century. Nationalists sought not only to defend Chinese sovereignty against external threats but also to assert the sovereignty of the national people who are equal in their status and civic participation. There were also nationalistic attempts to promote the concept of *guomin* (citizen) and use sports as a nationalistic tool in the nationalistic education of China. Upon establishing itself as a Communist country, socialist and communist ideas were engineered. Ideological and political education subjects were mandatory in primary and secondary schools and patriotic education centres were established throughout China in order to create socialist patriots among the students and the public. Patriotic education, however, may face challenges when clashes of ideologies and passive and active citizenship are taken into account in this globalized world. It would be interesting to see how Chinese citizenship education adapts and copes with the challenges of a globalization age which emphasizes multiple perspectives, flexibility, critical and independent thinking, and having a global identity. The Hong Kong and Macao SAR cases exhibited different pathways while developing the national education after reunification with China. Already globalized to a certain extent under colonial rules, Hong Kong and Macao face both the challenges of globalization and a need to develop nationalistic education since the handovers.

7
United Kingdom

Ian Davies

Introduction

The UK as a state has been characterized by violent relationships. The process of devolution has led to particular forms of governance in the 'four nations' of Northern Ireland, Scotland, Wales and England. The result of the 2014 referendum about Scottish independence signalled support for the continuation of the UK but it was a tense and closely fought contest. In this chapter, I describe and discuss historical and contemporary social and political contexts and relate these issues to education in general as well as regarding curriculum and pedagogy. Finally, I, briefly, make some recommendations and speculate on likely developments over the next 50 years about educating for the nation in the UK.

Background – the UK, its history and citizenship

There is much confusion among many citizens about what, precisely, is meant by the UK. Informal conversations quickly reveal, for example, that many British citizens feel unsure about the distinction between Great Britain and the UK. The former is, geographically, the largest of the British Isles. Most of the territories of England, Scotland and Wales exist on this island. The political state has been formed since 1922 by the United Kingdom of Great Britain and Northern Ireland. This complexity about the nature of British citizenship is recognized on the official government website (gov.uk) in its provision of a question and answer facility for people who wish to check if they are already British citizens. (The answer, incidentally, is that it is likely that people are citizens if they were born before 1983 within the UK or on one of the British overseas territories, except the sovereign base areas of Akrotiri and Dhekelia [in Cyprus]. There are, as one might imagine, some detailed comments about other possibilities.) In this uncertain context, the likelihood of diverse approaches to educating for the nation is very strong.

The key legislative background that is connected to British citizenship includes the British Nationality Act of 1948, which created citizenship of the UK and colonies. A variety of factors including fears about large-scale immigration and the changing nature of the relationship within the Commonwealth led to other acts of parliament including the 1971 Immigration Act and, importantly in light of its restrictions on who could be accorded the status of British citizenship, the British Nationality Act of 1981. Further relevant legislations which generally tighten the controls over immigration and limit rights of people to become citizens are the Immigration, Asylum and Nationality Act 2006 and the Borders, Citizenship and Immigration Act 2009. But, perhaps, for the purpose of this chapter, the most important recent legislation has been the Nationality, Immigration and Asylum Act of 2002 which, in addition to a language requirement, required citizens to show knowledge and understanding of 'Life in the UK'. Through this piece of legislation (as well as others) the connection between citizenship and education is very clearly demonstrated.

This legislative framework emerges from a specific historical context. The mixing of Celtic, Roman, Saxon, Norse, Norman and other peoples explains the deep-seated nature of the different traditions within the UK and goes some way towards explaining the desire to ensure that there is a recognizable overarching citizenship. Early attempts to establish a political state beyond the separate areas of the island of Britain include the actions of James VI of Scotland (who was also James I of England). In 1604 he declared himself to be the King of Great Britain (a title that was not accepted by the parliaments of England or Scotland). England conquered Wales in 1283 and united it to the English crown the following year. In 1536 the English and Welsh systems of law were united. The union between England and Scotland (1707) was followed by that of Britain and Ireland in 1801 with the establishment in 1922 of the Irish Free State and the separate

UK (including Northern Ireland). The idea of nation or nations does not, of course, necessarily match these political states.

The above brief overview of relevant recent and current legislation about citizenship and the historical background that has established the basis for that framework is open to interpretation. Linda Colley in a book interestingly titled *Britons: Forging the Nation 1707–1837* refers to the vitally important role of war in the creation of the modern state. The nation was *forged* on the anvil of war, anti-Catholicism, empire and trade. But also Colley is perhaps suggesting that Britain (and by extension the UK) is a *forgery*: an artificial combination created for political and economic purposes. In that sense the use of myth and supporting imagery becomes very important. Colley describes a portrait by Sir David Wilkie, 'Chelsea pensioners reading the gazette of the battle of Waterloo', which is full of characters and symbols from around Britain and shows 'the existence of a mass British patriotism transcending the boundaries of class, ethnicity, occupation, sex and age' (p. 365). There were in fact very high proportions of other nations involved in the anti-Napoleonic armies but such deliberate positioning of the four nations within a wider state can be seen as part of the invented traditions that Hobsbawn and Ranger (1983) reveal. An obvious example of such myth making is that Scottish tartans are of relatively recent origin and were first required in 1815 by the Highland Society of London.

This historical and legislative context provides a useful platform for describing the current situation. In recent years, debate about Britishness

> was prompted by a number of high-profile events and developments: by the increase in national sentiment in Scotland and Wales; by urban unrest in northern English towns in the summer of 2011; by the growth of Islamic fundamentalism and its link with terrorism, as experienced in the UK and wider international contexts; by the sustained debate about the numbers of immigrants arriving in Britain; and by continuing concerns about youth culture and youth crime. (Jerome and Clemitshaw, 2012, p. 22)

Some of these issues are explored below. But before that discussion about the levers and expressions of Britishness and its constituent elements I want, briefly, to define or characterize Britishness itself.

In the context of statements made about Britishness by high-profile politicians, there is now an official statement about this (which unsurprisingly given his advisory role at the Home Office is in line with views expressed by Crick (2008), as well, incidentally, of those of others who similarly describe other western democracies):

> To be British . . . mean[s] that we respect the laws, the elected parliamentary and democratic political structures, traditional values of mutual tolerance, respect for equal rights and mutual concern; and that we give our allegiance to the state (as commonly symbolized in the Crown) in return for its protection. To be British is to respect those over-arching specific institutions, values, beliefs and traditions that bind us all, the different nations and cultures together in peace and in a legal order. (Home Office, 2003, p. 11)

There are, as might easily be imagined given the comments above about the significance of myth-making and inventing traditions as well as empirically grounded arguments and individual lived experience, a wide range of reactions to such statements. Some search for an explanation of those things that bring the various groups within the UK together. Wallace Goodman argues:

> What does Britishness aspire to do? First, through citizenship tests, ceremonies, and language requirements, Britishness seeks to promote common values that reverse the 'diminution of citizenship'. Ceremonies are perfunctory, but can yield intangible levels of public confidence. Second, Britishness mandates a series of functional citizen skills for successful democratic (and labour market) participation. It is a functional instrument to improve integration among prior and potential immigrants. Finally, Britishness imposes integration expectations and requirements that make citizenship harder to obtain, especially for those who lack the skills or desire to meet these standards. Thus, immigrants and family members who would otherwise have access to entry are denied not because of economic demands or quotas, but because they are unwilling or unable to integrate. This strategic migration policy places the onus of integration on the individual, and protects the state against accusations of engaging in subjective rejection of immigrants. (Wallace Goodman, 2009 p. 170)

Some assert a cultural identity or at least distinctiveness within the UK that gives a collective sense of Britishness. Jerome and Clemitshaw (2012, p. 23) quote from the 2007 Green Paper Governance of Britain:

> [T]there is room to celebrate multiple and different identities . . . [but] none of these identities should take precedence over the core democratic values that define what it means to be British. (Green Paper, 2007, 57 in J and C, p. 23)

However, Devine and Logue (2002, p. 300) although acknowledging 'disparate and contradictory views' quote Billy Kay on the people of Scotland as demonstrating

> our human kindness in adversity, our rampant egalitarianism, our wild dark humour, the power of our stories, music and songs, our insatiable thirst for knowledge, our passionately shared desire for sense and worth over aw the earth tae bear the gree and aw that. (p. 299)

The idea of what is distinct exclusively to Britishness or more narrowly to one or more of the four nations is not straightforward.

Some of the key areas of discussion in, and concerning, the UK

The outline of historical, legislative and citizenship issues given above provides a broad account of the historical and contemporary context. But in order to have a clearer understanding of the nature of the UK which will inform the development of my argument about educational issues, it is necessary to explore a selection of discussion points in some greater depth. It should be admitted that there are very different issues that help characterize the UK: what applies in, say, Wales, does not apply in Scotland. It should also be noted that there is significant in-country variation in relation to social and political attitudes, ethnic diversity, wealth and many other things (Colley, 2014). The lowlands and highlands of Scotland; the north and south east of England; the Welsh speaking north and west and the cities of Cardiff and Swansea; and the strength of different language and religious groups in parts of Northern Ireland all attest to the dangers of drawing any simple conclusions about nationalism within and across the nations of the UK. Under the European Charter for Regional or Minority Languages, the Welsh, Scottish Gaelic, Cornish, Irish, Ulster Scots and Scots (or Lowland Scots) languages are officially recognized as Regional or Minority languages by the UK government. Generally, the decline of common patterns of life (e.g. in the regions across the UK where heavy industry dominated until the changes introduced by the Thatcher governments) and the growth of devolved decision-making may have led to reduced feelings of togetherness and increased desire for more local and regional power (Wintour and Mason, 2014). That said, I will explore three areas below (devolution, diversity, and relationships with countries beyond the UK) that allow for the nature of the characterization of the UK to be made clear.

Devolution

Although the debates over Welsh nationalism have at various times been violently expressed (e.g. in a high-profile attack near the time of the investiture of Charles as Prince of Wales in 1969 and in arson attacks against holiday homes owned by English people in the 1970s), there is currently, relative to other parts of the UK, little explicit agitation regarding Welsh independence. This however does not mean that the issue is completely inert. The long and violent history between the Welsh and English, the formation of Plaid Cymru (the National Party of Wales) in 1925 and various other political groups mean that it is unwise to ignore issues of identity. It is at times suggested that Welsh nationalism has a cultural rather than political element, but there were in 1997 and 2011 referenda relevant to separatism and the Government of Wales Acts of 1998 and 2006 have ensured law-making powers for the Welsh Assembly (and significant controversy about the ways in which this may or may not have privileged particular political groups). The debates occurring in 2014 about Scottish independence are likely to have had an impact on the strength of feeling about independence within Wales, and the 2015 general election was informed by a relatively higher profile than in previous elections of Plaid Cymru.

In Scotland there has been recent huge attention to the referendum of September 2014. The 2014 referendum was preceded by a series of highly significant developments. There had been in 1979 a referendum which was won (in terms of votes cast) by those favouring independence, but the result was dismissed in light of the low turnout. Another referendum in 1997 led to the establishment of the Scottish Parliament. Once the Scottish National Party won the 2011 Scottish election, it was decided that there would be a referendum on the question 'Should Scotland be an independent country?' A simple 'yes' or 'no' response was invited. The issues that were highlighted during the campaign include the impact on the currency, jobs and general economic development including the likely future effects of North Sea oil. There have for quite some time been debates about whether it is realistic to expect independence to create a new politics which allows for consensual social democratic decision-making and a closeness of the state and civil society as well as other issues about inclusive patriotism and a shared identity (McGarvey and Cairney, 2008). The tightly contested 2014 campaign has resulted in a victory for those who wish to maintain the union but debates continue, in very strong forms, about a wide range of issues.

In Northern Ireland from 1921 until 1972, the Parliament of Northern Ireland held political powers. From 1968 civil rights injustices and challenges to law and order and officially legitimated identity by various religious communities led to violent unrest. The unrest, labelled 'The Troubles', lasted for at least 30 years and perhaps it is reasonable to write in this highly controversial area that key issues are still not fully resolved. The 1998 Good Friday Agreement led to the establishment of the Northern Ireland Assembly and despite long periods of suspension there is now far greater – but not complete – stability in the area. It is perhaps particularly significant in the context of this book that the deputy first minister, Martin McGuinness, a senior figure in Sinn Féin (with alleged close associations with the Provisional wing of the Irish Republican Army) chose education as one of his principal areas of responsibility.

England has long been seen as the dominant partner within the UK, but here too there have been issues about the extent to which there is one overarching national identity. Regional difference (cultural, economic and political) is apparent as is resentment over the nature of the current devolved settlement in which members of the Westminster-based parliament who represent constituencies outside England are able to contribute to decision-making about matters that apply only in England. Fierce debates exist about the extent to which certain more generous health and welfare settlements that exist in various parts of the UK may be in part paid for by those who live in England, and, more particularly, in London. It is perhaps to be expected that sociologists and political scientists are engaged in these discussions, but the depth and extent of these conversations are revealed by the following quotation made by the poet Seamus Heaney in a discussion of the work of Ted Hughes, Geoffrey Hill and Phillip Larkin:

> The loss of imperial power, the failure of economic nerve, the diminished influence of Britain inside Europe, all this has led to a new sense of the shires, a new valuing of the native English experience. . . . English poets are being forced to explore not just the matter of England but what is the matter with England. (Heaney, 2002, p. 95)

The debate about the existence of the UK continues. The British Social Attitudes Survey of 2013 noted:

> One point is clear: devolution has certainly not proved to be the harbinger of any strengthening of Britishness. Rather that identity seems to have weakened somewhat in both England and Northern Ireland, while in Scotland it has remained as weak as it has ever been. (http://bsa-30.natcen.ac.uk/read-the-report/devolution/trends-in-national-identity.aspx)

Diversity and citizenship

The extent of the variation across the UK has been referred to above. It should be noted that this diversity informs the type and level of commitment to and identity with the UK. The decline of heavy industry has had significant impacts on those areas of Scotland, Wales and the north of England. The sense of detachment from the southeast of England has grown, in part along social class lines (although there is some tempering of this trend with the development of relatively prosperous cities such as Manchester, the attempt to develop regional assemblies and city mayors and proposals for high-cost technological initiatives including high-speed rail links). It is also the case that commitment to the UK varies in many ways in relation to gender and age. Although the data relating to British or UK identity are not entirely clear, there is some evidence from polling data to suggest that women's support for independence for Scotland is growing (Riddoch, 2014) and some evidence from the 2011 census (Easton, 2013) to suggest that Britishness is strongest amongst the young. The level of debate about Britishness in the context of a divided society has perhaps been most commonly discussed in relation to ethnicity. Over the last 20 years the number of people of a non-White ethnic background has grown from three to seven million (14% of the population in the UK) (Jivraj, 2012). Many including Blair in a speech in 2006 titled 'the duty to integrate: shared British values' emphasized the need for commonality. Phillips (2006) emphasized the extent to which ethnic communities and Parekh's view of Britain as a 'community of communities' (2000) was seen by some (e.g. McGhee, 2008) as being replaced by an emphasis on Britishness. It seemed to some as if the trends associated with a diverse population from the assimilation prior to the 1960s, the multiculturalism of the 1970s (that led to accusations of patronizing and exoticizing the foreigner), the anti-racism of the 1980s and the intercultural approaches of the 1990s were all being rejected in favour of a rather narrow conception. But Easton (2013) reviewed evidence from the 2011 census to suggest

> that those whose ethnicity is white British are the least likely to describe their identity as British – just 14%. About half of people with black or Asian ethnicity picked Britain. It was a similar story with religion – the faith group least likely to describe themselves as British are Christians (15%) and the most likely are Sikhs.

The UK is diverse economically, ethnically, in relation to religion, gender and age. But it would be a mistake to assume that this diversity is necessarily connected to separatism.

Relationships with other countries

The manner in which Britain interacts with other countries is also an extremely important matter that impacts on debates about educating for the nation. Broadly, it is possible to think about these connections as belonging to three types of relationship: international, transnational and global. All three conceptions of the relationship between the UK and others provide opportunities to clarify the nature of Britishness and all three are embraced by some sections of the population and rejected by others. There are also many differences about Britain from those people who live elsewhere. Business trading and other forms of exchange are, of course, essential features of the British economy and cultural life, but there are also complaints about levels of immigration (with the Conservative Party promising in their election manifesto of 2010 to bring about significant reductions and failing to do so when in government) and with opposition to those businesses that are accused of extracting resource from the country. Debates about transnational citizenship are even more tense. During recent years, the UK Independence Party (UKIP) has campaigned vigorously against membership of the European Union and (Conservative) Prime Minister David Cameron promised an in–out referendum during the 2015 general election.

Debates about globalism used to be, in the form of imperialism, the glue that some felt held Britain together. The empire has at times been given as one of the reasons why, unlike many other countries, Britain lacked a nation-based form of civic education (Davies, 1999). Despite the occasional suggestion for schools to have flags and other national (and nationalist) symbols and ceremonies to celebrate Britishness (Goldsmith QC, 2008), we are in this regard profoundly different from many other countries (including the US, many continental European nations and many nations in East Asia). Of course, perceptions about the British Empire are now fiercely debated. For those British people who are temporarily or permanently resident abroad (and/or hold formal, perhaps dual, citizenship) in places such as Chile, Canada and elsewhere, the nature of attachment is complex. And this complexity is, again, linked to the myth making referred to above – in a speech high on rhetoric and very low on historical accuracy, John Major in his 1992 speech to the Conservative Party Conference arguing for a positive approach to be taken to a limited form of European integration declared:

[A] thousand years of history should tell them: you cannot bully Britain . . . So let's be confident at home and in Europe. Let's not turn away and say: 'It's all too difficult.' Let's not hang back because we don't believe our voice will be heard. Right across Europe, now, in this critical hour, people are looking and listening to us and to what we have to say.

It won't always be easy. It won't always be comfortable. But in all we do, there is one thing I will never forget. This is our country.

What we do, we do for Britain. What we do, we do for the future of our children and for generations yet unborn. For their prosperity and their security – and never for short-term political advantage.

Let us have faith, and courage, and pride. Britain's interests will come first – for me, and this Party. First. Last. Always. (Major, 1992)

The connection between national identity and the role of the state in transnational and global contexts is for the UK controversial and contested.

Education and the nation in the UK: some brief overviews of the structure and processes of education in the four nations

Barton and Levstik argue, reasonably in my view, that '[s]ome form of identification is necessary for democratic life, because without attachment to community individuals would be unlikely to take part in the hard work of seeking the common good' (p. 46). There is though, of course, and as shown above a good deal of controversy as to what that identification should look like. In this part of the chapter, I make comments about the ways in which, generally, education operates within the four nations of the UK by drawing attention to issues of curriculum, learning, teaching and assessment. And this is developed, in line with the sentiments of Barton and Levstik, in a positive way. There are differences between nations that are worth paying attention to and, in a very practical sense, nation states provide what in most cases governs educational policy and practice. Not to take account of that position would be to fail to acknowledge current realities (Sears et al., 2011). That said, we need to be cautious about what is being done in an exploration of education in the nations. We need to be particularly cautious about the phrase 'national education':

The term 'National Education', as employed in the 19th century did not mean education for the whole nation, but rather an education organized and directed by the wealthy and powerful for the poor and unimportant. (Aldrich, 1996, p. 37)

This above historical point is useful as events in the UK over time have been tense and different in different locations. To choose only one example, the highly critical 'Reports of the commissioners of enquiry into the state of education in Wales' (or, Blue Books) in 1847 were negative about the Welsh language, nonconformity to the Church of England and about the people themselves who were seen as lazy, ignorant and immoral. This sort of historical baggage influences forms of education today.

The governance of education varies significantly across the UK. The UK government produces descriptive overviews of the different systems (see https://www1.oecd.org/edu/school/2635748.pdf, paragraphs 17–46). Education is organized in five stages (early years, primary, secondary, further education and higher education) and is compulsory for all children from 5 (4 in Northern Ireland) to 16, although in England young people must stay in some form of education or training until their 18th birthday if they were born on or after 1 September 1997. For post-16 education, students in Scotland, Wales and Northern Ireland can apply for Education Maintenance Allowance but those in England can apply only for a 16–19 Bursary Fund. Schools in Scotland and Wales are generally mixed in sex and ability and seen, largely, as being comprehensive (although there have been calls in Wales recently in light of OECD research that signalled poor assessment results relative to others in the UK for the reintroduction of grammar schools in which there is selection according to academic ability). In Northern Ireland it is legal for schools to use academic criteria to select students to secondary schools and faith-based schools are common. In Scotland, Wales and Northern Ireland, local authorities have considerable influence. Forms of the National Curriculum that applies to some schools in England apply in Wales and Northern Ireland but not in Scotland.

In England since 2010 major changes have been made to the ways in which education is provided. Michael Gove (the education minister 2010–2014) declared in his first speech as minister to the Conservative Party conference:

In every school year there are 600,000 children.

The very poorest are those eligible for free school meals – 80,000 in every year.

And out of those 80,000 how many do you think make it to the best universities?

Just 45.

More children from one public school – Westminster – make it to the top universities than the entire population of poor boys and girls on this benefit.

This waste of talent, this squandering of human potential, this grotesque failure to give all our fellow citizens an equal chance is a reproach to our conscience. It can't be allowed to continue.

And under this Government the injustice will end. (Gove, 2014)

In England the comprehensive school system has been from the start of the 21st century and perhaps earlier gradually dismantled. The power of local authorities in England has been considerably reduced in the face partly of austerity policies related to the economic crisis but also because of the current (writing in 2014) government's belief that the best way to raise standards is to increase the power of both the central government and individual schools. There has been a recent rapid increase in the number of schools that are Academies and 'Free Schools'. Academies and Free Schools do not have to follow the National Curriculum, may employ teachers who have not been trained, can set their own pay and conditions and are generally separated from local authority control. The inspection service Ofsted is – as formally stated in policy documents – independent of government, although some have expressed the opinion that in practice those schools that do not follow the government's policy preferences may found to be merely 'satisfactory' (which means that improvements must be made) or 'inadequate'. Such judgements have very serious consequences for schools including possible closure or, for those that have not already changed their status, redesignation as Academies. It is currently controversial as to whether these reforms are likely to increase standards for all or whether we are witnessing the release of energy that will favour those who are already best able to secure resources. This highly complex picture highlights two points: first, that there is no such thing as a national system across the UK and that education within the four nations already and may continue to work in favour of those who have more social capital than others.

In June 2014 there were some indications of how things have progressed:

> Although there has been progress over the last decade in the number of pupils eligible for free school meals achieving 5 GCSEs [examinations normally taken at 16] at grades A* – C, according to recent data, the gap between these pupils and their wealthier peers has remained either the same or has widened. (Gurney-Read, 2014)

Education for citizenship

The variation in policy and practice across and within the UK that has been referred to above also applies to citizenship education. This section of the chapter will address the overarching issues that are relevant to citizenship education; the curricular work in 'mainstream' or longer established subjects such as history and English that bear upon citizenship education; and the situation regarding discrete citizenship education programmes. A variety of work has been drawn upon and a good summary of issues and curricular developments may be seen in the web pages and events and papers organized by the Five Nations Network (see http://www.fivenations.net/).

There are many overarching features of the education systems in the UK that are relevant to citizenship education. In England the 1944 Education Act stipulated that education should be Christian in character. There are local and national arrangements that facilitate this as well as allowing for exceptions for schools that are based on faiths other than Christianity. Debates occasionally occur around this issue with, for example, the Bishop of Oxford suggesting in 2014 that the emphasis on a daily collective act of Christian worship could be counterproductive. In practice the legislation regarding worship may be interpreted by schools flexibly but the policy remains in place. This is important as the Church of England is the established church and the Queen as head of state retains the title (although initially granted to Henry VIII while England was still Roman Catholic by the Pope) of 'Defender of the Faith'. These examples of flexibility, however, have limits which emerge from time to time (one of the most recent occurring in the summer of 2014 in Birmingham with alleged attempts made by faith-based groups to change the character of schools).

Teacher education also shows issues relevant to the nation. Arrangements are devolved but broadly show attention to common issues regarding subject knowledge, planning, assessing and so on. In England, however, the current teachers' standards include the following requirements:

> Teachers uphold public trust in the profession and maintain high standards of ethics and behaviour, within and outside school, by: not undermining fundamental British values, including democracy, the rule of law, individual liberty and mutual respect, and tolerance of those with different faiths and beliefs. (Department for Education 2011, p.14)

Thus the government prefers tolerance to be enacted by people who currently reside in Britain. Whether or not that makes for 'British values' is debatable. Similarly, it is open to question whether education programmes actually cover such ground (as opposed to allowing for the monitoring of behaviour of those who are following teacher education courses) and whether it is reasonable to expect evidence to be provided of a person who reaches a professional standard of *not* doing something.

The situation about teacher education and Britishness relates to not only concerns about the views and opinions of teachers (Wilkins, 1999) but also the wider context in which acts of terrorism and disaffection from the mainstream community could be seen in violent unrest. The Ajegbo Report (DfES, 2007) explored issues of diversity in educational contexts and as a result the citizenship education programme of study (of which more below) was modified to include the strand of identity and diversity. And these matters connect to the ways in which established subjects such as history and English are taught. Throughout the UK there are long-standing controversies about what should be taught in those subjects. Phillips (1996) explored the extent to which cultural restorationism had, despite bold rhetoric from key figures such as Tate, largely little impact on the national emphasis in England. But in Wales, Phillips argued, this approach was 'more successful' (p. 393) with a separate curriculum Order for history and particular emphases in other subjects including art, geography and language. Elliott (2014) made a similar argument about the greater expression of national identity in curricula in relation to literature:

> In England, the rhetoric is more powerful than the actuality, so far. The curriculum reform has not kept up with the emphasis suggested by the Secretary of State's speeches, the most recent version of the curriculum merely suggesting that students will learn to appreciate 'our rich and varied literary heritage' . . ., and 'fiction from our literary heritage' appears in a list of text types for years 5 and 6 to study. In addition the new 'national' curriculum will only apply to the diminishing number of schools to which it has not been disapplied.
>
> However, in Scotland, the opposite situation obtains: the rhetoric has not been particularly strong, but a major change to the curriculum has been accomplished, which may prove its further significance in setting a precedent for governmental intervention in the English curriculum. If the inclusion of national literary heritage texts has its desired effect, they may represent still more an actual difference between the educational experiences of students within the systems of the two countries.

So, curiously, despite the protestations of Osler (2009) and Evans (2011) about the rhetoric of Conservative politicians (which included references to 'Our Island Story' as the prime minister's favourite children's book), we may in fact be witnessing some sections of the English political class struggling (and failing) to achieve change whilst others in the UK have already made things happen. There may be in these debates an absence of attention – in rhetoric or reality – to Britishness on all sides within the UK.

What then of citizenship education? The discrete curricular provision that helps young people to understand and develop the skills to take part in contemporary society is obviously directly relevant to questions and issues about national identity, about the UK and about the emphasis placed on the local and the national. Again there are differences across the four nations. The situation in England is easiest to describe as the 1998 Crick report focused on England. Crick made reference (controversially to some who accused him of reflecting institutional racism, see Osler, 2003) explicitly to the nation. And later (Crick, 2000) he reasserted the significance of countries by asserting through quotation of Arendt that 'a citizen is by definition a citizen among citizens of a country among countries' (p. 137).

Crick explained what he saw as the essence of citizenship:

> Civic education is about the civic virtues and decent behaviour that adults wish to see in young people. But it is also more than this. Since Aristotle it has been accepted as an inherently political concept that raises questions about the sort of society we live in, how it has come to take its present form, the strengths and weaknesses of current political structures, and how improvements might be made. . . . Active citizens are as political as they are moral; moral sensibility derives in part from political understanding; political apathy spawns moral apathy. (Qualifications and Curriculum Authority, 1998)

Crick suggested, using ideas from Hargreaves and others, that citizenship should encompass three related strands: social and moral responsibility, community involvement, and political literacy and was accepted by the Labour government who, under Prime Minister Blair and Secretary of State for Education Blunkett, was keen to promote the communitarianism associated with Giddens (1998) and others. In 2002 citizenship education became a National Curriculum subject. It was changed in a variety of ways in 2005 and then in 2008 (the latter changes including the additional strand of identity and diversity referred to above). In the version of the National Curriculum that existed from 2008 until 2014 students were expected to learn from a wide range of national and other content to learn about three pairs of concepts: democracy and justice, rights and responsibilities, and identity and diversity. They were expected to learn how to think critically; to advocate and represent the views of others; and to act responsibly. At the time of the 2010 general election, which led to a Conservative-led coalition government, many felt that citizenship education would be removed from the National Curriculum in England. There was certainly a diminishing of effort to support it with effectively the removal of key figures from Ofsted and the Department of Education, a lack of attention to youth voice with almost complete disregard of the Youth Citizenship Commission and a refusal to fund participation in both the 2016 International Civic and Citizenship Study and an extension of the citizenship education longitudinal study which had provided evidence about the progress of citizenship education. The evidence that had emerged from many different bodies (e.g. NFER, 2010; Ofsted, 2010; Whiteley, 2014) suggested that citizenship education had been a success (although also that there were still many important areas to work on).

Some sense of the changing attitudes within the government could be seen in the response by Cameron to the 2011 riots in English cities:

> Irresponsibility. Selfishness. Behaving as if your choices have no consequences. Children without fathers. Schools without discipline. Reward without effort.
>
> Crime without punishment. Rights without responsibilities. Communities without control. Some of the worst aspects of human nature tolerated, indulged – sometimes even incentivised – by a state and its agencies that in parts have become literally de-moralised.
>
> So do we have the determination to confront all this and turn it around? I have the very strong sense that the responsible majority of people in this country not only have that determination; they are crying out for their government to act upon it. And I can assure you, I will not be found wanting. (Stratton, 2011)

Few doubted that the removal of citizenship education was part of that determination, particularly when Michael Gove had referred to the need to remove 'pseudo-subjects' in his 2010 Conservative Party conference speech. The emphasis would in future be on the National Citizen Service (NCS) in which young people would be given an opportunity to undertake various forms of service learning.

Interestingly, however, citizenship education remains part of the National Curriculum. This may be due to the persuasiveness of Democratic Life, the organization that brought together the Citizenship Foundation, the Association for Citizenship Teaching and others. Or, it could have been retained in light of the realization that legislative difficulties would emerge as an Act of Parliament would be required for the removal or addition of any National Curriculum subject. Or, in light of the removal of the requirement to follow National

Curriculum in more than 50% of schools in England which are now Academies or Free Schools perhaps it was felt that the debate about the subject itself had been bypassed. The weak level of support by young people of NCS places and doubts that may be expressed about the value for money it represents receive very little attention. The National Curriculum itself now focuses on the rather curiously combined elements of constitutional and legal knowledge, personal and societal finance and the value of volunteering. Formally stated the curriculum specifies:

The National Curriculum for citizenship aims to ensure that all pupils:

1. acquire a sound knowledge and understanding of how the UK is governed, its political system and how citizens participate actively in its democratic systems of government;
2. develop a sound knowledge and understanding of the role of law in our society and how laws are shaped and enforced;
3. develop an interest in, and commitment to, volunteering that they will take with them into adulthood; and
4. are equipped with the financial skills to enable them to manage their money on a day-to-day basis as well as to plan for future financial needs.

The emphasis on the UK is stated but little elaborated.

In Wales Citizenship education is not taught separately but there are three features of education in that country that are relevant. Firstly, Personal and Social Education (PSE) is compulsory for students aged 7 to 19 although the detailed framework (which covers areas such as valuing diversity, understanding political processes and participating in community life as well as sustainable development and global citizenship) is not compulsory. Secondly (and similarly to PSE), Education for Sustainable Development and Global Citizenship is a policy for all levels of education across Wales and it is inspected (across all educational providers) by ESTYN (Her Majesty's Inspectorate). There are connections made with particular subjects such as Geography and RE. Thirdly, the Welsh Baccalaureate, which is relevant to 14- to 19-year-olds, includes topics that are connected to understanding and developing the skills for participating in contemporary society. Generally, discrete forms of citizenship education have not been widely debated in Wales.

In Scotland there are some similarities with the approach adopted in Wales (although citizenship education has perhaps received more attention). Crick moved to Edinburgh and involved himself strongly in civic life there as well as becoming Stevenson professor of citizenship at the University of Glasgow and working closely with Pamela Munn who was based at the University of Edinburgh. Munn chaired the Education for Citizenship Review Group whose report was published by Learning and Teaching Scotland in 2002. There was in that report a focus on knowledge and understanding, skills and competences, values and dispositions and creativity and enterprise emphasizing the need for schools to model a democratic community and to build connections with local communities. However, crucially in Scotland, perhaps in part because of the existence of the civics-related subject 'Modern Studies' (dating from 1959) citizenship education did not become a separate subject. The advantages of infusion and anticipated impact on the whole school community were favoured despite the English experience of the problems of that approach (lack of understanding or even awareness that citizenship was being taught (Whitty et al., 1994). Munn and Arnot (2009) suggest that the Scottish myth of education (that it is meritocratic and community minded), as well as the reaction against Thatcherite reforms influenced the National Debate of 2002 which included reflections about equality, consensus and thus citizenship. The governmental body *Learning and Teaching Scotland* provides guidance but there is less explicitly provided than is the case in England although there are web-based materials and Her Majesty's Inspectorate (not Ofsted) offers advice. Munn and Arnot suggest there has been some progress in citizenship education but in the absence of any systematically gathered evidence simply refer to the 'patchiness of developments' (Munn and Arnott, 2009, p. 452).

In Northern Ireland the situation regarding the discrete teaching and learning of citizenship has been strongly influenced by the wider social and political situation, the particular trajectory of policy decisions in education and the influence of curricular initiatives in England (Arlow, 1999; Kerr et al., 2002). Smith (2003) cites research to show that there is support for citizenship education and a need, partly evidenced by research showing that by the age of 6, 90% of children are aware of the divisions in the community. Policies on Integrating Education (1998) and Education for Diversity (1999) are discussed by Smith (2003) in the context of the development of 'education for mutual understanding' and 'cultural heritage'. The need for development in citizenship education is noticeable in light of work by Niens and McIlrath (2010) who reveal a positive approach but also some concern about tensions. As a result of interviewing stakeholders they argue that

> in Northern Ireland, despite involvement in the initial process, most interviewees indicated that their knowledge about the current status of citizenship education, the concepts currently included and its implementation was rudimentary. (p. 77)

The current situation allows for areas of learning at key stages 1 and 2 (for children aged 5–7) 'Personal Development and Mutual Understanding' – which incorporates some aspects of citizenship education. The Five Nations network (2015) has described this as follows:

> Personal Development and Mutual Understanding (PD&MU) focuses on encouraging each child to become personally, emotionally and socially effective, to lead healthy, safe and fulfilled lives and to become confident, independent and responsible citizens, making informed and responsible choices and decisions throughout their lives.

At key stage 3 and 4, there is an area called 'Learning for Life and Work' and within that is Local and Global Citizenship which is statutory at both key stages.

The future

The campaign – for and against – Scottish independence during the 2014 referendum process highlighted issues about national identity across the UK. In part a very sharp contestation occurred due to political ineptitude including the likely and misjudged calculation that the Scottish people would immediately and strongly recoil from the possibility of losing their UK citizenship, the botched process of devolution which led to inconsistencies and injustices in the management of English affairs, and the last-minute panic-ridden attempts by Westminster politicians to save the Union. But other things are more deep seated. The seismic shifts in economic policy since Thatcher, which disconnected the cables of union and the increasing and rampant concentration of capital in the south east of England, have led to a disunited kingdom. Relationships with other parts of Europe and the nature of the connection with the US and countries elsewhere in the world add to this complex picture. Issues about identity are deep-seated and not solely the result of economic change. In this context, education has had and may have in the future a role to play. The stark differences between what is studied by students in different parts of the UK mean that many young people lack understanding of basic geographical and historical facts and issues. It is not necessary to argue for a narrow concentration on knowledge, but it is surely no surprise that feelings of union are not strong when people simply do not know anything about their state (if not their nation). There has also been an approach to policymaking encouraged by what may be a form of neo-liberalism in England but which may also be characterized simply by muddle and fragmentation. The governmental fight against the supposed dead hand of the local authorities and the departments of education in universities in order to strengthen both centralism and localism may prove to be ill judged. The National Curriculum, teacher training, pedagogy and assessment (excluding formal examinations) seem now to be left to individual schools with the state intervening to correct errors. Such atomization in England is complemented culturally and politically in other parts of the UK.

Is it too late to save the state? Would people in the UK want to do so and would they be wise to do so? The movement towards devolution and perhaps independence may not stop. But for the reasons given above (Sears et al., 2011) about the need to understand one's own country, some careful thinking will need to be done about the standards debate and the need for professionalism. It seems straightforward to begin with a curricular framework; a professional – i.e. properly educated – teaching force; and an approach to assessment that goes beyond simplistic international benchmarks. This however is easily stated but presents very significant challenges and there are likely to be some very difficult discussions in the near future.

8
United States of America

Terrie Epstein and Debbie Sonu

Introduction

As in other nations, educational policies in the US related to teaching about the nation have reflected the broader economic and political contexts in which K-12 educational policies and programmes have developed. Unlike many nations, however, education in the US traditionally has been the responsibility of the 50 state governments, rather than the federal government. State governments determine elementary and secondary curricular frameworks and course sequences, as well as graduation requirements and state-wide assessment systems. Within the context of state regulations, however, there has also been a strong tradition of 'local' or 'community' control of the schools. As late as 2008, for example, eight years after the federal No Child Left Behind Act (NCLB) imposed significant federal requirements on public schools, 46% of adults still believed that local governments should have the greatest input into what schools teach (Manna, 2011).

Despite the tradition of local control, the federal government since the 1980s has exerted significant influence on the rationale, curricular frameworks, learning outcomes and teacher education policies related to teaching about the nation in US schools. We begin our discussion with contemporary policies that have shaped the landscape of teaching for and about the nation today. Then, we provide a history of the evolution of social studies education in public schools, with an emphasis on how stakeholders defined the purposes and contours of teaching about national history and citizenship. Next, we examine the state of teaching about the nation today and speculate on future directions. Overall, we argue that successive changes in policies related to teaching about the nation have reflected the dominance of one set of ideologies over others, shifting among liberal, progressive and conservative visions of what teaching about the nation ought to be about.

Contexts of contemporary educational landscape

The contemporary context of educational reform emerged in the 1980s. During the 1970s, globalization – the deregulation of markets and trade across international borders – increased economic competition between nations and decreased corporate profits in the US. The ensuing economic decline in the 1970s led to the rise of neo-liberalism as an economic–political ideology and set of policies intent on restoring the US position as a global economic leader. David Harvey (2007) defined neo-liberalism as

> a theory of political economic practices that proposes that human well-being can best be advanced by liberating individual entrepreneurial freedom and skills within an institutional framework characterized by strong private property rights, free markets and free trade. The role of the state is to create and preserve an institutional framework appropriate for such practices. . . . Furthermore, if markets do not exist (in areas such as land, water, education, health care, social security or environmental pollution) then they must be created, by state action if possible. (pp. 2–3)

Neo-liberalism challenged prevailing concepts and practices of the social welfare state in which governments had responsibility for providing public services and a safety net for the poor. Neo-liberals perceived the failure of the social welfare state to sustain corporate profits as an opportunity to promote policies to support corporate growth. Over time, neo-liberal policies eroded the social welfare state in the US and throughout Europe, as corporations and private–public ventures steadily replaced aspects of government responsibility (Ball, 2013; Hursh, 2007; Lipman, 2009).

The neo-liberal turn in educational policy – with a focus on the importance of education as a means to revitalize the US economy, as opposed to the federal government's previous welfare-state emphasis on mitigating financial inequalities among school districts – first appeared in 1983. The US Commissioner of Education released a report, entitled, *A Nation at Risk*. Its opening paragraph sets the terms in which the US was losing ground economically and its relation to educational policy:

> Our Nation is at risk. Our once unchallenged preeminence in commerce, industry, science, and technological innovation is being overtaken by competitors throughout the world. . . . while we can take justifiable pride in what our schools and colleges have historically accomplished and contributed to the United States and the well-being of its people, the educational foundations of our society are presently being eroded by a rising tide of mediocrity that threatens our very future as a Nation and a people. What was unimaginable a generation ago has begun to occur – others are matching and surpassing our educational attainments. (US Department of Education, 1983)

The last paragraph of the report appealed to citizens to stop the nation's economic slide by promoting more stringent educational policies:

> Americans like to think of this Nation as the preeminent country for generating the great ideas and material benefits for all mankind. The citizen is dismayed at a steady 15-year decline in industrial productivity, as one great American industry after another falls to world competition. The citizen wants the country to act on the belief . . . that education should be at the top of the Nation's agenda.

To stem the rising tide of mediocrity, *A Nation at Risk* called upon schools to implement more rigorous high school curricula and instruction, tougher high school graduation requirements and higher standards for post-secondary students entering the teaching profession. Several states revamped their curricular frameworks for subjects taught in secondary schools, while others enacted minimal competency tests for high school graduation and entry into teacher certification programmes. Notably, however, *A Nation at Risk* said nothing about federal-level accountability or choice. Federal involvement in the schools, beyond funding for schools with vulnerable populations (low income, English-language learners, special education, female students), was fairly limited and still left educational reform mainly to the states (Ravitch, 2013).

While *A Nation at Risk* used neo-liberal discourses about global competition to frame educational policies, the 1990s also witnessed the 'culture wars' over how national history was represented in curricular frameworks and popular culture. In the early 1990s, the Bush administration announced a set of National Education Goals, which included the establishment of voluntary national standards in core K-12 subjects. With federal support, a national panel of history professors and teachers, as well as education scholars, created a curricular framework for teaching US history that could serve as an outline for states to consider. Upon the publication of the standards, however, there was an outcry from the right and the left about the historical narrative put forward in the standards (Evans, 2004; Nash et al., 1997).

Conservative critics critiqued the standards for presenting a 'politically correct' history, one in which 'those who were "pursuing the revisionist agenda" no longer bothered to conceal their "great hatred for traditional history"' (Cheney, 1994). By this they meant that the standards maligned the white male leaders who had run the country for centuries and highlighted the victimization of 'the country's preferred minorities' (Krauthammer, cited in Nash et al., 1997). African American and Native American organizations protested that their groups' histories were not adequately represented by framing the national historical narrative around the theme of a 'nation of immigrants', rather than as a nation of colonizers and slaveholders. In the end, the US Senate voted 99 to 1 to denounce the US history standards, noting that they presented western civilization in a negative light (Nash et al., 1997). Although the US history standards were published and created sets of curriculum materials used by teachers across the nation, the political showdown over the standards ended the effort of creating national voluntary curricular standards.

One of the greatest federal interventions in education occurred when Congress passed the NCLB in 2001. Set against the nation's declining economic competitiveness and unequal educational achievement among ethnic groups, NCLB mandated that all states test all students in grades 3–8 in literacy and math. In addition, schools had to make 'adequate yearly progress' (AYP) in decreasing the achievement gap between what the Act defined as high-achieving ethnic groups (whites and Asian Americans) and lower-scoring groups (African Americans and Latinos). Schools that did not meet AYP goals could be closed, thereby creating opportunities for private groups to work with public schools. NCLB also expanded the number of charter schools, schools that received public monies and often corporate funding, yet could opt out of teacher union regulations and state laws (Darling-Hammond, 2007).

NCLB enabled powerful individuals and corporate entities with little or no scholarly expertise in education to exert significant influence over educational policies, particularly in communities of colour (Taubman, 2009). Through long-standing philanthropic organizations such as Carnegie Corporation, the Ford Foundation and the Rockefeller Foundation, as well as newer groups such as the Philanthropy Roundtable and the Business Roundtable, the business elite not just influenced school governance, they also shaped curricular, instructional and assessment systems. More in line with business interests than traditional forms of philanthropy, venture philanthropists such as Mark Zuckerberg, Bill and Melinda Gates, and Michael and Susan Dell donated millions of dollars to educational enterprises with the aim of privatizing education and divesting-money from public schools through alliances with organizations such as the Charter School Growth Fund. Such individuals are increasingly visible in educational goal setting, decision-making and processes of evaluation in K-12 education, as well as teacher certification at national levels (Ball, 2013, Lipman, 2009).

NCLB has been criticized on several counts. Some have critiqued the 'racial framing' (Leonardo, 2013) of the Act as disaggregating student populations into two competing racial groups: Asians and whites on the one hand, against Latinos and blacks on the other. These racial framings neglect the millions of individuals who disrupt generalizations about intelligence, that is, high-achieving black and Latino students, for example, and low-achieving white and Asian American students and have served less as a source of empirical study than a reason to enact slash-and-burn policies that shut down schools across the country. By reducing students to achievement measures without serious regard for context and resources, the Act has left in its wake a growing number of 'school deserts'; entire zip codes within which not a single school exists.

Darling-Hammond (2007) also critiqued NCLB for having narrowed the curriculum, emphasized low-level skills reflected on high-stakes tests, constructed inappropriate assessments for English Language Learners and special education students and encouraged schools to exclude low-scoring students. The legislation also led to punishment-driven assessment systems (i.e. students who did not pass literacy and math tests could be held back one grade). Most significant, the resources necessary to construct standards and assessment systems to measure NCLB's effects had drained resources from one of its stated goals: closing the racial/ethnic achievement gap.

When Barack Obama became president in 2008, his administration continued NCLB. In addition, the Obama administration created two new programmes. *Race to the Top* offered grants to states to ensure students succeed 'in college and the workplace and to compete in the global economy' by having K-12 teacher evaluations based in part on their students' achievement test scores. A second programme created in 2011 – *Our Teachers Our Future* (OTOF) – gave money to states to assess the performance of pre-service and in-service teachers. Like other neo-liberal reforms, OTOF's rationale was based on the fact that 'America is not following the lead of high-performing countries and recruiting the nation's best and brightest into teaching' (US Department of Education, 2011). OTOF assessed teacher education programmes based on how well their graduates' public-school students performed on standardized tests.

Through NCLB, *Race to the Top* and *Our Teachers, Our Futures*, the Obama administration has continued to enact a federal-level neo-liberal agenda in education. Accountability is the cornerstone of the policies; teachers, public schools and schools of education increasingly are assessed by student test scores and students who do poorly on tests continue to be marginalized. Driven by a vision of the nation in a life-or-death competition with other nations, neo-liberal educational policies have pushed administrators, teachers and students into a relentless 'race to the top' to ensure the nation's economic viability.

Teaching about the nation in historical contexts

Although US society prides itself on its diverse and democratic heritage, much of the nation's history has been marked by diverse people's exclusion from democracy. The founding governing document of the nation, the Constitution, excluded all but white men of property from citizenship. In 1840, white men without property gained the right to vote, but the vast majority of the population – all people of colour and women – still faced disenfranchisement. Even with the end of slavery, custom as well as violence prevented African Americans from equal citizenship, and US law continued to exclude people of colour. Women gained the right to vote in 1920 and the 1960s witnessed a Civil Rights Movement that extended greater rights to people of colour and the disabled. Despite the legal extension of political and civil rights to those formerly excluded, liberal and progressive critics still detail how US society today is separate and unequal in the distribution of income, rights and respect (Alexander, 2012; Smith, 1999).

Before 1900, most children in the US attended elementary school but most did not attend high school. As the country industrialized and the nation needed a more educated workforce, high schools and separate vocational schools began to grow in the first decades of the 20th century. In addition, the successive waves of immigrants from Southern and Eastern Europe in the late 19th century promoted an assimilationist vision of schooling, one in which immigrants would become 'Americanized' and loyal to their new nation through their experiences in the public schools. Civic education therefore had an important role to play in the Americanization of the children of the new immigrants and an even larger role to play in ensuring that young people understood the workings of government and responsibilities of citizenship in a democracy (Hertzberg, 1990).

In 1916, the National Education Association (NEA), the largest organization of public-school educators, released a report entitled *Commission on the Reorganization of Secondary Education*. The Report illustrated the inroads into educational theory and practice that progressive educators like John Dewey had made, moving school learning especially at the high school level from primarily preparation for college or career to preparation for living in a democratic society. In this vein, the Report recommended two separate secondary civics courses (Cogan, 1999). The first course for ninth grader was a combination of civics and economics meant to serve the majority of students who left school after the ninth grade. They also recommended a twelfth grade civics course to study 'the problems, issues, and conditions that students would face in their daily lives as citizens living in a democratic society' (p. 53). The Commission incorporated the two courses into a recommended 'social studies' sequence of courses and although the selection and sequencing of courses were voluntary, many states implemented the pattern that still embodies the social studies curriculum in many states today:

Grade 7: Geography or European History
Grade 8: US History
Grade 9: Community Civics
Grade 10: European History
Grade 11: US History
Grade 12: Problems of Democracy

In 1918, NEA commissioned a second report, *Cardinal Principles of Secondary Education*, which focused on the goals of secondary education as well as on how the goals might be met. One of the seven goals included civic education:

> The goal of civic education is to develop an awareness and concern for one's own community. A student should gain knowledge of social organizations and a commitment to civic morality. Diversity and cooperation should be paramount. The democratic organization of the school and classroom as well as group problem solving are the methods that this principle should be taught through. (NEA, 1918)

The two NEA reports established the aims and outlines of social studies curricula throughout most of the 20th century. With the rise of progressive politics nationally and educators like John Dewey and George Counts, the progressive turn in education permeated the interwar years. Progressive approaches placed greater emphasis on organizing learning around the child's interests and experiences, rather than on their roles as future college students, workers or citizens. During the 1930s, radical educators like George Counts gained a following promoting progressive ideas about the role of education generally, and civic education particularly, as a means to reform society rather than as a means to indoctrinate youth into the existing society. In 1935, the NEA and American Association of School Educators published recommendations for civic education based on more active participatory views of civic engagement in schools and using the classroom and the school as laboratories for democracy. They encouraged teachers to teach students to think critically, examine controversial issues, and question contemporary society.

After World War II, critics attacked progressive approaches to schooling, preferring conservative consensus-based approaches to teaching history and government, based in part on the Allies' victory in World War II and the rise of the US as the dominant world power. At the same time, however, the seeds of curricular reform had been planted. With the Soviet launching of the spacecraft Sputnik in 1957, US policymakers began to promote more inquiry problem-solving approaches to learning as a means to compete favourably with the Soviets. Jerome Bruner's popular *The Process of Education* (1960) made the case for disciplinary inquiry, an approach that children of any age could accomplish. Bruner's and others' work on inquiry led to the 'new social studies', where university professors developed inquiry-based approaches to history, geography and other social studies topics.

The political protest and cultural changes occurring during and after the 1960s had a significant influence on the social studies curriculum of the late 1960s and 1970s (Hertzberg, 1990). As the Civil Rights Movement and Vietnam War protests continued, African Americans and other people of colour, as well as progressive educators, demanded changes in the social studies curriculum. African Americans fought for greater and more accurate coverage of African American history in curricular materials, and progressives devised new courses like law-related education and values education to promote the study of past and contemporary problems. As the Civil Rights Movement and Vietnam War ended and with corporate profits slipping and the federal deficit burgeoning from the cost of the Vietnam War, the nation began to turn to more conservative policies, as evidenced in 1983 with the publication of *A Nation at Risk*.

Key features of the current education system

Today, all 50 states in the US have curricular standards related to civic education, based on standards either set out by the National Council for the Social Studies (NCSS) (the largest organization of social studies teachers and professors) or as set out in the non-profit Center for Civic Education's *National Standards for Civic and Government*

(Godsay et al., 2012). For example, all 50 states have standards related to learning about 'power, authority and government', as well 'civic ideals and practices'. As of 2013, 40 of the 50 states required one separate secondary course in government or civics. Also, 21 states required that secondary students take a state-level social studies test, of which 8 have state-wide, standardized tests specifically in government or civics that students must pass to graduate. In addition, 20 states have standards related to service learning (civic learning tied to service in the community) (Godsay et al., 2012).

Most state civics standards focus on how local, state and/or national governments operate, on how democracy compares with other types of political systems, on and the rights and responsibilities of citizenship. In addition, NCSS standards has as one of ten its standards learning about global connections and interdependence, while the *National Standards for Civics and Government* includes a standard on knowledge of the US relationship to other nations and the world. It is unclear, however, how much instruction on the US role in world affairs or on international issues actually takes place in the nation's classrooms.

A telling example of the significance that neo-liberal theory has had on teaching about the nation in the past decade is evident in the revisions of a highly publicized report. In 2002, the Carnegie Foundation and Center for Information and Research on Civic Learning and Engagement (CIRCLE) convened a national committee to advocate for civic education in schools. *The Civic Mission of the Schools (CMS)* (Carnegie Corporation, 2002) promoted more time and resources be spent on civic education. The Report claimed that young people were less interested in politics and public issues than either their older counterparts or young people of past decades. In addition, *CMS* was concerned with the civic opportunity and outcomes gaps among racial/ethnic groups. Closing the civic opportunity and achievement gaps among ethnic groups was a major goal of the 2002 Report.

In 2012, the Carnegie Foundation and CIRCLE revised the 2002 *CMS*, renaming it *Guardians of Democracy*. Whereas the 2002 document emphasized the lack of civic engagement among young people, as well as ethnic group civic opportunity and achievement gaps, the 2012 report emphasized civic education's connection to economic productivity. 'Interest is high on the part of the business community and the American public in the competencies that young people require to thrive in an economy that is rapidly changing and global in scope' (p. 20). Without those competencies, the Report warned, Americans will lose out to global competitors:

> We are at the beginning of an historic economic transformation as we move from an industrial, national economy to a technological, global one. The individual, economic, and societal impacts are already staggering, and few of our leaders have presented a plan that fully explains how we as a nation will emerge even stronger in the newly globalized world. Many wonder how we can restore the American Dream, as rates of social mobility in America fall behind those of our European counterparts. (pp. 9–10)

Whereas the goal of the 2002 *CMS* was greater civic knowledge and participation, the 2012 *Guardians of Democracy* considered these as narrow goals:

> Educators and advocates who are promoting the strengthening of civic learning in schools may be tempted to focus narrowly on the student's role as a future citizen who is grounded in knowledge of democratic principles and prepared to vote. This is vital, but it is also appropriate to pay attention to the student's future role as a productive and ethical worker who is grounded in positive attitudes toward work and the law, understands economic and democratic processes, is confident about expressing opinions, and can be collaborative with a diverse range of co-workers. Civic learning that blends interactive discussion with a strong content focus can contribute to a wide range of twenty-first century competencies. (p. 21)

While civic education has been part of the public school curriculum in the US for at least 100 years, the goals for civic understanding have changed drastically in the past decade. Throughout most of US history, the purpose of civic education has been to prepare young people for their political and civic responsibilities and rights as citizens. Even as the meaning of 'civic knowledge and participation' differed across the political spectrum, liberal and progressive educators promoted civil rights and/or activism, while traditional and conservative critics preferred civic knowledge and skills to promote nationalism

(Knight Abowitz and Harnish, 2006), teaching about the nation now has become justified for its ties to the economy.

One example of this turn to the right emerged during Obama's 2008 bid for the presidency. Obama had made 14 pledges about public service, including one that promised to expand service learning and community partnerships in schools by requiring middle and high school students to complete a minimum of 50 hours of service each year. By 2011, the proposed *Learn and Serve America* programme was completely eliminated. Some have argued that as globalization intensified and the US economic competitiveness declined, neo-liberalism invaded every aspect of the nation's educational system. Preparing young people for their roles as future citizens no longer was enough to rationalize the place of civic education in the schools. Now, school subjects, including civics, have to justify their existence based on their ability to train people for the workforce, a workforce that is in continual competition with the rest of the world.

Strategies used for educating about and for the nation

While the 2012 *Guardians of Democracy* used a neo-liberal rationale to make the case for the significance of civic education in the schools, its main findings about effective instructional strategies remained similar to those presented in *CMS* in 2002. There is a broad consensus in the civic education research community, based on years of research, about the pedagogical strategies that lead to greater civic knowledge, skills and engagement. While we use information from *Guardians of Democracy* to summarize the strategies and their effects below, several state civic education standards also make reference to the strategies.

Among the most often cited research findings is that an open classroom climate – one in which the teacher encourages students to express their opinions on current and/or controversial topics, and to treat others' opinions with respect, and responds to students' comments in non-judgemental ways – leads to higher levels of student knowledge, skills and engagement (Carnegie Corporation, 2012; Niemi and Junn, 2005). Respectful discussions of controversial issues, along with student voice in schools and service-learning experiences, result in a more positive school-wide climate. Other classroom and school experiences, such as participating in mock trials or elections and debates, as well as participation in student government, are correlated positively with student knowledge and engagement. This is particularly the case for students at risk: students who have experiences with interactive class discussions, engagement in extracurricular activities and/or service/community learning experiences are less likely to drop out than comparable students who did not have the experiences (Carnegie Corporation, 2012).

Curricular content also matters. Formal instruction in government, history and law increases young people's civic understanding, and *Guardians of Democracy* and state standards emphasize that content should be taught in ways that promote higher level thinking and student engagement (rather than rote memorization) (Carnegie Corporation, 2012). In addition, classroom and/or computer simulations – mock trials, elections, debates about current issues and international affairs – increase civic knowledge, skills and engagement. Computer simulations particularly increase student motivation to participate in civic activities (Carnegie Corporation, 2012).

Finally, service learning experiences – those that connect academic learning in the classroom to community-based projects that require students to analyse and solve community problems – have a positive effect on civic knowledge, skills and engagement, as well as raising student aspirations to pursue higher education (Carnegie Corporation, 2012). Not surprisingly, low-income students have less access to high-quality service learning experiences than others; yet service learning is a particularly effective pedagogy for use in low-income schools. Studies have shown that low-income students in service-learning classes achieved higher scores on standardized tests, had better school attendance and grades than low-income students who had no service learning experiences.

While there is a great deal of evidence on the pedagogical strategies that promote civic knowledge, skills and engagement, there is less evidence on what actually occurs in civic classrooms. Every few years, the US federal government gives assessments to a nationally representative sample of fourth, eighth and twelfth graders to determine achievement levels, instructional experiences and school environment measures associated with the particular school subjects. Called *The Nation's Report Card* (NCES, 2011), the Reports do not give scores for individual students or schools, nor are there any consequences attached to the scores. Rather, the federal government conducts the tests to gain a snapshot of student learning over time. The last *Nation's*

Report Card in civics education was published in 2010. The Report discussed the civic content/knowledge and classroom and school-wide activities that students had experienced in schools. They also presented data on student dispositions related to civic education.

According to *The Nation's Report Card: Civics* (NCES, 2011), the civic knowledge they tested covered five categories: civic life, politics and government; the foundations of the American political system; the principles, purposes and values of democracy as embodied in the US Constitution; roles of citizens in the US; and the relationship of the US to other nations and world affairs. Twenty per cent of the questions on the exam related to the relationship of the US to other nations and world affairs. Of the 35 questions that the report listed publicly, 4 were related to the US relationship to other nations or international affairs. Questions included naming one difference between national and international politics, identifying information relevant to and arguments for national or international military intervention, and identifying a change in international politics caused by World War II.

When asked what they had studied in their high school civics classes, almost 70% of twelfth graders reported they studied the US Constitution, Congress and the presidency; how laws are made; US political parties and elections; and state and local governments. Less than 50% of the students had studied other countries' governments or international organizations or issues (NCES, 2011). When asked on the 2010 exam about the type of pedagogical strategies students encountered in civics classes, about 36% of twelfth graders said they never or rarely discussed current events, heard outside speakers or took field trips, took part in simulations or debates or participated in group projects. On the other hand, 43% of students said they took part in these types of activities at least once or twice a week. Although *The Nation's Report Card* did not analyse which students or schools participated in more interactive classroom activities or outside experiences, other researchers (Kahne and Sporte, 2008) have found that students in low-income schools are less likely to participate in these types of activities than other students.

Likely and desirable futures for civic education

We end this chapter with a discussion of likely and desired futures, socially, economically and politically. In doing so, we nestle our imaginings within the rich landscape of American cultural diversity, one that is exponentially diversifying, and call for a teaching of nation that embraces its ever-changing vitality. As we have seen in the U.S., debates on teaching the nation have centred on the desirable qualities and disposition that young people are obliged to undertake if interested in fitting for participation within society. This includes having knowledge about governance, economic affairs, the founding fathers of colonial America, but in many cases, it does not emphasize the plural experiences of individuals as they engage, grapple and resist ideals of what nation comes to mean in the lived experiences of its people.

Public resistance against federal mandates may return focus to the very question of what constitutes a nation with the ability to empathize, critically examine and see oneself as in union with others. As civic engagement, protest and resistance continue to ignite spaces both in and out of school, we recognize that there is much to do for education to be rescued from the neo-liberalist agenda, at least not without changing the culture of neo-liberalism itself. We do, however, maintain faith that schools can become a precondition that enables further inquiry and modes of understanding, knowledge not as closed solution, but operational insofar as it opens up possibilities for newness and difference. One important starting point is to begin recognizing how resistance against the domestication of one particular kind of subjectivity is representative of a larger struggle for diversity and equity in the struggle over nation.

As we noted, citizenship education in the US has been long dominated by a primary emphasis on the knowledge, skills and values, each individual needs in order to function within the particulars of a nation state. This framework for teaching has led to an array of local, state and federal curricular standards through which teachers not only teach young people the skills and knowledge related to democratic equality, liberty, rights and civic duty, but also discipline them into the kinds of relationships they should have within systems and structures of government as well as the public sphere. In this view, schooling is driven by an explicit sociopolitical aim or objective. In the early years of primary schools, civic or social studies instruction for young children include months exploring the nation's rich yet difficult history of immigration. Teachers and students in New York, for example, trace the work of immigrants in building the Brooklyn Bridge, coming through Ellis Island, bringing with them the flavours and delicacies that have established the Lower East Side of New York City as a vibrant and dynamic food mecca.

As far back as the early 1920s, proponents of more culturally based definitions of citizenship have pushed to include the rights of non-dominant groups in American society (Banks, 2007). Fifty years later, African Americans, other communities of colour, women and those with disabilities galvanized their local powers in a monumental display of political empowerment. The way in which marginalized communities banded together to demand legislative rights for equality is a narrative sewn tight into the fabric of American culture, symbolizing a culturally based democracy that will not only grow in time, but also live on as a staunch reminder of how citizenship will always include the voice of its unique and individual people. The ever-expanding diversification of the term 'American' will ensure that, despite the pressures of neo-liberalism, social context matters and scholars are beginning to consider alternatives to neo-liberal federal policies, by calling attention to (opportunity, social capital and the educational debt) collective forms of educational opportunity for and debt owed to people of colour and other disenfranchised communities (Ladson-Billings, 2006).

The scholarship of multiculturalists, feminists, culturalists, reconstructionists and queer discourses of citizenship (Knight Abowitz and Harnish, 2006) makes the point that while multiculturally oriented citizenship understands group identification as healthy to attaining goals in political systems, liberalists and conservatives claim that individuals must detach from such divisions and exercise the free choice they are afforded by a modern democracy. Conservative proponents of education agree that the purpose of civic education should be to foster the kinds of individuals who, regardless of their ethnicity or culture, will respect and uphold the values and mores of the country to which they are officially bound. In the upper grades social studies education begins to shift from the 'colours' of diversity to the appearances of governmental structure and the need to understand oneself as part of a totalizing national identity.

Such clashes have led to recent policies that ban Mexican American studies in Arizona public schools, arguing that students should treat each other as individuals, not on the basis of race or as part of any racial or ethnic group. The contemporary context of teaching the nation faces direct attack by conservative ideologues who are constraining inclusive approaches to diversity by controlling curriculum. Take, for example, Florida where the governor passed a law charging revisionist history as 'newfangled relativism', banning anything other than 'genuine history' in Florida public schools, and also the Jefferson County, Colorado school board attempt to limit Adavnced Placement History content (courses for which high school students can receive university credit) by announcing that history courses should promote patriotism and the benefits of free enterprise, not encourage or condone civil disobedience and the disregard of the law. In the following week, 700 students participated in a protest; some appeared in school dressed as their favourite historical dissidents.

With a belief that education can contribute to a student's sense of self as a citizen, Westheimer and Kahne (2004) studied school-based programmes that aim to teach democratic citizenship and found them to yield three main types of citizens: the personally responsible, the participatory and the justice oriented. Programmes of this type, particularly for this last category, call for explicit attention to matters of injustice and aim to cultivate young people who are prepared to critically analyse social, political and economic structures and to consider collective strategies for addressing inequity and unfairness. In her book *Making Citizens: Transforming Civic Learning for Diverse Social Studies Classrooms*, Rubin (2012) presented three schools in their attempt to recapture the civic purpose of schooling by transforming classrooms into places where students study, ponder, discuss and take action. Rubin called into question what students were actually learning from social studies classrooms that use disengaging practices such as listening to lectures, reading from textbooks or completing worksheets and question sets of information. Through classroom narratives, she demonstrated how connecting classroom curriculum to the lives of students energized their interest and provided opportunities for meaningful civic learning. She concluded that young people have a variety of perspectives on civic action, some of which struggle between the proposed ideal and their realities. Such work emphasized the development of counter-discursive strategies and interventionist best practices, such as providing opportunities to discuss, write and speak on civic issues, all in the hopes that students move from complacent and discouraged dispositions towards more aware and empowered ways of being.

Understanding citizenship as occurring both in and out of school spaces calls for a reconceptualization that includes the diverse sites and modalities through which such engagements are expressed. As

Elizabeth Ellsworth (2005) argued, within informal sites, such as public monuments, artworks, parks and museums, learning often moves away from the cognitive processes commonly associated with education and towards notions of affect, aesthetics and presence. While schools are seen as inherently grounded within the language of the learning sciences, such that evaluation and measurement become ways to hold teachers and students accountable, public pedagogy provides unique grounds upon which to understand political engagement in less institutionalized ways. Within our contemporary society, knowledge becomes fixed and predetermined with schools oftentimes privilege certain ways of being over others. There is a need for more contextualized understandings in how young people are civically engaged both in and outside the parameters of schooling. Here, the capacity of the school as an instrument of democratic citizenship comes under question and the focus falls on the lived experiences of young people as they speak to the hopes, desires, frustrations and failures of becoming within a democratic society that at times seems anything but democratic.

In a nation rife with diversity, where labels are reductive and fleeting, where populations once marginalized are galvanizing powers of recognition, what does it mean to educate for nation? In a global age riddled by war and protest, with theories that defy national borders and threaten patriotism, what does it mean to be a human in the world? What of technology, and social media, and youth culture and global identity? Given the panoply of definitions surrounding global citizenship and nation, or an understanding of human existence outside the constructs of nation-state governance, it is also noteworthy to include in this discussion how global flows set into motion various forms of identity that are intersected as well as disjunctive. Within such networks, young people in the US are ignited through communities of sentiment with young people across the globe producing a kind of political engagement that cannot be examined in isolation (Savage and Hickey-Moody, 2010). Conceptions of citizenship, widely variable and always contingent, are being forced to contend with the ubiquitous nature of global forces and their pedagogical role in the formation of one's own understanding of self-in-society.

This area of needed study calls for new interpretations outside the binds of nation-state affiliation. Research, policies and practices need to make central the ways in which youth are making meaning of democracy, in more worldly and humanizing ways. It needs to take into account this era of great technological innovation, as it exists within the unconscionable reality of terror and violence. The current context of neo-liberalism, as well as the peculiarities of youth subcultures, pop culture and the like, forces a revitalization of interpretations about citizenship. The teaching of citizenship in a global age must then include an honest and complex understanding of the world. Forms of citizenship and civic education that are mechanical and emptied cannot account for the realities of social change and self-awareness in the global world. As young people come of age, in schools and on the streets, with peers and at home with families, we must believe in the strength of more relational approaches that cultivate a worldliness grounded in a love of self and others, grounded in the capacity to be mindful and compassionate to the unknown, and to examine oneself as connected to those seemingly far and distant.

To this end, we are concerned that the neo-liberal turn in education will lead to the further disenfranchisement of youth from communities that have long histories of racial and economic injustice and fear that designing policies and practices that best incline young people towards the global market will only result in further division and inequity in the world. Instead, we call for a kind of citizenship bent on the ideals and practices of inclusion, inclusion of a diverse people as well as a more diverse interpretation of engagement, agency and change. In this way, the education of young people is less about the characteristics needed to effectively run a particular kind of government or economy, and more about the ways in which youth understand and practise citizenship with others in their localized environments. We follow Lawy and Biesta (2006) in reconceptualizing citizenship as a process of transformation rather than a desirable outcome that is fixed to the fears and insecurities of the nation state. Such an interpretation honours the relational aspect of living with others, within a social context that is as well ever changing and anew. It invites experiences with civic engagement that occur inside as well as outside more formalized educational settings, acknowledging the subject as one that emerges from knowledge making across multiple spaces and contexts. The role of the teacher, then, is not to impart citizenship as something that is achievable or evaluated, but rather to cultivate a sophisticated and complex understanding of citizenship that moves us towards greater openness in the world and with others.

9
The European Union and Its Member States

Alistair Ross

Introduction

This chapter is necessarily rather different from the chapters that deal with individual countries. The EU consists of 28 states, each of which has considerable elements of sovereignty but is also a member of a political, economic and social union. Citizens of each member country are also citizens of the EU: this is additional to their country citizenship (and a consequence of it), and EU citizenship confers further – supranational – rights that can be enforced at the European level, which clearly compromises elements of state sovereignty. (Still more rights are given by the European Convention on Human Rights, established by the Council of Europe – which is a much larger body than the EU.) The EU is a mixture of being an intergovernmental institution, in which state governments meet, negotiate and compromise, and a 'supranational' institution, where pan-EU bodies can make policy and legislation that bind the individual countries. This makes a description and analysis of the educational policies and practices of 'educating for the nation' problematic. To analyse 28 state curricula and the various professional practices that are employed – and the EU's own supranational perspectives – would be either unduly long (and perhaps tedious) or meaninglessly concise. This chapter is thus rather more synoptic than some of its companions.

But the inclusion of the EU offers a particular and unique opportunity to examine the response of educational systems to the emerging post-national characteristics of the EU. There is a common acceptance that the nation should be understood as a social construct – an invention, as Hobsbawm and Ranger put it (1983); a forgery, as Colley describes it (1992). Also, most European countries should not be seen as nation states, in the original meaning of the term. Many political analysts, such as Rustow, inter-utilize the terms 'nation' and 'state' (e.g. 1967, p. 282), but Connor (1978) observed that just 9% of states in 1971 could justifiably be described as nation states: the proportion would be even smaller now (see Brubaker, 1996, p. 26). While there is often an assumption that citizens of a state are all in some way 'nationals' of that state, this is rarely the case in Europe, where there are in most cases a variety of nationalities and minorities within the political unit. These two factors have led some EU states to reappraise the place of the nation in their curriculum. EU citizenship itself compromises the near-exclusive national identities that some people (perhaps particularly elites of countries) require of the nation state. These innovations necessarily impact on the way in which young people learn about their nation and the characteristics of the national identity they may construct.

The EU is also in a near-permanent state of flux and change. As this chapter is being written, the various EU institutions and its member states are coming to terms with significant minorities expressing dissatisfaction with the Union, its centralizing tendencies and its responses to the series of economic crises since 2008. The results of the European parliamentary elections in May 2014, albeit with sometimes low levels of voter turnout, suggest that some Europeans see the supranational nature of the EU as endangering expressions of national identity. There were distinct xenophobic elements in many countries – though these, of course, are not unique to Europe.

The question 'what is a nation?' is particularly relevant in an analysis of what EU states offer in the way of teaching the nation (or not). This chapter attempts to analyse both this and the approaches to teaching 'the nation' in various individual EU states, supplemented with some evidence of what students appear to construct as the nation. But it does not attempt to be comprehensive: it merely draws on a range of countries and regions of the EU.

The context of the EU and its constituent countries

Just a hundred years ago, the political configuration of Europe was very different from what it is today. Most of the eastern area was divided between the large multinational empires of the Ottomans, Austria–Hungary and Russia: in the west, countries such as Great Britain combined European and global empires, while France, Portugal, Spain and the Netherlands had extensive overseas empires, Denmark a lesser empire, while Sweden had just lost its Norwegian dependency. Two new countries, Germany and Italy, had existed for little more than 40 years and were emulating their Western neighbours in attempting to find lands in Africa and beyond that might constitute their own empires, while Serbia, Romania and Bulgaria were fissiparous states that had no natural demographic borders and strove to expand at the expense of their neighbours. None could be called a nation state, though many claimed to be one: Massimo d'Azeglio, one of the architects of Italian unification, wrote *'s'e fatta l'Italia, ma non si fanno gl' Italiani'* (traditionally translated as 'we have made Italy: now we must make Italians') (d'Azeglio, 1867). This was echoed in the practice of the policymakers and educators of the dozens of new countries that have since been constructed in Europe (Green, 1990; Reid et al., 2010). The mid-19th-century nationalist movements claimed 'national' independence in many parts of the land-based European empires, but it was impossible to create borders that would respect the chequerboard of languages and ethnicities in these lands: almost every nationalist group made some irredentist claims for neighbouring territory that overlapped with and incorporated other groups (see Brubaker, 1996, on this). I have heard young people now still referring to *Magyarkodo* (Greater Hungary), the actions of the *Četnici* (who fought for a Greater Serbia) and the activities of the *Ustaša* (Greater Croatian activists) (Ross, 2015).

World War I threw its long shadow over Europe for the century that followed (Reynolds, 2014). As World War I drew to a close, the US President Woodrow Wilson set out principles he thought would settle the national territorial tensions that had helped precipitate the war. His Fourteen Points (USA, 1918) were to give autonomy to the peoples of Austria–Hungary (point 10); to restore Romania, Serbia and Montenegro, with access to the sea for Serbia, 'and the relations of the several Balkan states to one another determined by friendly counsel along historically established lines of allegiance and nationality' (point 11); and Poland was to be independent (point 13). None of these could be achieved without creating fresh tensions. Independent Poland's access to the sea through a free port shared with interwar Germany divided East Prussia from the rest of Germany. Finland and the Baltic states of Estonia, Latvia and Lithuania became independent. The ethnolinguistic communities or 'nations' within the dismantled Austro-Hungarian empire meant that there were no agreed 'historically established lines' to respect, and some communities were thought too small to be viable. The defeated powers of Austria and Hungary became rump nations. The northern Slavs were united through the creation of Czechoslovakia, and the southern Slavs were combined to eventually form Yugoslavia (Hoare, 2010, p. 113). An independent Albania left ethnic Albanian minorities in the Yugoslav provinces of Montenegro and Kosovo. In World War II, Nazi forces and their allies overran almost all of continental Europe: as these territories were recaptured, the allied governments acceded to Stalin's demand that the territories that the Soviet Union liberated would be predominantly under Soviet influence. The three Baltic states were reincorporated as Soviet Socialist Republics. Poland had both eastern and western borders moved westward, taking East Prussia and a swathe of eastern Germany into its territory but losing its own eastern provinces to Russia and Belarus. Germany was divided into two states: the Federal Republic (FDR) in the western sphere of influence and the Democratic Republic (DDR) in the Soviet sphere. There were many other, less dramatic, boundary changes. The Baltic states, Poland, Czechoslovakia, Hungary, Romania and Bulgaria all had communist regimes that were essentially imposed by the USSR, each with a repressive form of totalitarianism. They formed a buffer zone to 'protect' the USSR. It was not until 1985 that Mikhail Gorbachev, the USSR Party Secretary, introduced policies of *perestroika* ('restructuring' economic and political structures) and *glasnost* ('openness' or transparency in governmental institutions and activities). As soon as the Soviet Union allowed the Eastern bloc nations to freely determine their own internal affairs, the bloc rapidly fell apart. Poland held relatively free elections in early 1989, producing a victory for the trade union Solidarity party, *Solidarność*. Hungary disabled its physical border with Austria in August, and tens of thousands of East German 'tourists' migrated through this to the west. The Berlin Wall between the two sectors of the city was demolished, and the other countries shook themselves free: only in Romania was there significant violence in opposing these changes. The three Baltic Socialist Republics declared themselves independent of the USSR in 1991.

Yugoslavia fragmented over the following decade as Serbian hegemony was contested in a series of wars, and now comprises seven states, each of which contains a mix of nationalities.

While this was happening in *Mitteleuropa*, in 1951 western Europe, the French, German, Benelux and Italian post-war governments created the European Coal and Steel Community: the explicit aim of Robert Schuman in proposing this was 'to make any war between France and Germany not only unthinkable, but materially impossible' (European Community, 1967, p. 13; Schuman, 1950). The integration of the region's coal and steel production in a common market between the member states neutralized competition over both resources and markets. By 1957, this had become the European Common Market, based on the two principles of developing free access to goods, markets, services and employment between the member states and a commitment to democracy and the development and enforcement of agreed human rights. Ten years later, this was renamed the European Community (EC), and in 1973, three new member states joined: the UK, Ireland and Denmark. The democratic commitment of the EC meant that Greece was not able to join until 1981 (when the military junta had been overthrown), or Spain and Portugal till 1985, when their dictatorships had been replaced by democratic regimes. The reunification of East and West Germany in 1990 led to eastern Germany 'joining' by default. Cyprus and Malta were already in negotiations to join, so it was agreed in 1993 to create specific principles for future expansion. The 'Copenhagen criteria' required future members to have

1. stable political institutions that ensured democracy, the rule of law, human rights, and respect for and protection of minorities;
2. a functioning market economy sufficiently robust to cope with the competitive market forces of the Union; and
3. a commitment to the aims of political, economic and monetary union.

The European Community was renamed the European Union later in 1993.

The new criteria led to the expansion of the Union in 2004 to include Cyprus, the Czech Republic, Estonia, Hungary, Latvia, Lithuania, Malta, Poland, Slovakia and Slovenia. In 2007, Bulgaria and Romania joined, followed by Croatia in 2013. Currently, Macedonia, Montenegro, Serbia and Turkey are in negotiation over membership (Iceland's application being on hold), and Albania, Bosnia-Herzegovina and Kosovo have been recognized as potentially eligible candidates. Norway and Switzerland currently intend to remain outside the EU.

This historical background impacts on how – at both national and EU level – citizenship and the nation are taught. At different periods of the EU's history, the differing membership of the Union has stressed particular concepts. Citizenship education in Europe has been simply 'what states in Europe do', but has also developed as education *for* European citizenship. But what this means has changed in concept, partly as supranationalism has waxed and waned, and partly in response to the increase in the number and nature of the member states. What was originally a relatively small group of affluent Western countries with a long tradition of democratic norms has expanded to include, firstly, some poorer southern states that had only recently shaken off dictatorial regimes and, secondly, a much larger group of states that had been behind the Iron Curtain – very significantly poorer, with much weaker infrastructure, and lacking in traditions of civic participation.

What does 'educating for the nation' mean in these European contexts?

Citizenship has thus been a fundamental, if sometimes confused and contested, element of the EU project since the European Economic Community (EEC) was founded: the original treaty referred to the objective of 'ever closer union among the peoples of Europe', where decisions were made 'as closely as possible to the citizen' (EEC, 1957: Article 151, p. 308). European citizenship was established by the Maastricht Treaty (EU, 1992) in order to 'strengthen the protection of the rights and interests of the nationals of its Member States through the introduction of a citizenship of the Union' (EU, 1992: Article B) and was extended by the Treaty of Amsterdam (EU, 1997):

> Citizenship of the Union is hereby established. Every person holding the nationality of a Member State shall be a citizen of the Union. Citizenship of the Union shall be additional to and not replace national citizenship. (Article 20, p. 1)

By 2005, the European Commission produced a policy document *Citizens for Europe*, which set out the intention of the EU as 'involving citizens in the construction of a more united Europe and by fostering mutual understanding among European citizens' (EC, 2005b, p. 8).

Here, I would like to suggest three phases in the development of the EU's conception of European citizenship. In the first phase – the period before the Maastricht Treaty in 1992 – the EC can be seen as largely concerned with the harmonization of markets and the establishment of common understandings of values and rights.

The establishment of common citizenship at Maastricht opened a second phase (1992–2004), particularly with reference to education and the promotion of an understanding of the new and complementary citizenship established in the Treaty. Education policies within the EU had been to this point patchy and intermittent. The Union was predicated partly on the principle of subsidiarity, which meant that policy decisions were as far as possible devolved to the most local level possible. Education was seen as an area where policy should come from the country/state level (or even more locally), rather than the EU; moreover, education was seen as clearly having important implications for a country's culture and should, for this reason too, be kept at the state level. However, this was not easily reconciled with the overall objectives of the Union following Maastricht. How could a common conception of citizenship, democracy and human rights and respect for minorities be reconciled with individual state autonomy over curriculum policies?[1] How would intercultural understanding be fostered at the European level without effective common coordination? How could effective labour mobility be achieved when each country had its own system of recording educational attainment and professional and vocational qualifications? These inconsistencies had become particularly salient by this time: a Commission document of the same year as the Treaty (*New Prospects for Community Cultural Action*) concluded:

> Economic and social cohesion has been identified as a fundamental condition for the balanced development of the Community, and education and training have been identified as a crucial factor in achieving balanced social and economic development in all the Member States. (EC, 1992, pp. 11–12)

McCann and Finn (2006) analyse the various perceptions in this period:

> For the Commission it was quite clear that citizenship and economic integration were inexorably linked, that the prosperity of the people of the EU needed to be marked by a shared civic identity. From the member states' governments' point of view the question of national sovereignty was still a prominent reason for hesitating at the proposed progressive development of topics such as citizenship, and indeed the European dimension in education – viewing education as still primarily a national preserve. Attitudes did seem to soften however at national level throughout the 1990s and citizenship education in particular was to benefit from this attitudinal shift.

The issues of cohesion and diversity were particularly significant. Since the economic recovery after World War II, there had been flows of labour around Europe – from Italy, Spain and Portugal to the more northern countries, and from the various former overseas empires to the former colonial powers. This compounded issues around the multinational composition of most populations, which would be further accentuated with the inclusion of the new states in the 2000s, which had borders that were even less respectful of national identities. Banks (2006) has been quoted in Chapter 1 on the way in which 'multicultural societies are faced with the problem of creating nation-states that recognize and incorporate the diversity of their citizens and embrace an overarching set of shared values, ideals, and goals to which all citizens are committed'.

The EU was not seeking to unify a nation state around these values, but was concerned to unify the citizens of the Union around them. This was 'the key reason why the European dimension to education has taken such an indirect path to the curricula, yet has been given such prominence by the Commission' (McCann and Finn, 2006, p. 55). The Maastricht Treaty resonated with this evolving conception of a European-wide and more cohesive educational policy: the educational objectives that had been developed in preparation for Maastricht included promoting Europe as multicultural, with a distinctive European citizenship identity that included culture. Associated policies were the promotion of educational mobility at all levels through the Erasmus programme, encouraging training, life-long learning and inclusivity in education and developing citizens' levels of skills (EC, 1989, p. 236). The relationship between countries' own level of responsibilities and the role of the Commission remained somewhat opaque: Article 126 of the Treaty referred to the community 'contributing to the development of quality education by encouraging cooperation between Member States' – supporting their activities while still 'fully respecting the responsibility of the Member States' for the curriculum and organization of education. McCann and Finn refer to this as a successful 'symbiotic' relationship between the Commission and member states' education departments: 'the economic base of education was well aligned and the concept of citizenship was to become a new arena for integrated programmes within primary, secondary and indeed tertiary sectors' (2006, p. 58). The changing demographics of contemporary Europe, with greater diversity and plurality, have allowed the earlier foci of cultural, political and social education to transmute to make European identity a more distinctive element within education (EC, 2005b, p. 8–9). A decentred, post-national conception of what citizenship education consisted of emerged from both the intergovernmental structures and the supranational structures of the Union over the 1990s. A consensus developed – not without some tensions from within some countries – that citizenship education was not national, nor European, but was concerned with rights, participation and engagement, civic principles and the individual – and not historical processes and cultures. The 1996 report *Accomplishing Europe through Education and Training* (EC, 1996) defines European citizenship as

> based on a shared political culture of democracy . . . the route towards a 'postnational' model to which Europeans will feel that they belong as citizens, not because they subscribe to a common culture . . . or because of their specific origins, but because this sense of European citizenship will emerge from the new social relations that the Europeans establish between themselves. (1996, p. 21)

But during this stage, the composition of the EU was changing again: in the third phase (from 2004), the wide diversities in economic development and the different degrees to which civic values and cultural practices were embedded in the various states had to be acknowledged. Common citizenship of the EU focused in this phase on 'Unity in Diversity' as a rallying slogan. Citizenship became more concerned with civic values and practices – as expressed through the EU's programmes and policies – and less on a sense of cultural unity. As Keating observes (2014), this became critical in the Commission's educational responses to the inclusion of the new member states from 2004, where democratic traditions were perceived as less deep and young people were seen to need to understand pluralism and democracy. Citizenship education, in a particularly European sense, has become a means of understanding the relationship between the individual and society, understanding diversity, and general active civic engagement. The Commission's synoptic review *Citizenship Education at School in Europe* (2005a) characterized this meaning of citizenship as the enjoyment of rights and responsibilities in different communities that both 'encompasses the specific idea of political participation by members of a democratic state' and also 'embraces a range of participatory activities . . . that affect the welfare of communities . . . Citizenship is about making informed choices and decisions, and about taking action, individually and as part of collective processes' (EC, 2005a, p. 14).

In 2006, the European Parliament and the Council of the European Union defined eight key competences for lifelong learning, one of which was social and civil competence:

> Social competence refers to personal, interpersonal and intercultural competence . . . Civic competence, and particularly knowledge of social and political concepts and structures (democracy, justice, equality, citizenship and civil rights), equips individuals to engage in active and democratic participation. (EU, 2006, p. 16)

The concepts of civic and political engagement had become increasingly foregrounded in this decade: the term 'active citizenship' had been frequently used as an educational transversal theme (European Commission, 1995, 1997; for a discussion on various interpretations of 'active' citizenship, see Ross, 2008). These competences and themes, although they had no legislative power, became increasingly reflected in the educational policy documentation of the member states, as will be seen below. But there was also a continuing interest in the idea of some kind of cultural unity. It can thus be argued that three themes emerge as fundamental to the EU's conception of citizenship as it has developed in the decades since Maastricht. Firstly, that citizenship became a deterritorialized post-national concept of practice; secondly, that such practice was centred on 'common values of European civilization' that were at least potentially more universalistic than European:

> human rights/human dignity; fundamental freedoms; democratic legitimacy; peace and the rejection of violence as a means to an end; respect for others; a spirit of solidarity (both within Europe and vis a vis the world as a whole); equitable development; equal opportunities; the principles of rational thought; the ethics of evidence and proof; personal responsibility. (EC, 1996, p. 25)

The third theme was that of active citizenship. Together, these themes mean that the EU is attempting a number of interrelated objectives: the EU

1. sets itself the objective of extending supranationally, beyond the nation;
2. does this by stressing how EU citizens share particular rights and a specific civic (and to an extent cultural) identity by virtue of the common membership of the EU (rather than by developing unifying 'state-like' elements that go across countries); and
3. emphasizes multiple and coterminous citizenships, an important one of which is European.

Benedict Anderson strikingly referred to feelings of nationhood as belonging to *Imagined Communities* (1991), and for some young Europeans, this sense of belonging to such an EC is evident. I spoke with a 12-year-old young woman in Poland in 2011 who said that in Europe 'everywhere you go you are surrounded by your friends, people from the same group, natives. . . . They don't know you, but they know you – you are like a distant relative. In my opinion, being European means that everywhere you have neighbours' (Ross, 2015, p. 21).

But EU citizenship is not that of a state but of a supranational body that has a proper legal and political status and a commitment to common human rights values. This citizenship brings with it an expectation of shared knowledge, experiences and skills (e.g. in language learning). This implies some shared expectations of education, which leads to some conflict with those who would see education as an element of nation-building, and the curriculum as not simply educating *for* the nation but educating *about* the nation.

Some key features of educational practice in teaching about the nation in European countries

EU citizenship is directly a consequence of the formal status of being a citizen of a member state. But the conditions for state citizenship are determined at state level, and there have been significant variations in how citizenship is determined, notably the difference between by right of birthplace and by right of parentage (to which I will return).

This poses issues within and between the member states: while citizenship education in each of them has broadly reflected European-wide policies, they nevertheless maintain local specificities about what 'educating for the nation' might mean. These differences are only partially related to the realities of the norms and values of contemporary societies, which in most countries have coalesced around a set of democratic processes (such as the rule of law), human rights and values (such as respect for minorities and the abolition of the death penalty), a commitment to global development (not perhaps enough, but significantly greater than is found in the US and Japan), a sense of responsibility for environmental degradation, and so on. It thus becomes very hard to define what is specific about the national identity of any particular European state, other than aspects of its culture and sometimes language. Joppke (2010) analysed the tests for acquiring citizenship in a number of European states. These are supposed to ensure that aspiring new citizens understand the values and ethos of the country they seek to join: but in practice, there is very little difference between the various countries' tests. The exception is Germany, where one question displays a photograph of Chancellor Brandt kneeling at the site of the Warsaw Ghetto rising in 1970 (the *Warschau Kniefall*) and asks would-be citizens what significance this has for contemporary Germany. Joppke convincingly argues that no other European state has – or probably could have – such a unique marker.

Recent history is one of four possible areas that stand out in defining 'national' difference. The German conception of itself has been exceptionally defined by a sense of atonement that has been anti-militaristic, pacifist and eschewed any sense of patriotism. But younger people, at school now, are more inclined to see national patriotism as a (necessary-at-the-time) attitude of their parents and grandparents (Miller-Idriss, 2009). My own empirical study of young people in the new (post-2004) member states of the EU shows that while they have a strong and sympathetic sense of how the events between 1939 and 1989 affected their parents' and grandparents' conceptions of the country, they themselves say that they are liberated from the fears, memories and antagonisms that shaped the political orientations of earlier generations (Ross, 2013, 2015). This is similar to the argument put forward by Fulbrook in her study of German identities, which suggests that the significant differences in how identities are constructed by different generations are the consequence of political fractures and dissonance in national society: the 'construction of a collective identity on the basis of generationally defined common experiences' (2011, p. 11) explains the rise of National Socialism and the post-war politics of the Germans. Membership of a generational cohort, she suggests, can be 'crucial at times of transition, with respect to the ways in which people can become involved in new regimes and societies' (488). For young people, it is current political anxieties that contribute more to national identity: the concerns of young people in the Baltic states about Russian intimidation (Ross, 2012a, 2012b; Ross and Zuzeviciute, 2011), or perceptions of political differences from other states and nationalities in the Balkans and central-east European countries (i.e., the eastern countries of what is sometimes called Mittel Europa – Poland, Czech and Slovak Republics, former Yugoslav states and Romania and Bulgaria) (Ross, 2012b, 2014). One might expect to find a similar distancing from parental constructions of the nation in the former fascist states of Spain and Portugal, and perhaps in the Scandinavian countries, a detachment of young people raised in a more neo-liberal environment from some of their grandparents' attachment to a Nordic model of the social democratic state (Brandal et al., 2013).

The second area where 'national' differences may be apparent in citizenship education lies in the different ways in which citizenship is determined in the various countries of Europe. Two traditions of citizenship acquisition are found, *jus sanguinis* (citizenship by 'blood': by right of descent, determined by one's parentage) and *jus solis* (citizenship 'from the soil': by virtue of having been born in the country). An analysis by Brubaker (1996) contrasts the French republican tradition of birthplace, where every person born within the state becomes a French citizen with the German model of descent, where only those who can show German ancestry – even if it is very distant in time – can claim citizenship. Both models are found across Europe, though with various modifications and exceptions, and both the German and French models are no longer as precisely followed as was the case in the 20th century. Most states now allow both forms, but under fairly carefully defined conditions. The UK, which traditionally allowed either route, almost allowing the individual's preference, now has a complex set of conditions attaching to either route. *Jus solis* is found, for example, in Poland, to an extent in France (though *jus sanguinis* is now also permitted) and in Malta. *Jus sanguinis* is found in many more countries (and even more countries have various combinations with *jus solis*): in Germany, citizenship is open to member of recognized historical German community abroad (such as in the Balkans or in Kazakhstan) and also to the children and grandchildren of those deprived of citizenship by the Nuremberg Laws. Greece similarly grants citizenship to 'Pontic Greeks' from historical Greek communities abroad, for example, in countries of the former USSR. Hungary allows citizenship to anyone who can demonstrate they have at least one ancestor who was born within the borders of the 'Kingdom of Hungary' – without any limit as to the number of generations, or the precise location of these borders at that moment of history. These differing models of citizenship must have some impact on the ways in which the nation is constructed through citizenship education.

The third area of difference arises from the conception of the nature of the state, particularly in some of the newer countries of Eastern Europe, where (at least initially) in countries such as Slovakia and Macedonia, the constitution referred to the state as the embodiment of the nation. This conflation of nation and state caused grave difficulties – many fatalities in the case of Macedonia – when local national minorities (Hungarians in Slovakia and Albanians in Macedonia) protested at this disregard for their sense of identity. While constitutional changes have now accepted this, it is still the case that citizenship in the new EU member states of Eastern and

Southeastern Europe is 'closely linked to an ethnic interpretation of nationality, [in which] transmission to subsequent generations is exclusively based on descent, there is greater hostility towards multiple nationality, and greater emphasis is laid on citizenship links with ethnic kin-minorities in neighbouring countries' (Bauböck et al., 2007, p. 12). In the West, citizenship has become post-national: Soysal argues that it now involves rights that transcend the boundaries of the nation state (1994, p. 137).

The fourth potential area of national difference is that of religion. The great European religious wars of the post-Reformation period led to the settlement of *Cuius regio, eius religio* – that each region (state) would adopt the religious denomination of its ruler. This settlement, from the mid-1550s, largely ended conflicts between Catholics and Protestants, and also, to a lesser account, with Orthodox adherents. National borders still, to an extent, reflect particular denominations, but to a much less marked extent. Europe is becoming secularized, and particularly younger people are more secular, so this fourth area may be of decreasing significance (Hunter-Henin, 2011). A possible exception to this trend may be in the non-Christian faiths. Muslims have lived in Europe since 711CE (and Albania, Azerbaijan and Kosovo are predominantly Muslim), and since the 1950s, many more Muslims have migrated to Western Europe, and number of 'indigenous' Europeans have converted to the faith. There are about 44 million Muslims in Europe, many of whom may be less secular than many nominal Christians (Pew Forum, 2011).

While citizenship education may be supported by various EU programmes, it is realized in each country in ways that reflect both governmental priorities and the specifics of culture and recent history.

Citizenship education has thus been variously defined as to what it means in terms of 'educating for the nation'. In the newer states, particular emphasis is given to concepts of freedom and democracy, reflecting recent history: in Romania, a 14-year-old boy told me that the country had 'only been in [the EU for] four years – we have a lot of things to learn'. There is evidence of some demand for this, as when a 15-year-old Polish girl complained of the lack of political education: 'if we are to learn here in school, then we *should* talk about this! I miss it, I miss the opportunity' (both quotations in Ross, 2015). Conversely, in states with a longer tradition of democratic behaviour, there are other emphases – such as social integration and antisocial behaviour in France, or the nature of a multiethnic society and diversity in England.

Sometimes, there is a distinct inclusion of the European sense of the term. In Poland, the curriculum refers to the teaching of 'civic awareness'; in Latvia, this becomes 'civic attitudes'; and in Romania, 'civic involvement'. Germany and the Netherlands emphasize 'civic rights and duties'. The Irish Republic has linked it to the Council of Europe's conception of active citizenship, so the subject of civic, social and political education stresses intercommunity aspects of society, but the Northern Ireland government (which has educational jurisdiction for this part of the UK) has made the European dimension far less evident, with emphasis more on 'local and global' awareness and education for mutual understanding. The French republican model of citizenship is reflected in *l'éducation civique*.

'National' issues such as World War II and colonialism are treated differently in the history textbooks of different European countries. For example, the allied bombing raids of German cities are treated subjectively: in the textbooks of former western Germany (FDR), there was a less ideological perspective than those of eastern Germany (DDR). Polish textbooks concentrated on Warsaw, presenting an image of martyrdom, while American and British texts focus on the bombing of London and Coventry (Andrzejewski, 2005). Crawford (2008) found that English history textbooks up to 1960 displayed an 'anti-German rhetoric . . . entrenched into British culture that has matured and ossified into a form of hegemonic commonsense' (515), which he asserts is a form of emotional shorthand response to a crisis in a 'fragile [British] national identity', a phenomena that Ramsden (2007) asserts has continued into the current century (also Scully, 2012). Austrian history textbooks have, according to Wassermann (2005), approached the same period as a way of shaping a new national identity, focusing on democracy and education for democracy, developed within the Ministry of Education guidelines; on the other hand, Markova (2011) argues that such texts maintain a balance between portraying Austria as either a 'victim' or a 'perpetrator' of Nazism.

Colonialism and its aftermaths have also been treated ambivalently by different countries. Mish (2008) suggests that British textbooks presented decolonization as part of a national narrative of success well into the 1960s, a British-led process of constitutional reform:

it was not till the late 1980s that a more critical approach accorded agency to the colonized people. He also notes that colonialism and decolonization occupy only a very marginal place in the English curriculum. The same is largely true in France. Petter (2008) analyses French textbooks to 1962 as initially describing the country's 'civilising' imperial mission, and then portraying decolonization as a voluntary act of generosity. The Algerian War of Independence is simply discussed in the context of French domestic policies, according to a study by Oetting (2006) of grade 7 French textbooks. In German textbooks, on the other hand, the German colonial past is critically presented within the concept of the *Sonderweg* (the 'special path' that supposedly distinguished Germans from other 'races', culminating in the holocaust) (Baranowski, 2010; Grindel, 2008). The approach of Nordic textbooks is different again: Aamotsbakken notes their comparatively modest colonial heritage, and suggests that although Norwegian textbooks between 1970 and 2000 became 'more nuanced and balanced, and less Euro-centric' (2008, p. 763) in their depiction of colonialism, they used very similar pictorial materials. Elmersjö and Lindmark argue that Scandinavian textbooks have, for more than a century, made attempts to focus on cultural rather than military history, in order to 'promote international understanding [and] not propagate chauvinism' (2010, p. 63), but they still retain various national myths as central to each country's historical narrative.

Specific regional approaches to teaching about the nation

It might be helpful for analytic purposes to group various member states' approaches on the basis of when they joined the EEC/EC/EU, as there is some coherence between their approaches to European and national conceptions of citizenship and the nation and their accession to the Union. Below, I describe briefly how the various national curricula for history, geography and citizenship treat the issue of 'the nation' and of EU membership.

Considering firstly the older members of the EU – the original 1957 six, with Ireland and Denmark (who joined in 1973) (leaving the UK to Ian Davis in Chapter 7): these are countries with a relatively long democratic tradition. Most have had a strong extra-European colonial past, and most were devastated in World War II – and have made enormous economic developments since then, in no small measure kick-started by the Marshall Aid programme. All have also relatively high levels of post-war migration, either from parts of their former Empire or from southern Europe and Turkey.

Within these states, Germany presents a special case, particularly in terms of the nation. A strong sense of atonement for the consequences of the Nazi period permeates the German construction of the post-war state, and has considerably constrained expressions of nationalism and patriotism. The *Grundgesetz* or 'basic law' of 1949 put human rights, dignity and democracy at the core of the state. This underpins much of the curriculum: a 'national' curriculum has only emerged since 2002, when the *Länder* began to cooperate to harmonize provision. The history curriculum in the secondary school addresses the rise of Nazism and its defeat, but there are regional differences: the German Eurydice unit contrasts provision in Bavaria and Nordrhein-Westfalen: 'Bavaria attaches more significance to national history, except at the upper secondary level. The curricula of Nordrhein-Westfalen are balanced. About 40% of the topics are national and 50% international' (NFER, 2010, p. 16). The geography curriculum makes minimal reference to the nation, but has as an aim 'encouraging the development of democratic and tolerant viewpoints and responsible decision-making' (Curić et al., 2007, p. 485). In citizenship education, the Länder standing conference agreed on a document 'Strengthening Democratic Education' in 2009, on the 60th anniversary of the basic law and the 20th of reunification of the DDR and FDR (Eurydice, 2012a, p. 3). But the reunification of the 'nation' has not been unproblematic. Ku (2010) notes that German textbooks' coverage of Poland shifted in the late 1960s: before this, there was a largely negative depiction, which shifted very significantly after Brandt's *Ostpolitik* and the establishment of a German-Polish History Textbook Commission. However, an analysis of the use of literature texts in upper secondary schools (Steding, 2014) suggests that a different approach has been adopted with respect to the former East Germany (DDR): the books selected either focus on an ideological critique of the regime or ignore politics; 'both options result in a simplistic, even reductionist narrative of DDR literature' (p. 42).

France, on the other hand, has fewer inhibitions. The history curriculum sets out a sequence of historical periods, which are 'illustrated by key people and events in French history, which is a deliberate attempt to foster a sense of common national culture' (NFER, 2010, p. 12): this is then used 'to provide an access point to European and world history'. The civic education curriculum is part of the foundation competences (introduced in 2006) of humanistic culture, social and civic competences and autonomy and initiative (Eurydice, 2012a, p. 4).

The Italian history curriculum also includes many national references – to Greek and Roman civilizations in primary education, and in secondary to 'the fundamental steps of Italian history', and the 'cultural heritage of Italy and mankind': but this is set in a strongly European context, with references to globalization and understanding different cultures and opinions in the contemporary world (NFER, 2010, pp. 27–28). The Netherlands similarly combines national and European dimensions in the history curriculum: a 'timeline of Dutch [sic] history and culture, known as the canon, made up of fifty icons' (NFER, 2010, p. 29) is used in upper primary/lower secondary as a basis for connecting to the 20th century ('including the World Wars and the Holocaust'), to the environment, Europe and the world. The geography curriculum similarly includes many national references – to agriculture, industry, society – in the Netherlands, but also to how these relate to Europe and other parts of the world (Curić et al., 2007, p. 484). The citizenship curriculum is integrated to other social subjects, and has from 2007 included 30 hours of community service as part of the leaving certificate (Eurydice, 2012a, p. 6). In Luxembourg, a list of topics carries the caveat 'the history of Luxembourg is to be integrated into the study of these subjects, but they should also take into account the factors that unify European history and that of the rest of the world' (NFER, 2010, p. 25). Belgium offers 'a clear balance between national and international history' (NFER, 2010, pp. 3–4), and the citizenship curriculum in both French and Flemish communities refers strongly to human rights, genocide and democratic systems within European and international dimensions (Eurydice, 2012a, p. 2).

Ireland has a national history curriculum that aims 'to develop an enhanced understanding of their own country and the wider world': there are references to Ireland's roots in the ancient world and in Christianity, but also to international dimensions (NFER, 2010, pp. 22–23). The geography curriculum also appears to balance local, regional and international levels of study (Curić et al., 2007, p. 474).

The Danish history curriculum refers to students being 'able to make a stance on cultural meetings between Danish, European and World culture[s]', and to 'relating events from Danish history to world History' (NFER, 2010, p. 7).

These older nations thus tend to have quite discernible stresses on national elements within their curricula, but these are given a quite pronounced European flavour.

Between 1981 and 1986, the EC expanded to include Greece, Spain and Portugal. These states had previously been ineligible for membership: in Greece, there had been military rule, and in the Iberian Peninsula, long-standing dictatorships. Once these had been replaced with robust democratic institutions, they became eligible for membership, and enjoyed, at least for the first 20 years, sustained economic growth as well as the entrenchment of democratic norms.

In Greece, primary school history focuses almost exclusively on Greek national history; in lower secondary, there is a balance between Greek and European/international history, while in upper secondary, 'national history is incorporated in the European and international context' (NFER, 2010, p. 18). But within at least secondary education, there appears, in terms of classroom practice, to be an emphasis on the historically more distant periods, than the more modern: areas such as the period of the civil war, of military rule and the restoration of democracy tend to be avoided (Karakatsani, 2014). In contrast, Spanish post-16 education (*Bachillerato*) contains a compulsory course of eight units on the history of Spain, the last three of which cover the civil war, the Franco dictatorship and Spain's transition to democracy. The Eurydice unit in Spain comments 'As is to be expected, Spanish history concentrates exclusively on the history of Spain, from the roots of modern Spain in classical times to Spain's membership of the European Union' (NFER, 2010, p. 49). In the lower secondary school, however, there is a much clearer emphasis on international as well as national history. In Portugal, the basic educational law established after the fall of the dictatorship sets out the right to education and the promotion of democracy in education as a key feature of equality of opportunity, Education for Citizenship is present in an interdisciplinary manner at all stages, with references to democracy, social cohesion, diversity, interculturality, human rights and equity.

In these three countries, it appears that the transition to democracy is celebrated more in Spain and Portugal than it is in Greece, and that it does so in a way that does not particularly emphasize the nation.

In 1995, Austria, Finland and Sweden joined the EU. While Austria, as noted above, has the particular distinction of being positioned as both a victim and a perpetrator of Nazism, Finland and Sweden are long-standing democracies with a particular social welfare tradition since the 1930s.

In Austria, history is taught in primary education as part of *sachunterricht*: it is taught in secondary education in conjunction with social science and citizenship education. The Austrian Eurydice unit says 'historical citizenship education, which combines the teaching of contemporary history with its relevance to present and future issues, aims at showing that present societal problems are often connected with events in recent history' (NFER, 2010, p. 2), and that citizenship education includes human rights education: there is a 'reasonable balance' (ibid.) between national, European and international topics. A competency model has been adopted for citizenship education, following the EU model (above), and in the upper grades, a Democracy Initiative has been directed at newly enfranchised 16-year-olds for 'politico-democratic empowerment' (Eurydice, 2012a, p. 6). In the geography curriculum, there is a similar mix of the national and wider foci: only one year (grade 3) has an exclusive Austrian focus (Curić et al., 2007, p. 479).

Swedish schooling similarly places the national content firmly in a European and global perspective. While the history curriculum for early grades emphasizes the Swedish 'collective historical identity – Swedish and Nordic culture, including Sami and European culture', by the upper grades, students are expected to be making comparisons across Sweden, Europe and the world (NFER, 2010, pp. 51–52). Contemporary history has been a significant element of the history curriculum, following guidelines from the UNESCO and the Council of Europe (Nygren, 2012). Geography is similarly positioned in a global context (Curić et al., 2007, pp. 469–471).

In Finland, the history curriculum is described as aiming 'to guide students in becoming responsible players who know how to treat the phenomena of their own era and the past critically . . . it covers both Finish and general history' (NFER, 2010, pp. 9–10). A Youth

Participation Programme (2003–2007) complemented the citizenship curriculum, with an emphasis on engagement and participation in decision-making (Eurydice, 2012b, p. 9).

A more critical note is struck by Børhaug (2011), in his analysis of Norwegian (not strictly within this chapter's parameters) social studies textbooks, which he says attempt to encourage adolescent political engagement by focusing on individualism and the concept of an individual contract with the state, which he argues avoid 'real' political movements and are overly individualistic.

The countries that were formerly either within the Soviet Union or members of the Warsaw Pact – Estonia, Lithuania, Latvia, Poland, Czech Republic, Slovakia, Hungary, Slovenia, Croatia, Romania and Bulgaria (who joined the EU between 2004 and 2013) – form another, rather different, group. Many of the adult narratives continue to stress the achievement of independence (either from the USSR, in the case of the three Baltic states, from Yugoslavian/Serbian hegemony, in the cases of Slovenia and Croatia, or from Soviet dominance in the others; and from Communism in all cases). This nationalist discourse is reflected in a very much attenuated form by most young people, who have a strong and sympathetic sense of why their parents and grandparents acted as they did, and why these earlier generations constructed the post-1989 states in which they now live, but who are liberated from the fears, memories and antagonisms that shaped the political orientations of earlier generations (Ross, 2015).

In eastern Europe, school historical atlases are important required texts (Kamusella, 2010, also Ross, 2015, Chapter 4). Most perpetuate a model of ethnolinguistic nation states, which Kamusella argues uses graphical presentation to reinforce the '"natural" or "inescapable" overlapping of historical, linguistic and demographic borders . . . which produced the present-day ethnolinguistic nation-states' (113). There is a dominant model of the nation state that is based on primordialism, and – in the curriculum, at least – very little sense of the state or nation as a social construct.

Thus, for example, the Hungarian national history curriculum states,

> it is essential for students to know the peculiar features of the cultural heritage of our people and the historic values of our national culture. Students are expected to study the activities and the work of prominent Hungarian figures of history . . . to get

acquainted with the . . . everyday life of their country; 'important tasks' include 'laying down the foundations of national identity', deepening one's consciousness as a member of a nation and one's sense of patriotism, and, inseparably linked thereto, respect for the values, history and traditions of other peoples and ethnic groups living in the country. (NFER, 2010, p. 19)

The geography curriculum similarly includes as an aim 'developing the students' national and European identity, developing their patriotic feelings while respecting other nations and cultures' (Curić et al., 2007, p. 481). But the citizenship curriculum is, on the other hand, defined in terms of the European key competences: social and civic competences and the 'abilities, value orientations and attitudes related to education for active citizenship and democracy' (Eurydice, 2012a, p. 6).

In Poland, during the communist period, history textbooks and curriculum attempted to structure a national identity through a specific Marxist ideology, the portrayal of a 'scientific worldview', a justification of the post-war revision of Poland's frontiers and the creation of a new set of national role models (Wojdon, 2012). In contemporary Poland, history and civics are taught together in the primary school: the current history curriculum appears to be largely national in nature (though with reference to European and classical roots). In secondary education, history includes more European and world aspects, and has a greater emphasis on Poland since 1945, including references to the establishment of *Solidarność* 'and the building of the third Polish independent state' (NFER, 2010, p. 35). The post-2010 national curriculum has reduced the number of times the full cycle of Polish history is taught to twice. The citizenship curriculum echoes the European non-national approach, aiming to develop 'active, conscious and responsible participation in the social life of the country as well as in Europe' (Eurydice, 2012a, p. 7).

Czech history appears less focused on the nation: in primary education, there is an emphasis on moments in Czech history and the cultural wealth of the region and nation, but in secondary schools, there is greater emphasis on 19th and 20th centuries and 'the basic values of European civilisation': the 'history of the Czech countries [sic] is introduced in the European context' (NFER, 2010, pp. 5–6). And, as in Hungary, citizenship education is addressed (with ethical education) through the European key competencies (Eurydice, 2012a, p. 3).

There are other, rather different, responses to the nation within this group of countries. In Slovenia, for example, history is not introduced until the age of 11, and national history comprises only 40% of what is taught, the majority being international history (NFER, 2010, p. 42). In the area of citizenship education, a research project on 'Citizenship education for the multicultural and globalised world' in 2010–2011 suggested that the subject did not adequately address social and political issues, and needed more of a global and multicultural content: following public discussion, the curriculum was revised from 2012 'to reduce the emphasis on patriotism and enhance the political literacy component' (Eurydice, 2012a, p. 9).

Romanian history textbooks since the communist period have, according to Szakács (2007), become more synchronized with European trends towards multiculturalism and denationalization, but maintain an 'implicit and explicit construction of nationhood' (p. 23): national values and attitudes still permeate textbook construction. But in citizenship education, there is, yet again, reference to the European key competences that include civic and social competences (Eurydice, 2012a, p. 8). Similarly, in Bulgarian textbooks, there is 'an ethnic construction of the nation . . . maintaining the fiction of a homogeneous ethnic Bulgarian and religious Orthodox nation . . . effectively excluding minorities' (Katsarksa, 2007, p. 307).

These 'new' countries appear to be – as a very broad generalization – more nationalistic in their curricula approaches, reflecting the political experiences of the 1945–1990 period, during which nearly all political leaders, policymakers and teachers were born and largely brought up. But there have been changes since they have joined the EU, and boundary distinctions have become moderated and less pronounced, particularly for the younger generation.

Future potential development

The Education and Culture Directorate of the EU has given less attention to issues of citizenship since 2012, when it took a particularly marked neo-liberal shift. In the policy document *Rethinking Education: Investing in Skills for Better Socio-economic Outcomes* (EC, 2012), it defined the EU's most pressing mission as the need 'to address the needs of the economy and focus on solutions to tackle fast-rising youth unemployment' (p. 2). The EU was to focus on delivering employment skills and efficiency. While this objective was said to encompass active citizenship, there was very little emphasis on this.

Future developments are thus not easy to predict. The concept of European citizenship will almost certainly continue to grow and develop: many younger people in particular seem eager to use the EU's mobility programmes for education in differing member states, to consider using the labour market mobility possibilities, and to learn additional European languages (and in particular, English). National identity will continue, one suspects, for at least some generations to come, to have increasingly less significance in the lives of many of the Union's citizens. National identity is likely to become increasingly maintained and promoted by two particular groups: older people, who have been socialized and constructed their persona in more national-orientated eras, and national political and institutional elites, who may seek to preserve the concept of national identity in order to legitimize their authority. This latter group, of course, will control national educational systems, and we may see interesting rearguard exercises of imposing learning about 'the nation' on young people who are increasingly reluctant to accept this. The evidence appears to suggest that young people in the EU are becoming more willing to define themselves in European terms: a detailed analysis of the Eurobarometer data for 2010, for example, suggests that people in every country under the age of 20 were significantly more likely to say that they felt European 'somewhat' or 'to a great extent' than those over 20, and particularly those over 54 (Eurobarometer Ross, 2015, p. 24) (with the exception of Latvia).

But, to take the *longue durée*, a decline in feelings of national identity may be simply a reversion to an earlier position. At the beginning of this chapter, attention was drawn to the relatively recent creation of many European states – Massimo d'Azeglio's observation on the need to 'make Italians' was quoted. In France, recent historiography has suggested that before the 1880s, most peasants did not speak French or consider themselves as French (Weber, 1976, p. 6). From the opposite side of the continent, in 1920s' western Galicia (now divided between Poland, Slovakia and the Ukraine), most of the inhabitants had very weak national identities – Brubaker (1996, p. 100, citing Eley, 1990, p. 226) says that 'some identified themselves simply as *tuteshni* ("from here")'. National identity in Europe may yet prove to be a brief interlude in the continent's history.

10
Conclusions and Recommendations

Introduction

This part of the book allows us to go beyond description and analysis and into the development of what we consider should be done in key areas. In chapter 1, we referred to the need for proper consideration of the ways in which countries developed their national policies in the context of diverse populations and the obviously significant movements of people, goods, ideas and other resources around the world in part as a result – and expression – of globalization. Our individual case studies have given an indication of the particularity of what each country has and perhaps could and should do. We are now principally concerned with raising questions and making recommendations in four overlapping essential areas that frame what we should know, legislate for and do in globalizing education: policy (nationally framed and also in relation to international organizations, including NGOs, United Nations and others); research; teacher education; and education delivered to, with and by young people through schools as well as in informal and non-formal contexts. Our questions regarding policy are designed to allow us to avoid simplistic solutions to complex matters. By acknowledging explicitly that choices need to be made, our policy questions are then followed by more precisely framed recommendations (although not without recognition that choices need to be made in all matters that impact upon education, globalization and the nation).

Policy

Responsibilities for educational policy are generally distributed between at least agencies of national governments, regional and local authorities and schools. The implementation of policies is seen in the various practices of individual teachers and schools, and this may vary – sometimes significantly – from formal statements of policy, as practitioners respond to parental and other social and cultural pressures, as well as their judgement of the learning needs of their students. In a globalizing society, the cultural construction of an appropriate citizenship education will, inevitably, be contested and fluid. This seems to be entirely appropriate, given the range of understandings and practices described in this volume. Rather than lay down policies and principles, we here propose a set of questions that might be usefully addressed by policymakers and policy implementers as they construct, develop and modify educational policies for citizenship.

Policy Question 1: What should be the appropriate focal balance of citizenship education?

Most definitions of citizenship envisage it as 'a certain sort of membership in a political community' (Smith, 2001, p. 1857). This includes a range of possible foci: it may be a factual citizenship concerned with the membership of (normally) a singular state and the status this brings, or may be a normative concern, of how to behave in a sociopolitical context, with an understanding of how to exercise civil, political and social rights, and the obligations this entails; or it may focus on citizenship as a group and an individual sense of identity (Joppke, 2010). In most modern states, there seems to be a tendency for citizenship education policies to focus less on national status than would have been the case a hundred, or even fifty, years ago: 'nation building' is much less the purpose of schooling than it has been in the past. But new and emerging states may still see this as a priority, particularly if they arise from situations of conflict. The consequences for civil society of globalization and migration suggest that citizenship education policies should primarily engage with normative issues: How should we (including young people themselves) act towards each other in ways that respect and value a wide range of human rights that have been – to varying degrees – accepted across the globe through a variety of international conventions? What are our obligations to others – both those in our immediate social group and much wider – to ensure that these rights are cherished and appreciated for all members of society? How can this be achieved in a way that allows individual and group identities to be valued, particularly as most 'national' societies become increasingly diverse? And what implications does this bring for the conception of democracy that needs to be more than simply the dictates of a numerical majority?

Policy Question 2: What are the appropriate arenas for citizenship education to explore?

Citizenship conceptualized around these foci will be exercised in a number of geographical areas – in the classroom and school, in the local community, possibly regionally and nationally, and in wider areas – for example, the European Union or globally. Although these areas may be conveniently conceptualized as a set of nested concentric circles (and as nested identities), there is no logical or educational necessity to start at the most local and to progressively move outwards: a globalized community will provide familiar starting points for even young children. Deciding which of these arenas are appropriate will necessarily be linked to the foci selected in response to Question 1: issues of identity in a diverse society may be mapped on to different arenas, for example, so that identities are seen as varying contingently, multiple and plural, and sometimes shared. Issues of human rights are local and global, and can (and perhaps should) be discussed and explored in the context of organizations such as the United Nations and different systems of belief. Environmental concerns similarly lend themselves to a global–local dimension.

Policy Question 3: How should we best foster respect: for other people and for young people themselves?

Schools are not necessarily institutions that respect young people: educational policies that are overtly instrumental and designed to transmit received knowledge demean the experiences and aspirations of young people. Education about and for the foci and arenas suggested in Questions 1 and 2 will probably best be achieved not by telling students facts but by encouraging them to discuss issues and principles. Many adults would be surprised at the extent of young people's information about current events and the extent to which they are developing views and positions on these. As Charles Dickens wrote of his young character Pip in *Great Expectations*, this is for a child 'nothing so finely perceived, and finely felt, as injustice' (Dickens,

1861 [1894 ed., p. 48]). Dickens was writing of 'the little world in which children have their existence' (ibid.): today's globalized web-savvy children are even more aware of, and indignant about, inequities around the world. Sensitively listening to this, encouraging further exploration to perhaps correct some factual inaccuracies and asking questions about the views that have been expressed (rather than always setting the agenda): these are techniques that both palpably demonstrate respect for young people themselves and provide models for how they might respect 'others'.

Policy Question 4: How do we make citizenship a genuinely active process (and are we prepared to accept the consequences)?

True membership of a political community requires engagement with that community, and an effective policy for citizenship education might include an ambition of enhancing young people's active commitment to political processes. This might superficially appear very attractive to policymakers who are concerned with the apparent decline in young people's engagement in electoral politics. However, it might be argued that 'active citizenship' extends rather farther than voting, or even in taking part in voluntary community activities. Active engagement might involve lobbying, seeking support from others, involvement in pressure groups, 'single issue' engagement and so on, including participating (for example) in demonstrations. Policymakers might have some reservations about how educational professionals might support student engagement in such activities without being partisan; teachers themselves would need support – in service training, but more importantly, political support from criticism; and various entrenched interests might seek to halt or negate such involvement by young people (see, e.g. Mitchell, 2004). Of course, active citizenship would not preclude voting and participating in traditional political structures – but it should not be confined to these, because political processes and structures themselves need to develop and grow as globalization continues.

Research

In this section, we set out recommendations for research about education within and beyond nation states in a globalizing world. It is worth noting that these recommendations do not seek to detract from the existing research base. There has been significant research undertaken within national and supranational contexts that has sought to interrogate, investigate, and detail policy, curricular, as well as teaching, learning and assessment in these fields. This research has taken the form of countless small-scale localized studies as well as important large-scale national projects (see, e.g. ACARA, 2010; Keating et al., 2010) and international projects (see, e.g. Hoskins et al., 2011; Nelson and Kerr, 2006; Ross, 2015; Schulz et al., 2010; Torney-Purta et al., 2001). In light of the analysis provided to this point, we suggest that there are three areas upon which education research should focus if we are to understand better educating for and about the nation in a globalized world. In an important sense, the three recommendations are connected – our first recommendation is at a policy/ curricular level, our second concerns actual practices in educational settings, and our third relates to the sort of approaches that should shape research in this area.

Recommendation 1: A commitment to research on the relationship between shared identity/values and plural interests, including how these are operationalized in policy and curriculum

Perhaps the fundamental question facing nations today is how a sense of shared values can operate alongside the recognition of plural interests. The complex relationship between shared identity/values and the recognition of plural interests, including how this relationship is impacted upon by globalization, therefore requires more extensive research both within and across nations. Research is needed to interrogate the ways in which civic forms of shared identity have been constructed and enacted within policy and curricular. An important aspect of this research, and as Hahn (2010) has suggested, should be how different cultural, ethnic and religious groups within given civic polities – including indigenous populations – conceptualize shared identity in relation to their own interests and, in turn, how this impacts on civic learning. A range of globalizing factors have complicated the relationship between national constructions of shared civic identity. Given that each of these factors impacts on how education is constructed and experienced, these too need to be accounted for in and through research. Such factors include the global financial crisis in 2008, experiences of war and conflict affected by issues to do with nationhood, national determination and/or aggressive supranational foreign policies, the development of social and digital media, trends in religiosity (understood by some in terms of post-secularism), as well as concerns regarding radicalization and terrorism. For some, globalization renders the nation secondary to global structures (Garratt and Piper, 2008), while for others, nations themselves are too big and clumsy to respond adequately to globalization, meaning that we must look elsewhere for a political unit able to negotiate the challenges and opportunities that global interconnectedness and interdependence brings (e.g. see the work of Benjamin Barber (2013) on cities). We are reminded that nations are not, and indeed have never been, static but rather are constituted and shaped by a range of dynamic internal and external factors. There is a significant need, therefore, for education research to respond to this dynamism by being open to multiple understandings of the nation by exploring the ways in which multiple understandings are enacted through policy and curriculum.

Recommendation 2: A commitment to research about actual classroom practices

Existing research has taken various forms – philosophical investigation, critical policy analysis, exploration of curricular, as well as empirical research examining teaching, learning and assessment. While all of these are important, there is a particular and pressing need – expressed clearly in a number of the case study chapters – for us to understand more about what actually goes on in schools and classrooms (and indeed in other educational settings); that is, how schools and teachers construct and enact education for the nation in a globalized world and how this education is experienced and understood by students in a range of contexts (including, e.g. how this might be differentiated between classrooms that are themselves diverse or homogenous). As Reid et al. (2010, p. 5) assert in regard to global citizenship education, 'no matter how tightly the state seeks to prescribe educational practice to conform to the educational settlement, there is always "wriggle room" for educators . . . That is, there is never a one-to-one correspondence between the state's agenda and its realisation in the classroom.' A key role for education research is to interrogate the nature of this 'wriggle room' and to explore how teachers do, or do not, make use of their professional understanding and autonomy to pursue agendas which support, challenge or depart from those of intended policy. For teachers in some of our case study nations (most notably England, the US, Canada and Australia), for example, such teaching occurs within the context of an increasingly performative culture that prioritizes accountability, parental choice, competition and high-stakes testing alongside wider social and political aims of schooling. For this reason, it is important to recognize that schools and classrooms are sites of negotiation and struggle, where the aims of educating for the nation and globalization are not constructed and enacted in isolation from a range of other factors that simultaneously shape, limit, constrain and enable teachers' work.

Recommendation 3: A commitment to interdisciplinary and comparative research

As alluded to at the start of this section, research in the field of education for citizenship adopts many methodologies and methods. Whilst recognizing the value of diverse approaches, we need to ensure that research on educating about and for national and global citizenship is constituted by (and perhaps prioritizes) work that is interdisciplinary and comparative in nature. To fully understand the complexities involved requires insights from education, philosophy, psychology, political science, sociology and anthropology. By combining approaches within and across research studies, we will arrive at a more informed understanding of the complex nature of policy, curriculum, teaching, learning and assessment of national and global education. Similarly, further comparative work that seeks to draw out, interrogate and explain key similarities and differences between educational jurisdictions across nations is essential. While we recognize the range of excellent comparative research projects that exist, there is a need for still more research in this area, particularly research that is inclusive of nations and contexts which have to date remained under-represented in the research literature on national and global education.

Teacher education

We argue that there are key elements of teacher education programmes that need to be emphasized in a globalizing world.

Recommendation 1: The establishment of an international advisory professional and academic body to liaise with national agencies and communities

Teacher education like all other forms of education is always *for* something. We need to consider the various priorities – the means by which one can release the creative human potential held within a young learner; the need to prepare the young for economic contexts; the challenge of overcoming social and political injustice; the means by which one can identify and the best that has been thought and said. These need not be exclusively framed as discrete entities. But given that, understandably and appropriately, there are debates about the social and political nature of education, it is likely that there are biases that are usually applied to shape teacher education in particular ways. Heater (1999) has suggested persuasively that since the 18th century, citizenship and nationality have become very closely aligned. Prior to that point and again in the future, it is reasonable to suggest that the nation state may become relatively less important. If that is the case, we suggest the establishment not only of national bodies to establish and monitor standards but that these national bodies collaborate in an international forum where it is possible to learn from others, to develop policies and practices appropriate for specific locations, to allow for the necessary flexible dynamism associated with planning for progress within a context in which the essential nature of what we want from teacher education is considered in a global context. Of course, if such a recommendation were accepted, it would be vitally important to avoid the negative potential of developing something that was a simplistic homogenizing force directed towards control. If the initiative was successful, such a body would be able to consider various issues, including those that are outlined in the recommendations shown below.

Recommendation 2: A commitment to teaching as a profession

Teacher education within some national contexts is currently changing in ways which undermines professionalism. We are, of course, alert to the possibility that professional bodies may become inappropriately exclusive and bureaucratic, and we wish to emphasize that teacher education programmes always need to be creative and dynamic and schools should be open to those individuals and groups within local and other communities that have positive educational potential. In that context, we recommend that schools may occasionally need flexibility to meet staffing needs, but that teachers must in normal circumstances be qualified. These qualifications must be internationally recognized. We do not wish to accept a competence model that requires 'training' rather than education. We want to avoid a neo-liberal approach in which those who work in schools are simply enterprising individuals who reflect a market and not educational system. In this way, we wish to avoid what in its effects at least might not be neo-liberal, but instead is simply a muddle. When planning cannot occur and when standards cannot be maintained and developed, it is harder for teaching to be seen as being for the public good. This necessarily idealistic position is essential to safeguard vulnerable learners.

Recommendation 3: To promote teacher education as forms of partnership

Partnership is necessary in the development of professional teacher education programmes. The unhelpful position that higher education would provide theory and schools the practice is unacceptable. Teachers who help beginning teachers have theories that they favour and academics in higher education have practical experience and expertise. Partnership depends on identifying what each may contribute. The contributions that each of the key stakeholders (schools, parents, NGOs, local government and others) need to be identified so that progress is possible.

Recommendation 4: To promote appropriate forms of knowledge, understanding and action

We need to ensure that debates about narrowly framed national competences are not allowed to dominate. The simple performance of tasks is attractively simple as they are relatively easy to state and then to assess. But we suspect that there is something more than – or, something different from – competence that a professional needs. The knowledge and understanding that are essential for beginning teachers are related, of course, to their academic discipline, their pedagogical practice, and that should legitimately be relevant to their individual countries. But it should also include an understanding of how that relates more broadly to other contexts. We need to identify and promote what teachers should be able to understand and do in a globalizing world, demonstrating their knowledge of diverse societies and their ability to be interculturally competent. In making this recommendation, we wish both to recognize that teaching is a moral activity, but that we need to avoid the simplistic injunctions of those who feel that they have already identified the personal attributes of teachers and how they should be directed to the good of society. We need to avoid the simple insensitivities that are focused on individuals and see a form of national and global citizenship education at the heart of what teacher education is all about.

Education for, with and by youth

We do not wish, in highlighting youth in this section of the book, to suggest that we are not concerned with all learners and all forms of formal, non-formal and informal education. Indeed, youth itself is not something that is necessarily defined by age. It is, like much else, a social, historical, cultural and relational construction. It is a social condition and a kind of representation in which we need to consider the differences and similarities in socio-economic status, 'race', cultural diversity, gender and across territories. We need to think about youth in the plural and not singular (Dubet and Martuccelli, 1998). And, we need to acknowledge that in very obvious ways, those who have not lived very long are often the most vulnerable in society (UNICEF, 2012). It is for these reasons that we raise the following interlocking recommendations – for excellence and engagement – intending that they apply most straightforwardly to young people in schools and also to all learners in all contexts.

Recommendation 1: To achieve an appropriately characterized form of excellence

The pedagogy of Paulo Freire suggests that learners, challenged by the drama of the current time, need to think of themselves as both the problem and the solution. The education of young people in the context of globalization must have as a guiding principle the right of young people to knowledge of themselves and of the world. Education is not simply to be delivered to the young. Rather, education should be developed about, for and with the young. There should be recognition that learners are, as well as the analysts of knowledge, also its producers. As such, their right to be recognized in the world and to create the world is acknowledged. That world must be developed dynamically and with a commitment to equity and diversity. So, in addition to recommending a shift away from the forms of banking education so derided by Freire, there is the need to identify the goals to which those processes lead in a dynamically evolving society. Education is always *for* something, and our recommendation for co-construction, equity and diversity is how we wish to characterize what matters in learning.

Recommendation 2: Enhance opportunities for engagement

In the light of the recommendation given above, it is perhaps already clear that we are arguing that engagement is necessary in a globalizing world. If we are to achieve excellence, we need engagement. This means that two important principles should be recognized. The first is that there is a need for theoretical consideration about and for citizenship, such as exploring values and the civic and historical contexts for democracy. Another key aspect is the need for the school and other public spaces to create conditions for the everyday experimentation of democratic participation. Participation is important in part because it allows young people to experience the values of solidarity and democracy. These two principles mean that very specific and concrete matters may be explored in educational environments. There is a need for critical awareness in relation to knowledge and understanding. This will involve an appropriate respect for knowledge, but it will mean engagement with it by going beyond the transmission of content and values. The search for the underlying conceptual frameworks of any discipline or area of study is unlikely to lead to an immediate resolution or consensus about social and political issues, but it will allow learners to engage with problems that matter and be better equipped to understand and deal with them. Those underlying concepts should be globally framed: that does not necessarily mean that all issues will be illustrated through geographically diverse subject matter (often the emphasis on international matters serves only to highlight the nation), but it does mean that education is not only associated with patriotism, nationalism and exclusion of 'the other'. And these acts of participation should be constructed in a variety of ways which allow for the respect and tolerance of and towards individuals and also to allow for group dynamics.

At times, that engagement will occur virtually. These forms of youth experiences are mediated by symbolic matters in which cybercultures and the culture of social networks present in the Internet have great relevance. And there should also be opportunities for a face-to-face interaction across ages, genders and involving those who may be perceived to occupy different positions in the school and other hierarchies. An informed and interactive approach to a globalized world will allow for the realization of its democratic potential.

Conclusion

Educating for the nation in a globalizing world is intensely complex and controversial. We do not claim in this book to have provided a comprehensive analysis of the issues. But we do argue that the key points raised throughout this book allow us to suggest that our recommendations should be given some consideration. The idea that nation states should simply proceed in a limited possibly blinkered way as international ambitions and globalizing forces shift political and economic realities is bizarre. Our argument in this book – shown very clearly by our detailed examination of our country case studies – is that the nation matters a very great deal, but that it is no longer sufficient as a way of making sense of or of creating practice. We already know much of what is needed in order to make educational progress in a globalizing world. Whether or not we seize, that potential is – at least to some extent – in our own hands. We invite readers of this book to consider what their own contribution might be.

Notes

2   Key Contexts and Challenges

1   Former prime minister of Canada, Joe Clark, used the phrase community of communities to describe Canada in his book *A Nation Too Good to Lose: Renewing the Purpose of Canada* (Clark, 1994).

5   Canada

1   Essentially French Canadians in Québec.

9   The European Union and Its Member States

1   These issues are not, of course, unique to the EU: they also are found in states that have extensive federal and provincial powers, as can be seen in several other chapters in this book.

References

Aamotsbakken, B. (2008). The Colonial Past in Norwegian History Textbooks. *Internationale Schulbuchforschung*, 30(3): 763–776.

Abbott, T. (2013). '*Weary' Dunlop Lecture*. University of Melbourne, 5 December. Retrieved from http://asialink.unimelb.edu.au/calendar/Recent_Events/2013_asialink_chairmans_dinner_the_weary_dunlop_lecture_and_launch_of_the_pwc_melbourne_institute_asialink_index,_keynote_by_the_honourable_tony_abbott_mp/2013_weary_dunlop_lecture_by_the_honourable_tony_abbott_mp; accessed 05.09.2014.

Aikins, S. J. (1919, October 20–22). Opening Address. Paper presented at the *National Conference on Character Education in Relation to Canadian Citizenship*, Winnipeg.

Ajegbo, S. K., Kiwan, D., & Sharma, S. (2007). *Diversity and Citizenship Curriculum Review*. London: Department for Education and Skills.

Alberta Education (2005). *Social Studies K-12*. Retrieved from http://www.education.gov.ab.ca/k_12/curriculum/bySubject/social/sockto3.pdf; accessed 29.08.2005.

Alberta Education (2007). *Social Studies 20-1: Perspectives on Nationalism*. Edmonton: Alberta Education.

Aldrich, R. (1996). *Education for the Nation*. London: Cassell.

Alexander, M. (2012). *The New Jim Crow: Mass Incarceration in the Age of Color Blindness*. New York: New Press.

Allen, J. (1997). *Seeing Red – China's Uncompromising Takeover of Hong Kong*. Singapore: Butterworth-Heinemann Asia.

Alomes, S. (1988). *A Nation at Last? The Changing Character of Australian Nationalism 1880–1988*. North Ryde, NSW: Angus & Robertson.

Alomes, S., & Jones, C. (1991). *Australian Nationalism: A Documentary History*. North Ryde, NSW: HarperCollins.

Anderson, B. (1991). *Imagined Communities: Reflections on the Origins and Spread of Nationalism*. London, UK: Verso.

Andrzejewski, M. (2005). Der Bombenkrieg gegen deutsche Städte in Geschichtslehrbübuchern. *Internationale Schulbuchforschung*, 27(3): 255–277.

Araújo, Ricardo Benzaquem. Guerra e Paz. Casa-Grande & Senzala e a obra de Gilberto Freyre nos anos 30. (1994). Rio de Janeiro: Editora 34.

Arlow, M. (1999). Citizenship Education in a Contested Society. *The Development Education Journal*, 6(1) (October): 14–15.

Asian Education Foundation (2014). *Australian Curriculum Review: Asia Education Foundation*. Retrieved from http://www.asiaeducation.edu.au/verve/_resources/AEFAustCurrReview_SUB_PDF.pdf; accessed 05.09.2014.

Auguste, I. (2010). Rethinking the Nation: Apology, Treaty and Reconciliation in Australia. *National Identities*, 12(4): 425–436.

Australian Curriculum, Assessment and Reporting Authority (2010). *National Assessment Program – Civics and Citizenship Years 6 & 10 Report*. Sydney, NSW: ACARA.

Australian Curriculum, Assessment and Reporting Authority (2013a). *Draft Years 3 to 10 Australian Curriculum: Civics and Citizenship*. Retrieved from http://consultation.australiancurriculum.edu.au/Static/docs/HSS/Draft%20 Years%203%20-%2010%20Australian%20Curriculum%20-%20Civics%20 and%20Citizenship%20-%20May%202013.pdf; accessed 01.09.2014.

Australian Curriculum, Assessment and Reporting Authority (2013b). *Years 3 to 10 Australian Curriculum: Civics and Citizenship*. Retrieved from http:// www.australiancurriculum.edu.au/humanities-and-social-sciences/civics-and-citizenship/Curriculum/F-10?layout=1; accessed 01.09.2014.

Australian Government (2014). *Review of the Australian Curriculum: Final Report*. Canberra, ACT: Australian Government Department of Education.

Ausubel, D. P. (1968). *Educational Psycology: A Cognitive View*. New York: Holt, Rinehart and Winston.

Ball, S. (2013). *The Education Debate: Policy and Politics in the Twenty-first Century* (2nd ed.). Bristol, UK: Policy Press.

Banks, J. (2006). Democracy and Diversity: Principles and Concepts for Educating Citizens in a Global Age. *Comparative and International Education Society Newsletter*, 141 (May). Retrieved from http://www.cies.us/newsletter/may%2006/banks1.htm

Banks, J. (2007). *Educating Citizens in a Multicultural Society*. New York: Teachers College Press.

Banks, J. (2008). Diversity, Group Identity, and Citizenship Education in a Global Age. *Educational Researcher*, 37(3): 129–139.

Bannerji, H. (2000). *The Dark Side of the Nation: Essays on Multiculturalism, Nationalism and Gender*. Toronto: Canadian Scholars' Press.

Baranowski, S. (2010). *Nazi Empire: German Colonialism and Imperialism from Bismarck to Hitler*. Cambridge: Cambridge University Press.

Barber, B. (2013). *If Mayors Ruled the World*. New Haven, CT: Yale University Press.

Barton, K. C., & Levstik, L. S. (2004). *Teaching History for the Common Good*. Mahwah, NJ: Lawrence Erlbaum Associates.

Battiste, M. (2013). *Decolonizing Education: Nourishing the Learning Spirit*. Saskatoon: Purich Publishing.

Battiste, M., & Semaganis, H. (2002). First Thoughts on First Nations Citizenship Issues in Education. In Y. Hébert (Ed.), *Citizenship in Transformation in Canada* (pp. 93–111). Toronto: University of Toronto Press.

Bauböck, R., Perching, B., & Sievers, W. (Eds.) (2007). *Citizenship Policies in the New Europe*. Amsterdam: Amsterdam University Press.

Beech, J. (2005). *International Agency, Educational Discourse, and the Reform of Teacher Education in Argentina and Brazil (1985–2002): A Comparative Analysis*. Tese (Doutorado) – Institute of Education, University of London (mimeo).

Beech, J. (2012). Quem está passeando pelo jardim global? Agências educacionais e transferência educacional. In R. Cowen, M. Kazamias & E. Unterhalter (Eds.), *Educação comparada. Panorama internacional e perspectivas* (vol. 1, pp. 414–433). Brasilia: UNESCO, CAPES.

Beijing Times (2014). Nanjing Massacre: Nanjing Announced That Massacre Is a Required Course in Secondary and Primary Schools, 20.11.2014. (In Chinese)

Bellah, R., Madsen, R., Sullivan, W. M., Swidler, A., & Tipton, S. M. (1986). *Habits of the Heart: Individuals, and Commitment in American Life*. New York: Harper Collins.

Berlin, I. (1979). Nationalism: Past Neglected and Present Power. In H. Hardy and A. Kelly (Eds.), *Against the Current: Essays in the History of Ideas* (pp. 333–355). London: Hogarth Press.

Berlin, I. (1997). *The Sense of Reality: Studies in Ideas and Their History* (Ed. Henry Hardy) (pp. 232–248). London: Pimlico.

Bernstein, R., & Munro, R. H. (1997). The Coming Conflict with America. *Foreign Affairs*, 76(2): 18–32.

Bew, J. (2009). *The Glory of Being Britons: Civic Unionism in 19th Century Belfast*. Dublin: Irish Academic Press.

Bhabha, H. (2001). *The Location of Culture*. London: Routledge.

Bickley, G. (2002). *The Development of Education in Hong Kong 1841–1897*. Hong Kong: Local Printing Press.

Bickmore, K. (2005). Teacher Development for Conflict Participation: Facilitating Learning for 'Difficult Citizenship' Education. *Citizenship Teaching and Learning*, 1(2): 2–16. Retrieved from http://www.citized.info/pdf/ejournal/ Vol%201%20Number%202/007.pdf

Bickmore, K. (2014). Citizenship Education in Canada: 'Democratic' Engagement with Differences, Conflicts, and Equity Issues? *Citizenship Teaching and Learning*, 9(3): 257–278. doi:10.1386/ctl.9.3.257_1

Bishop, J. (2006). *Australia History Summit*. Media Release. Canberra, ACT: Department of Education, Science and Training.

Bittencourt, C. (1990). Pátria, civilização e trabalho. São Paulo: Edições Loyola.

Blainey, G. (1993). Drawing Up a Balance Sheet of Our History. *Quadrant*, 37(7–8) (July–August): 10–15.

Blair, T. (2006). The Duty to Integrate: Shared British Values, 8 December. Retrieved from http://www.prime-minister.gov.uk/output/Page10563.asp; accessed 09.12.2006.

Børhaug, K. (2011). Justifying Citizenship Political Participation in Norwegian Political Education. *Journal of Educational Media, Memory and Society*, 3(2): 23–41.

Boron, A. (1999). *A coruja de Minerva. Mercado contra democracia no capitalismo contemporâneo*. Rio de Janeiro: Vozes.

Brandal, N., Bratberg, O., & Thorsen, D. (2013). *The Nordic Model of Social Democracy*. London: Palgrave Macmillan.

BRASIL (1996). *Lei 9.394, de 20 de dezembro 1996. Estabelece as diretrizes e bases da educação nacional*. Diário Oficial da Republica Federativa do Brasil. Brasilia, DF, 20 dez. 1996. Retrieved from http://www.planalto.gov.br/ccivil_03/ LEIS/19394.htm (Conhecimento como Lei de Diretrizes e Bases da Educação – LDB).

BRASIL (2003). *Lei n.10.639, de 9 de janeiro de 2003. Altera a Lei 9.394, de 20 de dezembro de 1996, que estabelece as diretrizes e bases da educação nacional, para incluir no currículo oficial da Rede de Ensino a obrigatoriedade da temática*

"História e Cultura Afro-Brasileira", e dá outras providências. Diário Oficial da República Federativa do Brasil. Brasilia, DF, 9 jan. 2003. Retrieved from http://www.planalto.gov.br/ccivil_03/leis/2003/L10.639.htm

BRASIL (2004). *Ministério da Educação.* Diretrizes curriculares nacionais para a educação das relações étnico-raciais e para o ensino de história e cultura afro-brasileira e africana. Brasília: MEC (.). Retrieved from http://portal.mec.gov.br/cne/

BRASIL (2008). *Ministério da Educação/Organização das Nações Unidas para a Educação, a Ciência e a Cultura.* Contribuições para a implementação da Lei 10.639/2003. Brasília: MEC, November. Retrieved from www.acordacultura.org.br/

BRASIL CNE/CEB (1998). *Diretrizes para o Ensino Médio. Parecer n. 15 jun. 1998.* Retrieved from www.cefetce.br/Ensino/Cursos/Medio/parecerCEB15htm; accessed 28.05.2013.

BRASIL Constituição (1988). Constituição da República Federativa do Brasil. *Brasília: Senado Federal, 1988.* Retrieved from http://www.senado.gov.br/sf/legislacao/const/

BRASIL/MEC/SESu (2010). *Referenciais Curriculares Nacionais dos Cursos de Bacharelado e Licenciatura.* Brasília: MEC/SESu, abril.

BRASIL/MECFNDE/PNLD (2014). *Programa Nacional do Livro Didático. Anos Finais do Ensino Fundamental. Edital 2014.* Retrieved from portal.mec.gov.br/index.php?Itemid=668id=12391option=com . . .

Bray, M. (1997). Higher Education and Colonial Transition in Macau: Market Forces and State Intervention in a Small Society. In M. Bray & W. O. Lee (Eds.), *Education and Political Transition: Themes & Experiences in East Asia* (pp. 139–161). Hong Kong: Comparative Education Research Centre, The University of Hong Kong.

Brean, J. (2013, July 30). *Critics Accuse the Conservative Party of 'Politicizing History' as National Museum Mandates Change.* Retrieved from http://news.nationalpost.com/2013/07/30/critics-accuse-the-conservative-party-of-politicizing-history-as-national-museum-mandates-change/; accessed 01.08.2013.

Breuilly, J. (1982). *Nationalism and the State.* Chicago: Chicago University Press.

Broome, R. (2010). *Aboriginal Australians: A History since 1788.* Crow's Nest, NSW: Allen & Unwin.

Brown, G. (2006). Speech to the Fabian Society, January. Retrieved from http://news.bbc.co.uk/1/hi/uk_politics/4611682.stm; accessed 14.08.2014.

Brown, G. (2014). *My Scotland, Our Britain.* London: Simon and Schuster.

Brubaker, R. (1996). *Nationalism Reframed: Nationhood and the National Question in the New Europe.* Cambridge: Cambridge University Press.

Bruner, J. (1960). *The Process of Education.* Cambridge, MA: Harvard University Press.

Bruno-Jofré, R., & Aponiuk, N. (Eds.) (2001). *Educating Citizens for a Pluralistic Society.* Calgary: Canadian Ethnic Studies.

Cardoso, M. L. (Ed.) (2008). Programa Diversidade na Universidade. Avaliação final. *Brasilia: MEC/SECAD. Educação para a Diversidade e cidadania,* 18 March. Retrieved from http://pronacampo.mec.gov.br/images/pdf/bib_

volume29_o_programa_diversidade_na_universidade_e_a_construcao_de_
uma_politica_educacional_anti_racista.pdf

Carnegie Corporation (2002). *Civic Mission of the Schools*. New York: Carnegie Corporation.

Carnegie Corporation (2012). *Guardians of Democracy: The Civic Mission of the Schools*. New York: Carnegie Corporation.

Carvalho, José Murilo de (2002). *Cidadania no Brasil. O longo Caminho* (3ª ed.). Rio de Janeiro: Civilização Brasileira.

Castles, S., Cope, B., Kalantzis, M., & Morrissey, M. (1990). *Mistaken Identity, Multiculturalism and the Demise of Nationalism in Australia*. Sydney, NSW: Pluto Press.

Castro-Gómez, S., & Gosfoguel, R. (2007). *El giro decolonial. Reflexiones para una diversidad epistémico más allá del capitalismo global*. Bogotá: Siglo del Hombre.

CBC News (2006). Quebecers from a Nation Within Canada: PM. Retrieved from http://www.cbc.ca/canada/story/2006/11/22/harper-quebec.html; accessed 10.03.2009.

Chang, M. H. (1998). Chinese Irredentist Nationalism: The Magician's Last Trick. *Comparative Strategy*, 17(1): 83–101.

Cheney, L. (1994, October 20). The End of History. *Wall Street Journal*. Retrieved from http://www.personal.umich.edu/~mlassite/discussion261/cheney.html; accessed 26.11.2014.

Childress, S. (2014). Why Voter Id Laws Aren't Really about Fraud. *Frontline*. Retrieved from http://www.pbs.org/wgbh/pages/frontline/government-elections-politics/why-voter-id-laws-arent-really-about-fraud/; accessed 23.03.2015.

China Education Daily (2009). The General Office of the Communist Party of China forwarded the requirement of "Opinions from the Publicity Department of the Communist Party of China of Carrying out mass patriotic education activities to celebrate the 60th anniversary of the founding of New China, 27.04.2009. (In Chinese)

Christou, T., & Sears, A. (2014). Rapprochement: Toward an Inclusive Approach to History and Citizenship Education in Canada. *Canadian Issues/ Thèmes Canadiens* (Fall): 17–21.

Civics Expert Groups (1994). *Whereas the People: Civics and Citizenship Education*. Canberra: Australian Government Printing Service.

Clark, A. (2008). *History's Children: History Wars in the Classroom*. Sydney, NSW: University of New South Wales Press.

Clark, J. (1994). *A Nation Too Good to Lose: Renewing the Purpose of Canada*. Toronto: Key Porter Books.

Clayton, C. H. (2009). *Sovereignty at the Edge: Macau & the Question of Chineseness*. Cambridge, MA and London: Harvard University Asia Center.

Cleverley, J. (1985). *The Schooling of China: Tradition and Modernity in Chinese Education*. Sydney, Australia: Allen & Unwin.

Cogan, J. (1999). Civic Education in the United States: A Brief History. *International Journal of Social Education*, 14(1): 52–64.

Colley, L. (1992). *Britons: Forging the Nation 1707–1837*. London: Pimlico.

Colley, L. (2014). *Acts of Union and Disunion. What Has Held the UK Together and What Is Dividing It?* London: Profile Books.

CONFERÊNCIA REGIONAL DA AMÉRICA LATINA E CARIBE PREPARATÓRIA PARA A CONFERÊNCIA MUNDIAL DE DURBAN. Brasilia. 2008. Anexo ao documento da posição brasileira. *Brasilia.MEC, 2008.* Retrieved from https://pt.scribd.com/doc/162814345/De-Durban-a-Lei-10639

Connor, W. (1978). A Nation Is a Nation, Is a State, Is an Ethnic Group, Is a . . . *Ethnic and Racial Studies,* 1(4): 379–388.

Conrad, M., Ercikan, K., Friesen, G., Létourneau, J., Muise, D., Northrup, D., & Seixas, P. (2013). *Canadians and Their Pasts.* Toronto: University of Toronto Press.

Crabb, A., & Guerrera, O. (2004). PM Queries Values of State Schools. *The Age,* 20 January. Retrieved from http://www.theage.com.au/articles/2004/01/19/1074360697635.html; accessed 01.09.2014.

Crawford, K. (2008). A Vicious and Barbarous Enemy: Germans and Germany in British History Textbooks, 1930–1960. *Internationale Schulbuchforschung,* 30(1): 515–534.

Crick, B. (2000). *Essays on Citizenship.* London: Continuum.

Crick, B. (2008). The Four Nations: Interrelations. *The Political Quarterly,* 79(1): 71–79.

Criddle, E., Vidovich, L., & O'Neill, M. (2004). Discovering Democracy: An Analysis of Curriculum Policy for Citizenship Education. *Westminster Studies in Education,* 27(1): 27–41.

Crowe, D. (2014). We Have to Learn from the Best, Says Kevin Donnelly. *The Australian,* 11 January. Retrieved from http://www.theaustralian.com.au/national-affairs/education/we-have-to-learn-from-the-best-says-kevin-donnelly/story-fn59nlz9-1226799423153; accessed 01.09.2014.

Curić, Z., Vuk, R., & Jakovčić, M. (2007). Geography Curricula for Compulsory Education in 11 European Countries – Comparative Analysis. *Metodika,* 15: 467–493.

Curran, J. (2004). *The Power of Speech: Australian Prime Ministers Defining the National Image.* Melbourne: Melbourne University Press.

Curriculum Development Council (CDC) (2002). *Basic Education Curriculum Guide – Building on Strengths (Primary 1–Secondary 3).* Hong Kong: Curriculum Development Council.

Curthoys, A. (2007). History in the Howard Era. *Teaching History,* (March): 4–9.

Curtis, B. (2013). Debate on the Teaching of History. *Historical Studies in Education: Historical: Epistemology Meets Nationalist Narrative,* 25(2): 115–128.

Dale, R. (2004). Globalização e educação: demonstrando a existência de uma 'Cultura Educacional Mundial Comum' ou localizando uma 'Agenda Globalmente Estruturada para a Educação'? In *Revista Educação & Sociedade. Dossiê Globalização e Educação: Precarização do trabalho docente.* Campinas, vol. 25, no. 87, may/aug. 2004. Retrieved from http://dx.doi.org/10.1590/S0101-73302004000200007; accessed 10.06.2013.

Darling-Hammond, L. (2007). Race, Inequality and Educational Accountability: The Irony of 'No Child Left Behind'. *Race, Ethnicity and Education,* 10(3): 245–260.

Davies, I. (1999). What has Happened in the Teaching of Politics in Schools in England in the Last Three Decades, and Why? *Oxford Review of Education*, 25(1&2): 125–140.

Davies, I., Gregory, I., & Riley, S. C. (1999). *Good Citizenship and Educational Provision*. London: Falmer Press.

D'Azeglio, M. (1867). *I Miei Ricordi: Origine e scope dell' Opera*. Florence: Barbera Edizione di riferimento, p. 4. Retrieved from http://www.letteraturaitaliana. net/pdf/Volume_8/t207.pdf

Deane, W. (1996). Some Signposts from Daguragu. *The Inaugural Vincent Lingiari Memorial Lecture*. Northern Territory University. August. Kingston, ACT: Council for Aboriginal Reconciliation.

Department for Education (2011). *Teachers' Standards. Guidance for School Leaders, School Staff and Governing Bodies*, DFE-00066-2011. London: Department for Education.

Department of Education, Science and Training (2005). *National Framework for Values Education in Australian Schools*. Canberra, ACT: Commonwealth of Australia.

Department of Education, Science and Training (2007). *Guide to the Teaching of Australian History in Years 9 and 10*. Canberra, ACT: Commonwealth of Australia.

Department of Immigration and Border Protection (2012). *Factsheet 8 – Abolition of the 'White Australia' Policy*. Retrieved from https://www.immi. gov.au/media/fact-sheets/08abolition.htm; accessed 01.09.2014.

Department of Justice (1982). Constitution Acts 1867–1982. Retrieved from http://laws.justice.gc.ca/en/const/annex_e.html#I; accessed 10.03.2009.

Devine, T., & Logue, P. (2002). *Being Scottish: Personal Reflections on Scottish Identity Today*. Edinburgh: Polygon.

DfES (Department for Education and Science) (2007). *Diversity and Citizenship Curriculum Review* (The Ajegbo Report), DFES-00045-2007. London: DfES.

Dickens, C. (1861) (1894 edition). *Great Expectations*. London: Chapman and Hall.

Dickson, B. J. (2003). Whom Does the Party Represent? From 'Three Revolutionary Classes' to 'Three Represents'. *American Asian Review*, 21: 1–24.

Direcção dos Serviços de Educação e Juventude (DSEJ) Curriculum Reform Working Team (1999). *Civic Education*. Macau: DSEJ.

Donnelly, K. (2005). The Culture Wars in the School. *Quadrant*, 49(4) (April): 56–61.

Doppen, F. H. (2010). Citizenship Education and the Dutch National Identity Debate. *Education, Citizenship and Social Justice*, 5(2): 131–143.

Downer, A. (1999). *Australia and Asia – A New Paradigm for the Relationship*. Speech Made to the Foreign Correspondents Association, 16 April. Retrieved from http://www.foreignminister.gov.au/speeches/1999/990416_aust_asia. html; accessed 28.08.2014.

Dubet, F., & Martuccelli, D. (1998). *En la escuela. Sociologia de la experiencia escolar*. Buenos Aires: Losada.

Duquette, C. (2014). Through the Looking Glass: An Overview of the Theoretical Foundations of Québec's History Curriculum. In R. Sandwell & A. von Heyking (Eds.), *Becoming a History Teacher: Sustaining Practices in*

Historical Thinking and Knowing (pp. 139–157). Toronto, ON: University of Toronto Press.

Durham, L. (1839). *Lord Durham's Report on the Affairs of British North America.* Retrieved from http://faculty.marianopolis.edu/c.belanger/quebechistory/docs/durham/1.htm; accessed 10.03.2009.

Easton, M. (2013). How British Is Britain? Retrieved from http://www.bbc.co.uk/news/uk-24302914; accessed 20.08.2015.

Education and Manpower Bureau (2001). *Learning for Life Learning through Life: Reform of the Education System in Hong Kong.* Hong Kong: Education and Manpower Bureau.

EEC (1957). *TRAITÉ instituant la Communauté Economique Européenne*, Fait à Rome, le vingt-cinq mars mil neuf cent cinquante-sept (Treaty Establishing the European Economic Community) (Not available in print form or in English: Retrieved from http://old.eur-lex.europa.eu/LexUriServ/LexUriServ.do?uri=CELEX:11957E/TXT:FR:PDF).

Eley, G. (1990). Remapping the Nation: War, Revolutionary Upheaval and Sate Formation in Eastern Europe, 1914–1923. In H. Aster & P. Potichnyi (Eds.), *Ukrainian-Jewish Relations in Historical Perspective* (pp. 205–246). Edmonton: Canadian Institute of Ukrainian Studies.

Elliott, V. (2014). The Treasure House of a Nation? Literary Heritage, Curriculum and Devolution in Scotland and England in the Twenty-First Century. *The Curriculum Journal*, 25(2): 282–300.

Ellsworth, E. (2005). *Places of Learning: Media, Architecture and Pedagogy.* New York: Routledge.

Elmersjö, H., & Lindmark, D. (2010). Nationalism, Peace Education and History Textbook Revision in Scandinavia, 1886–1940. *Journal of Educational Media, Memory and Society*, 2(2): 63–74.

Erebus Consulting Group (1999). *Evaluation of the Discovering Democracy Program.* Canberra: Erebus Consulting Group.

Éthier, M.-A., & Lefrançois, D. (2010). Learning and Teaching History in Québec: Assessment, Context, Outlook. In P. Clark (Ed.), *New Possibilities for the Past: Shaping History Education in Canada* (pp. 325–343). Vancouver, BC: UBC Press.

Éthier, M.-A., & Lefrançois, D. (2011). Learning and Teaching History in Quebec: Assessment, Context, Outlook. In P. Clark (Ed.), *New Possibilities for the Past: Shaping History Education in Canada* (pp. 325–343). Vancouver, BC: UBC Press.

Eurobarometer (2010). *Eurobarometer 73.3, March–April 2010. TNS Opinion & Social: ZA5233*, dataset version 2.0.0. Cologne: GESIS/Brussels: European Commission. doi:10.4232/1.10709

European Commission (1989). *Education and Training in the EC: Guidelines for the Medium Term 1989–92*, COM (89), 236. Brussels: EC.

European Commission (1992). *New Prospects for Community Cultural Action*, COM (92), Brussels: EC.

European Commission (1997). *Study Group on Education and Training: Report. Accomplishing Europe through Education and Training.* Luxembourg: Office for Official Publications of the European Communities.

European Commission (2005a). *Citizenship Education at School in Europe.* Brussels: EC.

European Commission (2005b). *Citizens for Europe,* COM (2005) 116 Final. Brussels: EC.

European Commission (2012). *Rethinking Education: Investing in Skills for Better Socio-economic Outcomes,* COM (2012) 669. Strasbourg: EC.

European Parliament and the Council of the European Union (2006). *Recommendation 2006/962/EC of the Council of 18 December 2006 on Key Competences for Lifelong Learning* [Official Journal L 394 of 30.12.2006].

European Union (1992). Treaty on European Union [The Maastricht Treaty]. *Official Journal* C 191, 29 July. Brussels: European Union.

European Union (1997). Treaty of Amsterdam Amending the Treaty on European Union, the Treaties Establishing the European Communities and Related Acts. *Official Journal* C 340, 10 November: Art 17§. Brussels: European Union.

European Union (2006, December 30). Recommendation of the European Parliament and of the Council of 18 December 2006 on Key Competences for Lifelong Learning (2006/962/EC). *Official Journal of the European Union, L 394,* 49: 18–20.

Eurydice (2012a). *Citizenship Education in Europe: Appendix for Internet: Main Reforms in Citizenship Education since 2005.* Retrieved from http://eacea.ec. europa.eu/education/eurydice/documents/thematic_reports/139EN_RA.pdf

Eurydice (2012b). *Citizenship Education in Europe.* Retrieved from http://eacea. ec.europa.eu/education/eurydice/documents/thematic_reports/139EN.pdf

Evans, R. J. (2011). The Wonderfulness of Us. *London Review of Books,* 33(6): 9–12.

Evans, R. W. (2004). *The Social Studies Wars: What Should We Teach the Children?* New York: Teachers College Press.

Faden, L. Y. (2012). Teachers Constituting the Politicized Subject: Canada and U.S. Teachers' Perspectives on the 'Good' Citizen. *Citizenship Teaching and Learning,* 7(2): 173–189.

Fairbank, J. K. (1987). *The Great Chinese Revolution 1800–1985.* New York: Harper Perennial.

Fitzgerald, J. (2006). Nationalism, Democracy, and Dignity in Twentieth-Century China. In S. Y. S. Chien & J. Fitzgerald (Eds.), *The Dignity of Nations – Equality, Competition, and Honor in East Asian Nationalism.* Hong Kong: Hong Kong University Press.

Five Nations Network (2015). *Citizenship and Values Education in England, Ireland, Northern Ireland, Scotland and Wales.* Retrieved from http://www.five-nations.net/northern-ireland.html; accessed 20.08.2015.

Freire, P. (1987). *Pedagogia do Oprimido.* Rio de Janeiro: Paz e Terra.

Freyre, G. (1988). *Casa-Grande e Senzala.* Rio de Janeiro: Livraria José Olympio.

Friedman, E. (1997). Chinese Nationalism, Taiwan Autonomy and the Prospects of a Larger War. *Journal of Contemporary China,* 6(14): 5–33.

Fukuyama, F. (1992). *The End of History and the Last Man.* New York and Toronto: Avon Books/Free Press, Maxwell Macmillan Canada.

Fullbrook, M. (2011). *Dissonant Lives: Generations and Violence through the German Dictatorships.* Oxford: Oxford University Press.

Galloway, G. (2013). *Ottawa Ordered to Find and Release Millions of Indian Residential School Records*. Retrieved from http://www.theglobeandmail. com/news/politics/ottawa-ordered-to-find-and-release-millions-of-indian-residential-school-records/article8001068/; accessed 02.10.2014.

Garratt, D., & Piper, H. (2008). *Citizenship Education, Identity and Nationhood: Contradictions in Practice*. London: Bloomsbury.

Geddes, J. (2013, July 29). *How Stephen Harper Is Rewriting History*. Retrieved from http://www2.macleans.ca/2013/07/29/written-by-the-victors/; accessed 01.08.2013.

Gellner, E. (1983). *Nations and Nationalism*. Oxford: Basil Blackwell.

Gersema, E. (2012, January 6). Ethnic Studies Case: District's Funds Cut. *The Arizona Republic*. Retrieved from http://www.azcentral.com/arizonarepublic/news/articles/2012/01/06/20120106arizona-ethnic-studies-case-funds-cut.html

Giddens, A. (1998). *The Third Way: The Renewal of Social Democracy*. Cambridge: Polity Press.

Giddens, A. (2002). *Runaway World: How Globalization Is Reshaping Our Lives*. New York: Routledge.

Gill, J., & Howard, S. (2009). *Knowing Our Place: Children Talking About Power, Identity and Citizenship*. Camberwell, VIC: ACER Press.

Gill, J., & Reid, A. (1999). Civics Education: The State of Play or the Play of the State? *Curriculum Perspectives*, 19(3): 31–40.

Gilroy, P. (2002). *O Atlântico negro: Modernidade e Dupla Consciência*. Rio de Janeiro: Editora 34/UCAM.Centro de Estudos Afro-Asiáticos.

Ginwright, S., & Cammarota, J. (2007). Youth Activism in the Urban Community: Learning Critical Civic Praxis within Community Organizations. *International Journal of Qualitative Studies in Education*, 20(6): 693–710.

Godsay, S., Henderson, W., Levine, P., & Littenberg-Tobias, J. (2012). *State Civic Education Requirements*. Medford, MA: Center for Information and Research on Civic Education (CIRCLE).

Goldburg, P. (2013). Values and Religion in Education: An Australian View. In J. Arthur & T. Lovat (Eds.), *The Routledge International Handbook of Education, Religion and Values* (pp. 124–134). London: Routledge.

Goldsmith QC, L. (2008). *Citizenship: Our Common Bond*. London: Citizenship Review, Ministry of Justice.

Gooda, M. (2011). *Constitutional Reform: Creating a Nation for All of Us*. Sydney, NSW: Australian Human Rights Commission.

Gove, M. (2014). *Speech to the 2010 Conservative Party Conference*. Retrieved from http://centrallobby.politicshome.com/latestnews/article-detail/newsarticle/speech-in-full-michael-gove/

Government of Saskatchewan (2014). *Treaty Education*. Retrieved from http://www.education.gov.sk.ca/treaty-education/; accessed 03.10.2014.

Granatstein, J. (1998). *Who Killed Canadian History?* Toronto: Harper-Collins.

Green, A. (1990). *Education and State Formation: The Rise of Education Systems in England, France and the USA*. London: Macmillan.

Green Paper (2007). *The Governance of Britain*. Presented to Parliament by the Secretary of State for Justice and Lord Chancellor by Command of Her Majesty. CM 7170. London, HMSO.

Gries, P. (2004). *China's New Nationalism*. Berkeley, CA: University of California Press.

Grindel, S. (2008). Deutscher Sonderweg oder europäischer Erinnerungsort? Die Darstellung des modernen Kolonialismus in neueren deutschen Schulbüchern. *Internationale Schulbuchforschung*, 30(3): 695–716.

Guerra Pratas, M. H. (2009). An Experience of Education for Peace and Human Rights in Teacher Training. In P. Cunningham (Ed.), *Human Rights and Citizenship Education* (pp. 329–331). London: CiCe.

Gurney Read, J. (2014). Educational Divide Still Blighting Our Society. *The Daily Telegraph*, 20 June. Retrieved from http://www.telegraph.co.uk/education/educationnews/10913754/Educational-divide-still-blighting-our-society.html

Hahn, C. (1998). *Becoming Political: Comparative Perspectives on Citizenship Education*. New York: State University of New York Press.

Hahn, C. (2010). Comparative Civic Education Research: What We Know and What We Need to Know. *Citizenship Teaching and Learning*, 6(1): 5–23.

Hall, S. (2003). New Ethnicities. In L. Martín Alcoff & E. Mendieta (Eds.), *Identities: Race, Class, Gender, and Nationality* (pp. 90–95). London: Blackwell.

Harvey, D. (2007). *A Brief History of Neoliberalism*. London: Oxford University Press.

Hasenbalg, C., & Silva, Nelson do Valle (1990). *Raça e Oportunidades Educacionais*. Estudos Afro-Asiáticos. Rio de Janeiro: no. 18, pp. 73–89.

Hastings, A. (1997). *The Construction of Nationhood: Ethnicity, Religion, and Nationalism*. Cambridge: Cambridge University Press.

Heaney, S. (2002). Englands of the Mind. In *Finders Keepers. Selected Prose 1971–2001* (pp. 77–95). London: Faber and Faber.

Heater, D. (1999). *What Is Citizenship?* Cambridge: Polity Press.

Heath, A., & Roberts, J. (2008). *British Identity: Its Sources and Possible Implications for Civic Attitudes and Behaviour*. London: Citizenship Review, Ministry of Justice.

Henderson, H. (2000). Transnational Corporations and Global Citizenship. *The American Behavioral Scientist*, 43(8): 1231–1261.

Hertzberg, H. (1990). *Social Studies Reform: 1880–1980*. Boulder, CO: Social Science Education Consortium.

Hess, D. E. (2009). *Controversy in the Classroom: The Democratic Power of Discussion*. New York: Routledge.

Hoare, M. (2010). The War of Yugoslavian Succession. In S. Ramet (Ed.), *Central and Southeast European Politics since 1989* (pp. 111–135). Cambridge: Cambridge University Press.

Hobsbawn, E., & Ranger, T. (Eds.) (1983). *The Invention of Tradition*. Cambridge: Cambridge University Press.

Hocking, J. (2008). *Gough Whitlam: A Moment in History*. Carlton, VIC: Melbourne University Publishing.

Hodgetts, A. B. (1968). *What Culture? What Heritage? A Study of Civic Education in Canada*. Toronto: OISE Press.

Hodgetts, A. B., & Gallagher, P. (1978). *Teaching Canada for the '80s*. Toronto: Ontario Institute for Studies in Education.

Home Office (2003). *The New and the Old: The Report of the 'Life in the UK' Advisory Group*. London: Home Office. Retrieved from http://ec.europa.eu/ewsi/UDRW/images/items/docl_19546_997974966.pdf

HORTA, José Silvério Baía (1994). *O hino, o sermão e a ordem do dia: a educação no Brasil (1930–1945)*. Rio de Janeiro: Editora da UERJ.

Hoskins, B., Janmaat, J. G., & Villalba, E. (2011). Learning Citizenship through Social Participation Outside and Inside School: An International, Multilevel Study of Young People's Learning of Citizenship. *British Educational Research Journal*, 38(3): 419–446.

Houle, F. (2004). Canadian Citizenship and Multiculturalism. In P. Boyer, L. Cardinal, & D. Headon (Eds.), *From Subjects to Citizens: A Hundred Years of Citizenship in Australia and Canada* (pp. 215–228). Ottawa: University of Ottawa Press.

Howard, J. (1996). *Speech on Racial Tolerance*. Hansard. Retrieved from http://parlinfo.aph.gov.au/parlInfo/search/display/display.w3p;db=CHAMBER;id=chamber%2Fhansardr%2F1996-10-30%2F0071;query=Id%3A%22chamber%2Fhansardr%2F1996-10-30%2F0000%22; accessed 30.08.2014.

Howard, J. (2006). *Address to the National Press Club – Australia Day Address*, January 25. Retrieved from http://www.theage.com.au/news/national/pms-speech/2006/01/25/1138066849045.html?page=fullpage#contentSwap2; accessed 30.08.2014.

Howard, S., & Gill, J. (2005). Learning to Belong: Children Talk about Feeling 'Australian'. *Childrenz Issues*, 9(2): 43–49.

Hughes, A., Print, M., & Sears, A. (2010). Curriculum Capacity and Citizenship Education: A Comparative Analysis of Four Democracies. *Compare: A Journal of Comparative and International Education*, 40(3): 293–309.

Hughes, A. S., & Sears, A. (2006). Citizenship Education: Canada Dabbles While the World Plays On. *Education Canada*, 46(4): 6–9.

Hughes, A. S., & Sears, A. (2008). The Struggle for Citizenship Education in Canada: The Centre Cannot Hold. In J. Arthur, I. Davies, & C. Hahn (Eds.), *The Sage Handbook of Education for Citizenship and Democracy* (pp. 124–138). London: Sage.

Hunt, T. C. (2002). *The Impossible Dream: Education and the Search for Panaceas*. New York: Peter Lang.

Hunter-Henin, M. (Ed.) (2011). *Law, Religious Freedoms and Education in Europe*. Farnham: Ashgate.

Huntington, H. (1993). The Clash of Civilizations? *Foreign Affairs*, 72(Summer): 22–49.

Hursh, D. (2007). 'No Child Left Behind' and the Rise of Neoliberal Education Policy. *American Educational Research Journal*, 44(3): 493–518.

Hurst, D. (2014). Christopher Pyne Is on 'Brainwashing and Propaganda Mission', Critic Claims. *the.guardian.com*, 16 January. Retrieved from http://www.theguardian.com/world/2014/jan/10/christopher-pyne-is-on-brainwashing-and-propaganda-mission-critic-claims; accessed 01.09.2014.

Ibbitson, J. (2013). *For Tories, Rewriting History Is Just One of the Perks of Power*. Retrieved from http://www.theglobeandmail.com/news/politics/globe-politics-insider/for-tories-rewriting-history-is-just-one-of-the-perks-of-power/article11744087/

Ignatieff, M. (1996). Nationalism and Toleration. In R. Caplan & J. Feffer (Eds.), *Europe's New Nationalism* (pp. 213–232). New York: Oxford University Press.

IPEA (2008). *Desigualdades raciais, racismo e políticas públicas*. Brasília, Instituto de Pesquisa Economica e Aplicada, 2008. Retrieved from www.ipea.gov.br

Jaenen, C. J. (1981). Mutilated Multiculturalism. In J. D. Wilson (Ed.), *Canadian Education in the 1980s* (pp. 79–96). Calgary: Destelig.

Jenkins, R. (1996). Ethnicity Etcetera: Social Anthropological Points of View. *Ethnic and Racial Studies*, 19(4): 807–822.

Jerome, L., & Clemitshaw, G. (2012). Teaching (about) Britishness? An Investigation into Trainee Teachers' Understanding of Britishness in Relation to Citizenship and the Discourse of Civic Nationalism. *The Curriculum Journal*, 23(1): 19–41.

Jivraj, S. (2012). *How Has Ethnic Diversity Grown 1991–2001–2011? Dynamics of Diversity: Evidence from the 2011 Census*. Manchester: Centre on Dynamics of Ethnicity, University of Manchester. Retrieved from www.ethnicity.ac.uk/census/869_CCSR_Bulletin_How_has_ethnic_diversity_grown_v4NW.pdf

Johnson, C. (2007). John Howard's 'Values' and Australian Identity. *Australian Journal of Political Science*, 42(2): 195–209.

Johnson, L., & Joshee, R. (Eds.) (2007). *Multicultural Education Policies in Canada and the United States*. Vancouver, BC: UBC Press.

Joppke, C. (2010). *Citizenship and Immigration*. Cambridge: Polity Press.

Joshee, R. (2004). Citizenship and Multicultural Education in Canada: From Assimilation to Social Cohesion. In J. A. Banks (Ed.), *Diversity and Citizenship Education: Global Perspectives* (pp. 127–156). San Francisco: Jossey-Bass.

Joshee, R., & Johnson, L. (Eds.) (2007). *Multicultural Education Policies in Canada and the United States*. Vancouver, BC: UBC Press.

Kahne, J., & Sporte, S. (2008). Developing Citizens: The Impact of Civic Learning Opportunities to Students' Commitment to Civic Participation. *American Educational Research Journal*, 45(3): 738–766.

Kamusella, T. (2010). School Atlases as Instruments of Nation-State Making and Maintenance: A Remark on the Invisibility of Ideology in Popular Education. *Journal of Educational Media, Memory and Society*, 2(1): 113–138.

Kan, L. F. (2007). *Hong Kong's Chinese History Curriculum from 1945: Politics and Identity*. Hong Kong: Hong Kong University Press.

Karakatsani, D. (2014). History Teaching and Citizenship in a Time of Crisis: History Teachers' Attitudes to Teaching Controversial and Traumatic Topics in Secondary Education in Greece. Paper presented at the *16th Children's Identity and Citizenship in Europe Conference*, June 2014, Olsztyn, Poland.

Katsarksa, M. (2007). National Identity in Textbooks and Marginalizing Practices: A Case Study from Bulgaria. *Internationale Schulbuchforschung*, 29(3): 307–322.

Keating, A. (2014). *Education for Citizenship Education in Europe: European Policies, National Adaptations and Young People's Attitudes*. Basingstoke: Palgrave Macmillan.

Keating, A., Kerr, D., Benton, T., Munday, E., & Lopes, J. (2010). *Citizenship Education in England 2001–2010: Young People's Practices and Prospects for the Future: The Eighth and Final Report from the Citizenship Education Longitudinal Study*. Research Brief. London: DfE.

Keating, P. (1992). Redfern Park Speech, 10 December. In M. Ryan (Ed.), *Advancing Australia: The Speeches of Paul Keating* (pp. 227–228). Sydney, NSW: Big Picture Publications.

Kelly, P. (2011). *The March of the Patriots: The Struggle for Modern Australia*. Carlton, VIC: Melbourne University Press.

Kempe, F. (2006). Fevered Pitch. *Wall Street Journal*, 13 June, A4.

Kennedy, K., Watts, O., & McDonald, G. (1993). *Citizenship Education for a New Age*. Toowoomba, QLD: University of Southern Queensland Press.

Kerr, D., McCarthy, S., & Smith, A. (2002). Citizenship Education in England, Ireland and Northern Ireland. *European Journal of Education*, 37(2): 179–191.

Kiwan, D. (2008). *Education for Inclusive Citizenship*. London and New York: Routledge.

Knight Abowitz, K., & Harnish, J. (2006). Contemporary Discourses of Citizenship. *Review of Educational Research*, 76(4): 653–690.

Knightley, P. (2000). *Australia: A Biography of a Nation*. London: Random House.

Korff, J. (2014). Would a Treaty Help Aboriginal Self-determination. *Creative Spirits*. Retrieved from http://www.creativespirits.info/aboriginalculture/ selfdetermination/would-a-treaty-help-aboriginal-self-determination; accessed 01.09.2014.

Ku, Y. (2010). The Politics of Historical Memory in Germany: Brandt's Ostpoltik, the German-Polish History Textbook Commission and Conservative Reaction. *Journal of Educational Media, Memory and Society*, 2(2): 75–92.

Kumashiro, K. (2012). *Bad Teacher! How Blaming Teachers Distorts the Bigger Picture*. New York: Teachers College Press.

Kymlicka, W. (1998). *Finding Our Way: Rethinking Ethnocultural Relations in Canada*. Toronto and New York: Oxford University Press.

Kymlicka, W. (2003). Being Canadian. *Government and Opposition Ltd.*, 38(3): 357–385.

Kymlicka, W., & Norman, W. (2000). *Citizenship in Diverse Societies*. Oxford and New York: Oxford University Press.

Kymlicka, W., & Opalski, M. (2001). Introduction. In W. Kymlicka & M. Opalski (Eds.), *Can Liberalism be Exported? Western Political Theory and Ethnic Relations in Eastern Europe* (pp. 1–10). Oxford: Oxford University Press.

Laborde, C. (2002). From Constitutional to Civic Participation. *British Journal of Political Science*, 32: 591–612.

Ladson-Billings, G. (2006). From the Achievement Gap to the Education Debt: Understanding Achievement in U.S. Schools. *Educational Researcher*, 35(7): 3–12.

Lawy, R., & Biesta, G. (2006). Citizenship-as-Practice: The Educational Implications of an Inclusive and Relational Understanding of Citizenship. *British Journal of Educational Studies*, 54(1): 34–50.

Lee, W. O. (2001). Educational Insight from May Fourth Movement. In W. O. Lee, J. Fang, & T. Y. J. Lo (Eds.), *Education about Freedom in China* (pp. 19–28). Hong Kong: Longman.

Lenaerts, K. (1994). Education in European Community Law after Maastricht. *Common Market Law Review*, 31: 7–41.

Leonardo, Z. (2013). *Race Frameworks: A Multidimensional Theory of Racism and Education*. New York: Teachers College Press.

Létourneau, J. (2004). *A History for the Future: Rewriting Memory and Identity in Quebec* (P. Aronoff & H. Scott, Trans.). Montreal: McGill-Queen's University Press.

Létourneau, J. (2011). The Debate on History Education in Quebec. In P. Clark (Ed.), *New Possibilities for the Past: Shaping History Education in Canada* (pp. 81–96). Vancouver, BC: UBC Press.

Lévesque, S. (2008). *Thinking Historically: Educating Students for the Twenty-First Century*. Toronto: University of Toronto Press.

Li, C. S. (2010). *A History of Foreign Press in Contemporary Macao*. Guangzhou: Guangdong People's Press. (In Chinese)

Liberal Party of Australia (1988). *Future Directions: It's Time for Plain Thinking*. Canberra, ACT: Liberal National Party.

Lipman, P. (2009). *The New Political Economy of Urban Education*. New York: Routledge.

Macintyre, S., & Clark, A. (2004). *The History Wars* (New ed.). Carlton, VIC: Melbourne University Press.

MacMillan, M. (2008). *The Uses and Abuses of History*. Toronto: Viking.

Maguire, K. (2014). Let's Stay Together: Gordon Brown's My Scotland, Our Britain, 18 July, *New Statesman*. Retrieved from http://www.newstatesman.com/politics/2014/07/let-s-stay-together-gordon-brown-s-my-scotland-our-britain; accessed 15.08.2014.

Major, J. (1992). Leader's Speech. *Conservative Party Conference*, Brighton. Retrieved from http://www.britishpoliticalspeech.org/speech-archive.htm?speech=138; accessed 14.08.2014.

Manna, P. (2011). *Collision Course: Federal Educational Policy Meets State and Local Realities*. Thousand Oaks, CA: CQ College Press.

Markova, I. (2011). Balancing Victimhood and Complicity in Austrian History Textbooks: Visual and Verbal Strategies of Representing the Past in Post-Waldheim Austria. *Journal of Educational Media, Memory and Society*, 3(2): 58–73.

Martinsson, J., & Lundqvist, L. J. (2010). Ecological Citizenship: Coming Out 'Clean' Without Turning 'Green'. *Environmental Politics*, 19(4): 518–537.

McAndrew, M. (2001). *Immigration et diversité à l'école: le débat québécois dans une perspective comparative*. Montréal: Presses de l'Université de Montréal.

McCann, G., & Finn, P. (2006). Identifying the European Dimension in Citizenship Education. *Policy & Practice: A Development Education Review*, 3(Autumn): 52–63.

McGarvey, N., & Cairney, P. (2008). *Scottish Politics: An Introduction*. Basingstoke: Palgrave Macmillan.

McGhee, D. (2008). *The End of Multiculturalism? Terrorism, Integration and Human Rights*. Maidenhead: Open University Press.

Mckenna, M. (1997). Different perspectives on Black Armband History. Research Paper 5. Retrieved from http://www.aph.gov.au/About_Parliament/Parliamentary_Departments/Parliamentary_Library/pubs/rp/RP9798/98RP05; accessed 15.09.2014.

McLachlan, N. (1989). *Waiting for the Revolution: A History of Australian Nationalism*. Ringwood, VIC: Penguin.

McLean, L. (2007). Education, Identity, and Citizenship in Early Modern Canada. *Journal of Canadian Studies*, 41(1): 5–30.

Mellor, S. (2003). Comparative Findings from the IEA Civic Study and Their Impact on the Improvement of Civic Education in Australia. *Journal of Social Science Education.* Retrieved from http://www.jsse.org/index.php/jsse/article/viewFile/468/384; accessed 10.08.2015.

Miller-Idriss, C. (2009). *Blood and Culture: Youth, Right Wing Extremism and National Belonging in Contemporary Germany.* Durham, NC: Duke University Press.

Milner, A. (2011). A History Curriculum for Our Times? *Teaching History,* 45(4) (December): 24–29.

Ministerial Council for Employment, Education, Training and Youth Affairs (2008). *Melbourne Declaration on Educational Goals for Young Australians.* Canberra, ACT: MCEETYA.

Ministry of Education (ROC) (1990). *History of National Reconstruction of the Republic of China,* 4: 1055–1058 [Taipei: Guoli bianyiguan].

Ministry of Education (2013). *Instruction on Delivering 'Recommendations on Thinking and Morality Courses in Junior High School and Ideological and Political Courses in High School to Act the Spirit of the 18th Party Congress'.* Beijing: Ministry of Education.

Ministry of Justice (2008). *Citizenship: Our Common Bond.* Report to the Prime Minister by Lord Goldsmith. Retrieved from http://image.guardian.co.uk/sys-files/Politics/documents/2008/03/11/citizenship-report-full.pdf; accessed 14.08.2014.

Mish, C. (2008). Die Dekolonisation des Empire in britischen Geschitsbüchern seit 1947. *Internationale Schulbuchforschung,* 30(3): 741–762.

Mitchell, K. (2004). Educating the National Citizen in Neoliberal Times – From the Multicultural Self to the Strategic Cosmopolitan. *Transactions of the Institute of British Geographers NS,* 28: 387–402.

Morris, P. (1997). Civics and Citizenship Education in Hong Kong. In K. J. Kennedy (Ed.), *Citizenship Education and the Modern State* (pp. 107–125). London: Falmer.

Muecke, S., & Shoemaker, A. (2004). *Aboriginal Australians: First Nations of an Ancient Continent.* Fisherman's Bend, VIC: Thames and Hudson.

Mundine, W. (2014). *Special Broadcasting Service,* 27 January. Retrieved from http://www.sbs.com.au/news/article/2014/01/27/mundine-calls-indigenous-treaties; accessed 01.09.2014.

Munn, P., & Arnot, M. (2009). Citizenship in Scottish Schools: The Evolution of Education for Citizenship from the Late Twentieth Century to the Present. *History of Education, Journal of the History of Education Society,* 38(3): 437–454.

Mycock, A., McGlynn, C., & Andrews, R. (2011). Understanding the 'History Wars' in Australia and the UK. In C. McGlynn, A. Mycock, & J. W. McAuley (Eds.) *Britishness, Identity and Citizenship: The View from Abroad* (pp. 313–334). Oxfordshire, UK: Peter Lang.

Mycock, A., Tonge, J., & Jeffery, B. (2012). Does Citizenship Education Make Young People Better-Engaged Citizens? *Political Studies,* 60(3): 578–602.

Nash, G., Crabree, C., & Dunn, R. E. (1997). *History on Trial: The Culture Wars and the Teaching of the Past.* New York: Knopf.

National Center for Educational Statistics (2011). *The Nation's Report Card: Civics.* Retrieved from http://nces.ed.gov/nationsreportcard/itmrlsx/search. aspx?subject=civics; accessed 23.09.2014.

National Curriculum Board (2009). *Shape of the Australian Curriculum: History.* Retrieved from http://www.acara.edu.au/verve/_resources/Australian_ Curriculum_-_History.pdf; accessed 31.08.2014.

National Education Association (1916). *Commission on the Reorganization of Secondary Education.* Washington, DC: National Education Association. Retrieved from https://www3.nd.edu/~rbarger/www7/cardprin.html; accessed 26.11.2014.

National Education Association (1918). *The Cardinal Principles of Secondary Education.* Washington, DC: National Education Association. Retrieved from http://www.ux1.eiu.edu/~cfrnb/cardprin.html; accessed 22.09.2014.

National Inquiry into the Separation of Aboriginal and Torres Strait Islander Children from Their Families (1997). *Bringing Them Home.* Canberra: Commonwealth of Australia.

National Museum of Australia (n.d.). *Programmed to be White.* Retrieved from http://www.nma.gov.au/exhibitions/from_little_things_big_things_grow/ behind_the_scenes/programmed_to_be_white; accessed 30.08.2014.

Need to Know Editor (2010, March 24). *Texas School Board Approves Controversial Textbook Changes.* Retrieved from http://www.pbs.org/wnet/need-to-know/ culture/texas-school-board-approves-controversial-textbook-changes/954/

Nelson, J., & Kerr, D. (2006). *Active Citizenship in International Review of Curriculum and Assessment Countries: Definitions, Policies, Practices and Outcomes.* Retrieved from https://www.youtube.com/watch?v=i3q0JsFNmHQ; accessed 14.08.2014.

NFER (2010). *History in the Curriculum.* Survey by the NFER Eurydice Unit for England, Wales and Northern Ireland. Retrieved from https://www.nfer.ac. uk/shadomx/apps/fms/fmsdownload.cfm?file_uuid=9788BD95-C29E-AD4D-0F52-03EC523CD31B&siteName=nfer

Ng, S. W. (2011). The Contradictions in Values of National Education. *Mingpao*, 24 June. (In Chinese)

Niemi, R., & Junn, J. (2005). *Civic Education: What Makes Students Learn?* New Haven, CT: Yale University Press.

Niens, I., & McIlrath, L. (2010). Understandings of Citizenship Education in Northern Ireland and the Republic of Ireland: Public Discourses among Stakeholders in the Public and Private Sectors. *Education, Citizenship and Social Justice*, 5(1): 73–87.

Nuhoglu, Y., & Wong, S. Y. (2006). Educating Future Citizens in Europe and Asia. In A. Benavot & C. Braslavsky (Eds.), *School Knowledge in Comparative and Historical Perspective – Changing Curricula in Primary and Secondary Education* (pp. 73–88). Hong Kong: Comparative Education Research Centre, The University of Hong Kong.

Nygren, T. (2012). The Contemporary Turn: Debate, Curricula and Swedish Students' History. *Journal of Educational Media, Memory and Society*, 4(1): 40–60.

Oetting, B. (2006). Bruch mit der kolonialen Vergangenheit? Der Algerienkreig und die Entkolonisierung in französischen Geschichtsschulbüchern der Troisième. *Internationale Schulbuchforschung*, 28(1): 25–41.

Ofsted (2010). *Citizenship Established? Citizenship in Schools 2006/09*. London: Ofsted.

Ontario Ministry of Education (2013). *The Ontario Curriculum Grades 9 and 10 Canadian and World Studies: Geography, History, Civics (Politics)*. Toronto: Ontario Ministry of Education.

Orr, J., & Ronayne, R. (2009). Indigeneity Education as Canadian First Nations Citizenship Education. *Citizenship Teaching and Learning*, 5(2): 35–49.

Osborne, K. (1987). To the Schools We Must Look for Good Canadians: Developments in the Teaching of History in Schools since 1960. *Journal of Canadian Studies*, 22(3): 104–125.

Osborne, K. (2000). Our History Syllabus Has Us Gasping: History in Canadian Schools – Past, Present and Future. *Canadian Historical Review*, 81(3): 404–435.

Osborne, K. (2001). Democracy, Democratic Citizenship, and Education. In J. P. Portelli & R. P. Solomon (Eds.), *The Erosion of Demoracy in Education* (pp. 29–61). Calgary: Detselig.

Osborne, K. (2004). History and Social Studies: Partners or Rivals. In A. Sears & I. Wright (Eds.), *Challenges and Prospects for Canadian Social Studies* (pp. 73–89). Vancouver, BC: Pacific Educational Press.

Osborne, K. (2005). Political and Citizenship Education: Teaching for Civic Egagement. *Education Canada*, 45(1): 13–16.

Osborne, K. (2011). Teaching Canadian History: A Century of Debate. In P. Clark (Ed.), *New Possibilities for the Past: Shaping History Education in Canada* (pp. 55–96). Vancouver, BC: UBC Press.

Osborne, W. F. (1919, October 20–22). Preface. Paper presented at *The National Conference on Character Education in Relation to Canadian Citizenship*, Winnipeg.

Osler, A. (2003). The Crick Report and the Future of Multiethnic Britain. In L. Gearon (Ed.), *Learning to Teach Citizenship in the Secondary School*. London: RoutledgeFalmer.

Osler, A. (2008). Citizenship Education and the Ajegbo Report: Re-imagining a Cosmopolitan Nation. *London Review of Education*, 6(1): 11–25.

Osler, A. (2009). Patriotism, Multiculturalism and Belonging: Political Discourse and the Teaching of History. *Educational Review*, 61(1): 85–100.

Osler, A., & Starkey, H. (2003). Learning for Cosmopolitian Citizenship. *Educational Review*, 55(3): 243–254.

Ou, T. C. (1977). Education in Wartime China. In P. K. T. Sih (Ed.), *Nationalist China during the Sino-Japanese War, 1937–1945* (pp. 99–103). Hicksville, NY: Exposition Press.

Paradise, J. F. (2009). China and International Harmony: The Role of Confucius Institutes in Bolstering Beijing's Soft Power. *Asian Survey*, 49(4): 647–669.

Parekh, B. (2000). *The Future of Multi-ethnic Britain (The Parekh Report)*. London: Profile Books and the Runnymede Trust.

Pashby, K., Ingram, L. A., & Joshee, R. (2014). Discovering, Recovering, and Covering-up Canada: Tracing Historical Citizenship Discourses in K–12 and Adult Immigrant Citizenship Education. *Canadian Journal of Education*, 37(2): 1–26.

Peace, T. (2014, March 24). *Lessons from the Past, Promises for the Future: Reflections on Historical Thinking in Canadian History.* Retrieved from http://activehistory.ca/2014/03/lessons-from-the-past-promises-for-the-future-reflections-on-historical-thinking-in-canadian-history/

Pearson, N. (2008). *Contradictions Cloud the Apology to the Stolen Generations,* 12 February. Retrieved from http://www.theaustralian.com.au/news/features/when-words-arent-enough/story-e6frg6z6-1111115528371; accessed 02.09.2014.

Peck, C. L. (2010). 'It's Not Like [I'm] Chinese and Canadian. I Am in between': Ethnicity and Students' Conceptions of Historical Significance. *Theory and Research in Social Education,* 38(4): 575–617.

Peck, C. L., Sears, A., & Donaldson, S. (2008). Unreached and Unreasonable: Curriculum Standards and Children's Understanding of Ethnic Diversity in Canada. *Curriculum Inquiry,* 38(1): 63–92.

Peck, C. L., Thompson, L. A., Chareka, O., Joshee, R., & Sears, A. (2010). From Getting Along to Democratic Engagement: Moving toward Deep Diversity in Citizenship Education. *Citizenship Teaching and Learning,* 6(1): 61–75. doi:10.1386/ctl.6.1.61_1

People for Education (2014). *Measuring What Matters.* Retrieved from http://www.peopleforeducation.ca/measuring-what-matters/the-goal/; accessed 06.10.2014.

Petter, D. (2008). Bilder imperialen Abschieds: Die französische Dekolonisation im Spiegel von öffentlichen Debatten und Geschichtsschulbüchern (1954–1962). *Internationale Schulbuchforschung,* 30(3): 717–740.

Pew Forum (2011). The Future of the Global Muslim Population. Retrieved from http://www.pewforum.org/2011/01/27/the-future-of-the-global-muslim-population/

Phillips, D. (2006). Parallel Lives? Challenging Discourses of British Muslim Self-segregation. *Environment and Planning D: Society and Space,* 24(1): 25–40. Retrieved from http://www.envplan.com/epd/fulltext/d24/d60j.pdf

Phillips, R. (1996). History Teaching, Cultural Restorationism and National Identity in England and Wales. *Curriculum Studies,* 4(3): 385–399.

Print, M. (1995a). Introduction: Context and Change in Civics Education. In M. Print (Ed.), *Civics and Citizenship Education: Issues from Practice and Research* (pp. 7–12). Canberra, ACT: Australian Curriculum Studies Association.

Print, M. (1995b). *Political Understanding and Attitudes of Secondary Students.* Canberra, ACT: Commonwealth of Australia.

Print, M. (2001). Teaching Discovering Democracy: The National Perspective 1999 to 2000. In M. Print, W. Moroz, & P. Reynolds (Eds.), *Discovering Democracy in Civics & Citizenship Education* (pp. 134–148). Katoomba, NSW: Social Science Press.

Ptak, R. (2014). Foreword. In C. X. G. Wei (Ed.), *Macao – The Formation of a Global City* (pp. xvi–xviii). Abingdon, Oxon: Routledge.

Pyne, C. (2014). *Press Conference – Adelaide,* 10 January. Retrieved from http://ministers.education.gov.au/pyne/press-conference-adelaide-1; accessed 01.09.2014.

Qualifications and Curriculum Authority (1998). *Education for Citizenship and the Teaching of Democracy in Schools.* Final Report of the Advisory Group on Citizenship. London: QCA.

Ramsden, J. (2007). *Don't Mention the War: The British and the Germans since 1890 – The British and Modern Germany.* London: Abacus.

Ravitch, D. (2013). *Reign of Error: The Hoax of Privatization Movement and the Danger to America's Public.* New York: Knopf Doubleday.

Reed, G. G. (1997). Looking in the Chinese Mirror: Reflecting on Moral-Political Education in the United States. In W. K. Cummings & P. G. Altbach (Eds.), *The Challenge of Eastern Asian Education – Implications for America* (pp. 51–64). New York: State University of New York Press.

Reid, A., & Gill, J. (2010). In Whose Interest? Australian Schooling and the Changing Contexts of Citizenship. In A. Reid, J. Gill, & A. Sears (Eds.), *Globalization, the Nation-State and the Citizen: Dilemmas and Directions for Civics and Citizenship Education* (pp. 19–34). London: Routledge.

Reid, A., Gill, J., & Sears, A. (Eds.) (2010). *Globalization, the Nation-State and the Citizen: Dilemmas and Directions for Civics and Citizenship Education.* New York and London: Routledge.

Reynolds, D. (2014). *The Long Shadow: The Great War and the Twentieth Century.* London: Simon and Schuster.

Riddoch, L. (2014). Why Women Are Saying Yes. *The Guardian,* 12 September, p. 42.

Robertson, H.-J. (2006). An Idea Whose Time Keeps Coming. *Phi Delta Kappan,* 87(5): 410–412.

Robinson, J., & Parkin, G. (1997). Discovering Democracy: A Missed Opportunity. *The Social Educator,* (December): 16–20.

Rodrigues, N. R. (2011). *Os africanos no Brasil.* Rio de Janeiro: Centro Edelstein de Pesquisas Sociais.

Roots of Empathy (2012). Roots of Empathy: Changing the World Child by Child. *History and Milestones.* Retrieved from http://www.rootsofempathy.org/images/documents/Roots_of_Empathy_History_and_Milestones_Nov2012.pdf

Roots of Empathy (n.d.). *Roots of Empathy: Mission, Goals, and Values.* Retrieved from http://www.rootsofempathy.org/en.html; accessed 05.10.2014.

Roskam, J. (2011). Bad History Now a National Problem. *The Institute of Public Affairs Review: A Quarterly Review of Politics and Public Affairs,* 63(2): 33–35.

Ross, A. (2008). Organising a Curriculum for Active Citizenship Education. In J. Arthur, I. Davies & C. Hahn (Eds.), *The SAGE Handbook of Education for Democracy and Citizenship* (pp. 492–505). London: Sage.

Ross, A. (2012a). Controversies and Generational Differences: Young People's Identities in Some European States. *Educational Sciences,* 2(2): 91–104.

Ross, A. (2012b). Communities and Others: Young Peoples' Constructions of Identities and Citizenship in the Baltic Countries. *Journal of Social Science Education,* 11(3): 22–42.

Ross, A. (2013). Identities and Diversities among Young Europeans: Some Examples from the Eastern Borders. In S. Gonsalves & M. Carpenter (Eds.), *Diversity, Intercultural Encounters and Education* (pp. 141–163). London: Routledge.

Ross, A. (2014). Intersecting Identities: Young People's Constructions of Identity in South-East Europe. In K. Bhopal & U. Maylor (Eds.), *Educational Inequalities in Schools and Higher Education* (pp. 247–466). London: Routledge.

Ross, A. (2015). *Constructions of Identities by Young New Europeans: Kaleidoscopic Identities*. London: Routledge.

Ross, A., & Zuzeviciute, V. (2011). Border Crossings, Moving Borders: Young People's Constructions of Identities in Lithuania in the Early 21st Century. *Profesinis Rengimas: Tyrimai ir Realijos*, 20 (Kaunus, Lithuania): 38–47.

Rubin, B. (2007). 'There's Still Not Justice': Youth Civic Identity Development amid Distinct School and Community Contexts. *Teachers College Record*, 109(2): 449–481.

Rubin, B. (2012). *Making Citizens: Transforming Civic Learning for Diverse Social Studies Classrooms*. New York: Routledge.

Rudd, K. (2008). Apology to Australia's Indigenous Peoples, 13 February. Retrieved from http://australia.gov.au/about-australia/our-country/our-people/apology-to-australias-indigenous-peoples; accessed 02.09.2014.

Rudd, K. (2012). We must Strive to Make Our Own Luck in Asia. *Australian Financial Review*, 29 October. Retrieved from http://www.afr.com/p/opinion/we_must_strive_to_make_own_luck_aUXAHDS3RiyJEbrhBSH6cL; accessed 05.09.2014.

Rüsen, J. (2012). Temporalizing Humanity: Towards a Universal History of Humanism. In M. I. Spariosu & J. Rusen (Eds.), *Exploring Humanity – Intercultural Perspectives on Humanism* (pp. 29–44). Taiwan: National Taiwan University Press.

Rustow, D. (1967). *A World of Nations*. Washington, DC: Brookings.

Said, E. (1995). *Orientalism*. London: Penguin Books.

Sandwell, R., & von Heyking, A. (2014). *Becoming a History Teacher: Sustaining Practices in Historical Thinking and Knowing*. Toronto: University of Toronto Press.

Santos, R. G., Chartier, M. J., Whalen, J. C., Chateau, D., & Boyd, L. (2011). Effectiveness of School-Based Violence Prevention for Children and Youth: Cluster Randomized Field Trial of the Roots of Empathy Program with Replication and Three-Year Follow-Up. *Healthcare Quarterly*, 14: 80–91.

Saskatchewan Ministry of Education (2013). *Treaty Education Outcomes and Indicators*. Saskatoon: Government of Saskatchewan, Ministry of Education.

Sautman, B. (1997). Racial Nationalism and China's External Behavior. *World Affairs*, 160(2): 78–96.

Savage, G., & Hickey-Moody, A. (2010). Global Flows as Gendered Cultural Pedagogies: Learning Gangsta in the 'Durty South'. *Critical Studies in Education*, 51(3): 277–293.

Schattle, H. (2008). Education for Global Citizenship: Illustrations of Ideological Pluralism and Adaptation. *Journal of Political Ideologies*, 13(1): 73–94.

Schonert-Reichl, K. A., Smith, V., Zaidman-Zait, A., & Hertzman, C. (2012). Promoting Children's Prosocial Behaviours in School: Impact of the 'Roots of Empathy' Program on the Social and Emotional Competence of School-Aged Children. *School Mental Health*, 4(1): 1–12.

Schulz, W., Ainley, J., Fraillon, J., Kerr, D., & Losito, B. (2010). *ICCS 2009 International Report: Civic Knowledge, Attitudes and Engagement among Lower Secondary School Students in Thirty-Eight Countries*. Amsterdam: IEA.

Schuman, R. (1950). *Europe – A Fresh Start: The Schuman Declaration 1950–1990*. Luxembourg: Office for Official Publications of the European Community, pp. 13–14.

Schwarcz, L. M. (1993). *O espetáculo das raças. Cientistas, Instituições e questão racial no Brasil. 1870–1930.* São Paulo: Companhia das Letras.

Schwarz, K. C. (2011). Mandated Community Involvement: A Question of Equity. *Education Canada,* 51(2): 7. Retrieved from http://www.cea-ace.ca/education-canada/article/mandated-community-involvement-question-equity

Scully, R. (2012). *British Images of Germany: Admiration, Antagonism and Ambivalence, 1860–1914.* Basingstoke: Palgrave Macmillan.

Sears, A. (1997). Instruments of Policy: How the Federal State Influences Citizenship Education in Canada. *Canadian Ethnic Studies,* 29(2): 1–21.

Sears, A. (2010). Possibilities and Problems: Citizenship Education in a Multinational State, The Case of Canada. In A. Reid, J. Gill, & A. Sears (Eds.), *Globalization, The Nation-State and the Citizen: Dilemmas and Directions for Citizenship Education* (pp. 191–205). New York: Routledge.

Sears, A. (2011). Historical Thinking and Citizenship Education: It Is Time to End the War. In P. Clark (Ed.), *New Possibilities for the Past: Shaping History Education in Canada* (pp. 344–364). Vancouver, BC: UBC Press.

Sears, A. (2014, January 23–25). A History Educator Looks Forward. In *From the Curriculum to the Classroom: More Teachers, More Students, More Thinking.* A Report on the Annual Meeting of the Historical Thinking Project, Toronto.

Sears, A., Clarke, G. M., & Hughes, A. S. (1999). Canadian Citizenship Education: The Pluralist Ideal and Citizenship Education for a Post-Modern State. In J. Torney-Purta, J. Schwille, & J.-A. Amadeo (Eds.), *Civic Education Across Countries: Twenty-Four National Case Studies from the IEA Education Project* (pp. 111–135). Amsterdam: IEA.

Sears, A., Davies, I., & Reid, A. (2011). From Britishness to Nothingness and Back Again. In C. McGlynn, A. Mycock, & J. W. McAuley (Eds.), *Britishness, Identity and Citizenship: The View From Abroad* (pp. 291–311). New York: Peter Lang.

Seixas, P. (2014). History and Heritage: What's the Difference. *Canadian Issues Thèmes Canadiens* (Fall): 12–16.

Seixas, P., & Morton, T. (2013). *The Big Six Historical Thinking Concepts.* Toronto: Nelson Education.

Senate Select Committee on Employment, Education and Training (1989). *Education for Active Citizenship in Australian Schools and Youth Organisations.* Canberra: Australian Government Printing Service.

Shen, S. C., & Chien, S. Y. S. (2006). Turning Slaves into Citizens: Discourses of Guomin and the Construction of Chinese National Identity in the Late Qing Period. In S. Y. S. Chien & J. Fitzgerald (Eds.), *The Dignity of Nations – Equality, Competition and Honor in East Asian Nationalism* (pp. 49–69). Hong Kong: Hong Kong University Press.

Smith, A. D. (1983). *Theories of Nationalism* (2nd ed.). New York: Holmes & Meier.

Smith, A. D. (1991). *National Identity.* Reno, Las Vegas, and London: University of Nevada Press.

Smith, A. D. (1995). *Nations and Nationalism in a Global Era.* Cambridge: Polity Press.

Smith, A. D. (1998). *Nationalism and Modernism: A Critical Survey of Recent Theories of Nations and Nationalism*. London: Routledge.

Smith, M. (2003). Citizenship Education in Northern Ireland: Beyond National Identity? *Cambridge Journal of Education*, 33(1): 15–32.

Smith, R. (1999). *Civic Ideals: Conflicting Visions of Citizenship in U.S. History*. New Haven, CT: Yale University Press.

Smith, R. (2001). Citizenship: Political. In N. Smelser & P. Baltes (Eds.), *International Encyclopedia of the Social and Behavioural Sciences* (pp. 1857–1860). New York: Pergamon.

Sobanski, Adriane de Quadros (2008). *Como os professores e jovens estudantes do Brasil e de Portugal se relacionam com a ideia de África*. Curitiba: UFPR/ Programa de Pós Graduação em Educação. Dissertação de Mestrado.

Souza Neto, Cláudio Pereira de (2008). Considerações sobre a juridicidade das políticas de ação afirmativa para negros no Brasil. In J. Zoninsein & J. Feres Junior (Org.). *Ação afirmativa no ensino superior brasileiro* (pp. 303–328). Rio de Janeiro: Iuperj; Belo Horizonte: EdUFMG.

Soysal, Y. (1994). *Limits of Citizenship: Migrants and Postnational Membership in Europe*. Chicago, IL: University of Chicago Press.

Stanley, T. J. (2000). Why I Killed Canadian History: Towards an Anti-racist History in Canada. *Histoire sociale/Social History*, 33(65): 79–103.

Stearns, P., Seixas, P., & Wineburg, S. S. (Eds.) (2000). *Knowing, Teaching, and Learning History: National and International Perspectives*. New York and London: New York University Press.

Steding, E. (2014). What Stories Are Being Told? Two Case Studies of (Grand) Narratives from and of the German Democratic Republic in Current *Oberstufe* Textbooks. *Journal of Educational Media, Memory and Society*, 6(1): 42–58.

Stratton, A. (2011). David Cameron on Riots: Broken Society Is Top of My Political Agenda. *The Guardian*, 15 August. Retrieved from http://www. theguardian.com/uk/2011/aug/15/david-cameron-riots-broken-society

Sweeting, A. (1990). *Education in Hong Kong – Pre-1841 to 1941: Fact & Opinion*. Hong Kong: Hong Kong University Press.

Sweeting, A. (2004). *Education in Hong Kong, 1941 to 2001: Visions and Revisions*. Hong Kong: Hong Kong University Press.

Symons, T. H. B., Page, J. E., & Commission on Canadian Studies (1975). *To Know Ourselves: The Report of the Commission on Canadian Studies*. Ottawa: Association of Universities and Colleges of Canada.

Szakács, S. (2007). Now and Then: National Identity Construction in Romanian History. A Comparative Study of Communist and Post-Communist School Textbooks. *Internationale Schulbuchforschung*, 29(1): 23–47.

Tang, W. F., & Darr, B. (2012). Chinese Nationalism and Its Political and Social Origins. *Journal of Contemporary China*, 21(77): 811–826.

Taubman, P. (2009). *Teaching by the Numbers: Deconstructing the Discourse on Standards and Accountability in Education*. New York: Routledge.

Taylor, C. (1993). *Reconciling the Solitudes: Essays on Canadian Federalism and Nationalism*. Montrêal: McGill-Queen's University Press.

Taylor, T., & Collins, S. (2012). The Politics Are Personal: The Australian vs the Australian Curriculum in History. *Curriculum Journal*, 23(4): 531–552.

Theodoro, M. (Org.) (2008). *As políticas públicas e a desigualdade racial no Brasil 120 anos após a abolição*. Brasilia: IPEA.

Tomkins, G. S. (1986). *A Common Countenance: Stability and Change in the Canadian Curriculum*. Scarborough, ON: Prentice-Hall Canada.

Torney-Purta, J., Lehmann, R., Oswald, H., & Schulz, W. (2001). *Citizenship and Education in Twenty-Eight Countries: Civic Knowledge and Engagement at Age Fourteen*. Amsterdam: IEA.

Trudeau, P. E. (1971). *Multiculturalism*. Retrieved from http://www.canadahistory. com/sections/documents/Primeministers/trudeau/docs-onmulticulturalism. htm; accessed 28.07.2014.

Tupper, J. (2012). Treaty Education for Ethically Engaged Citizenship. *Citizenship Teaching and Learning*, 7(2): 143–156. doi:10.1386/ctl.7.2.143_1

UNESCO (1990). Declaração mundial sobre educação para todos: satisfação das necessidades básica de aprendizagem, Jomtien, 1990. Brasilia: UNESCO. Retrieved from http//www.interlegis.gov.br/processo/legislativo

UNESCO (2002). Educação na América Latina: análise de perspectivas. Brasilia: UNESCO, OREALC. Retrieved from http://www.brasilia.unesco.org/ publicacoes/livros/educamericalatina

UNESCO/MEC (2008). *Contribuições para Implementação da Lei 10.639/2003*. Grupo de Trabalho Interministerial Instituído por Meio da Portaria Interministerial Mec/Mj/sePPIr No 605 de 20 de Maio de 2008. Brasília: MEC. Proposta de Plano Nacional de Implementação das Diretrizes curriculares Nacionais da educação das relações Étnico-raciais e para o ensino de História e cultura Afro-Brasileira e Africana – Lei 10.639/2003.

Ungerleider, C. (2003). *Failing Our Kids: How We Are Ruining Our Public Schools*. Toronto: McClelland & Stewart.

UNICEF (2012). *Access, Permanence, Learning and Completion of Basic Education at the Right Age. Right of All and of Each One of the Children and Adolescents*. Brasilia: UNICEF.

USA (1918). Woodrow Wilson: Speech to a Joint Session of Congress, 8 January. Washington, DC: Congressional Record.

U.S. Department of Education (1983). *A Nation at Risk: The Imperative for Educational Reform*. Retrieved from http://www2.ed.gov/pubs/NatAtRisk/ index.html; accessed 23.09.2014.

U.S. Department of Education (2001). *No Child Left Behind*. Retrieved from http://www2.ed.gov/policy/elsec/leg/esea02/index.html; accessed 23.09.2014.

U.S. Department of Education (2008). *Race to the Top*. Retrieved from http:// www2.ed.gov/programs/racetothetop/index.html; accessed 23.09.2014.

U.S. Department of Education (2011). *Our Teachers, Our Future: The Obama Administration's Plan for Teacher Education Reform and Improvement*. Retrieved from http://www.ed.gov/teaching/our-future-our-teachers; accessed 23.09.2014.

van Krieken, R. (1999). The 'Stolen Generations' and Cultural Genocide: The Forced Removal of Australian Indigenous Children from Their Families and the Implications for the Sociology of Childhood. *Childhood*, 6(3): 297–311.

Varma-Joshi, M., Baker, C. J., & Tanaka, C. (2004). Names will Never Hurt Me. *Harvard Educational Review*, 74(2): 175–208.

Viana, F. O. (2005). *Evolução do Povo Brasileiro*. Brasília: Senado Federal. Conselho Editorial.

Wallace Goodman, S. (2009). *Civic Integration Requirements and the Transformation of Citizenship*. Unpublished PhD Thesis, Georgetown University, Washington, DC.

Wang, W. G. (2011). The Great Victory of Marxism in China. *Social Sciences in China*, XXXII(4): 5–18.

Wassermann, H. (2005). Wissens- und Gewissensbildung, Wie Geschichtsbücher historische Realitäten am Biespiel von Faschismus and Nationalsozialismus generieren. *Internationale Schulbuchforschung*, 27(3): 292–318.

Weber, E. (1976). *Peasants into Frenchmen: The Modernization of Rural France, 1870–1914*. Stanford, CA: Stanford University Press.

Wei, C. X. G. (Ed.) (2014). *Macao – The Formation of a Global City*. New York: Routledge.

Westheimer, J., & Kahn, J. (2004). What Kind of Citizen? The Politics of Educating for Democracy. *American Educational Research Journal*, 41(2): 237–269.

Wherry, A. (2015, March 17). Larry Miller and the Case against the Niqab. *Maclean's*. Retrieved from http://www.macleans.ca/politics/further-arguments-in-the-case-of-the-niqab/; accessed 23.03.2015.

Whiteley, P. (2014). Does Citizenship Education Work? Evidence from a Decade of Citizenship Education in Secondary Schools in England. *Parliamentary Affairs*, 67(3): 513–535.

Whitty, G., Rowe, G., & Aggleton, P. (1994). Subjects and Themes in the Secondary School Curriculum. *Research Papers in Education*, 9(2): 159–181.

Whyte, B. (1988). *Unfinished Encounter: China and Christianity*. New York: Fount Paperbacks.

Wilkins, C. (1999). Making 'Good Citizens': The Social and Political Attitudes of PGCE Students. *Oxford Review of Education*, 25(1): 217–230.

Williams, G. (2013). Treaty with Australia's Indigenous People Long Overdue. *Sydney Morning Herald*, 23 November. Retrieved from http://www.smh.com.au/comment/treaty-with-australias-indigenous-people-long-overdue-20131112-2xeel.html; accessed 01.09.2014.

Willis, C. (2002). *China and Macau: Portuguese Encounters with the World in the Age of the Discoveries*. Aldershot: Ashgate.

Wilson, J. (2015, March 23). *Je Ne Suis Pas Charlie Hebdo*. Retrieved from http://labourlist.org/2015/01/je-ne-suis-pas-charlie-hebdo/

Windschuttle, K. (1996). *The Killing of History: How Literary Critics and Social Theorists Are Murdering Our Past*. Paddington, NSW: Encounter Books.

Wintour, P., & Mason, R. (2014). Clegg Urges Greater Devolution for All UK. *The Guardian*, 12 September, p. 6.

Wojdon, J. (2012). The Impact of Communist Rule on History Education in Poland. *Journal of Educational Media, Memory and Society*, 4(1): 61–77.

Xu, G. Q. (2008). *Olympic Dreams – China and Sports 1895–2008*. Cambridge, MA: Harvard University Press.

Yee, H. S. (2001). *Macau in Transition: From Colony to Autonomous Region.* New York: Palgrave.

Yip, K. C. (2003). *Guomindang*'s Refugee Relief Efforts, 1937–1945. In C. Y. Y. Chu & R. K. S. Mak (Eds.), *China Reconstructs* (pp. 83–102). Lanham, MD: University Press of America.

Yoshida, T. (2007). Advancing or Obstructing Reconciliation? Changes in History Education and Disputes over History Textbooks in Japan. In E. A. Cole (Ed.), *Teaching the Violent Past: History Education and Reconciliation* (pp. 51–79). Lanham, MD: Rowman & Littlefield.

Yu, Y. S. (1996). *Democracy and Nationalism.* (In Chinese). Retrieved from http://www.hornbill.cdc.net.my/e-class/culture/democ01.htm

Zhao, S. S. (2004). *A Nation-State by Construction: Dynamics of Modern Chinese Nationalism.* Stanford, CA: Stanford University Press.

Zhao, S. S. (2008). The Olympics and Chinese Nationalism. *China Security,* 4(3): 48–57.

Zhao, S. S. (2013). Foreign Policy Implications of Chinese Nationalism Revisited: A Strident Turn. *Journal of Contemporary China,* 22(82): 535–553. Retrieved from http://dx.doi.org/10.1080/10670564.2013.766379

Index

Printed and bound in Great Britain by
CPI Group (UK) Ltd, Croydon, CR0 4YY